Biological and
Social Factors in
Psycholinguistics

Biological and
Social Factors in
Psycholinguistics

Edited by
John Morton
MRC Applied Psychology Unit
Cambridge

Logos Press Limited

Published by Logos Press Limited
in association with Elek Books Limited
2 All Saints Street, London N1

Printed by Blackfriars Press Limited
Smith Dorrien Road
Leicester

Contents

References and footnotes at the end of each chapter

Contributors

Dr Bernard Campbell
Duckworth Laboratory of Physical Anthropology
University of Cambridge, England

Dr John Marshall
MRC Speech and Communication Research Unit
University of Edinburgh, Scotland

Professor D. McNeill
Department of Psychology, University of Chicago, USA

Dr Roger Wales
Department of Psychology, University of Edinburgh
Scotland

Dr John Morton
MRC Applied Psychology Unit, Cambridge
England

Dr I. M. Schlesinger
Hebrew University of Jerusalem, and the
Israeli Institute of Applied Social Research
Jerusalem, Israel

Professor A. A. Leontiev
Institute of Linguistics of the Academy of Science
Moscow, USSR

Dr Rugaiya Hasan
Sociological Research Unit
University of London Institute of Education
England

Professor Thomas G. Bever
Department of Psychology, Rockefeller University
New York, USA

Editor's Introduction

This volume is the result of a symposium entitled *Biological, Social and Linguistic Factors in Psycholinguistics* which I had the honour to convene at the XIXth International Congress of Psychology held in London during the summer of 1969. There is only a slight resemblance to the actual proceedings of that symposium, as four of the original speakers were unable to attend. Their papers were much too good to miss though, and I am grateful to Logos Press for the opportunity of presenting them to a wider audience. In addition the discussants at the symposium have expanded their remarks to full articles.

When I set out to assemble the symposium, my feeling was that some kind of unity of theme should be apparent to prevent the audience, who were not specialists in the area, from becoming too overwhelmed. Accordingly, in my original invitations to the contributors I enclosed a brief statement of what I hoped the symposium might accomplish. This statement formed the basis of my introduction to the symposium the beginning of which is printed below.

"We are all agreed on one thing if no more—that there is something about language which is unique to man. The concern of this symposium will be to discuss both the nature of this uniqueness and its origins. Some of what will be said is highly speculative; our hope is that the gaps in our knowledge or in our reasoning will become apparent and that the most profitable lines of future enquiry will suggest themselves.

"There are three clearly distinguishable factors which we can accept as playing some role in the evolution of language both in the individual and in the species. These are:
1. The physical make-up of man.
2. The relation between man and the outside world.
3. The relationship between individuals—the social factor.
What is not clear is the way in which these factors operate, the way in which they interact, and which, if any, is dominant. Any controversy which appears to be generated among the speakers today is to be related mainly to the different emphases placed on the factors. On the platform at any rate, we are agreed that human language

behaviour cannot be usefully discussed merely as a quantitative extension of other forms of behaviour of other species."

The rest of my introduction was expanded into a paper which was delivered at the 2nd International Congress of Applied Linguistics in Cambridge, which I have included in this volume.

The chapters need no additional commentary or introduction except for references by Campbell and Marshall to Washoe. In the past a number of attempts have been made to teach chimpanzees to speak. The failure of these attempts—the most serious of which involved bringing the chimp up in a household with a human baby of about the same age—has reinforced our belief in the special relationship between man and language. Washoe, however, is a chimpanzee which has been taught Sign Language (the gestural system of communication used by the deaf, see Chapter 6), the form of communication used by her human companions. While the available information is still relatively scanty, being limited to one published paper (Gardner and Gardner, 1969) and a few unpublished reports, it is sufficient to force us to reappraise the capabilities of chimps and to think very carefully about the nature of the special relationship between man and language. It may turn out that we cannot in the end easily claim that language is unique to man, although we must be careful neither to accept Washoe's performance too readily as linguistic nor reject it too glibly (note the warnings in Marshall's article in this volume). However, I anticipate a long, acrimonious and largely futile debate over the next few years as more information becomes available.

To Washoe's achievements: it is apparent that, at the age of about three years she could perform the following feats.

1. She can use signs reliably to indicate:

    (a) objects—'toothbrush', 'hat', 'key', 'napkin-bib'.

    (b) commands or requests—'tickle', 'hurry', 'open', 'out'.

    (c) internal states (or complex situational concepts) — 'funny', which is used during games and occasionally "when being pursued after mischief"; 'sorry', used "after biting someone or when someone has been hurt in another way (not necessarily by Washoe), and when told to apologise for mischief".

    (d) people—'you' and 'I-me' as well as at least two signs appropriate to particular individuals.

Her vocabulary was over 60 signs and her rate of acquisition was increasing.

2. She could understand (that is react appropriately to) well over 100 signs including 'Bad Washoe'.

3. She engaged in exchanges which might be called conversations such as — Washoe: 'Tickle'. Person: 'Who tickle?' W: 'Tickle Washoe'. P: 'Who?' W: 'You'.

4. She spontaneously generalised from the particular to the general— the sign for 'dog' was used for pictures and for the sound of an unseen dog barking.

5. She produced strings of signs in combinations. A large proportion of these involve what the Gardners call *emphasisers*—'please', 'come-gimme', 'hurry' and 'more'; as in 'please open hurry' and 'gimme drink please'. Other examples include the following which are not imitations; 'listen eat' (at the sound of the alarm clock signalling mealtime', 'gimme tickle' and 'open food drink' (for the refrigerator which her human companions always call the 'cold box').

As I remarked earlier it is premature to come to any firm conclusions except that both Washoe and the Gardners are to be congratulated on their achievements. What follows may help the reader to form a framework from which these feats may be evaluated.

JOHN MORTON
Cambridge, April 1970

1

The roots of language

Bernard Campbell

Duckworth Laboratory of Physical Anthropology,
University of Cambridge,
England

A. Introduction
B. The anatomy of language
C. Words and things
D. The evolution of language
E. Discussion and summary

A. Introduction

Speculation on the evolution of language has been based on linguistic history (eg Révész, 1956) and on minute features of the skulls and jaws of fossil men. Today, in place of these traditional and often ill-founded conjectures (Vallois 1961, 217; DuBrul and Reed 1960), we are obtaining valuable new data from comparative studies of the brain and of the anatomy and behaviour of living primates, in particular the Old World monkeys and apes—our nearest relatives in the animal world. Some of these data are briefly reviewed in the following pages.

Communication is a necessary part of social adaptation whether it is found in bees or birds; and in primates—the most social of social animals—it has evolved far beyond the levels found elsewhere in the animal kingdom. The primate troop appears to be the ideal social unit for the evolution of communication. Here we find the phylogenetically old olfactory signalling systems being replaced by highly evolved visual, and vocal-auditory signals. At one extreme of the visual range we have the purely physiological signal of the sexual skin of the baboon and mandrill, while at the other we have the evolution of complex facial musculature among the African apes (which we share) which makes possible a range of emotional expression quite comparable with our own, as Darwin (1872) and Köhts (1935) have observed. Gesture with hands and body posture are common and appear as complex as our own, and very similar; especially, for example, those that serve the mother-infant bond and in ourselves signify affection. The mother chimpanzee clasps her child to her, greets her siblings, and approaches her consort with quite recognisable gestures, as anyone who has seen the wonderful films taken at the Gombe Stream Reserve will admit. The gentlest touch of finger to finger gives complete reassurance to a frightened child, a touch reminiscent of Michelangelo's famous fresco on the ceiling of the Sistine chapel. So complex and so delicate is this language of gesture in the chimpanzee that it cannot be said to be less evolved than our own.

It is characteristic of primates, however, that communication is multimodal (Marler, 1965) and to some extent sounds seem to have the function of drawing attention to the expression or gestures of the subject (Rowell, 1962); but the sounds themselves have also reached a new level of complexity. The proportion of gesture and sound varies in different species and, of course, relates to the environment. A dense leafy environment means more reliance on sounds to carry a full content of information; in an open savannah habitat more information will be passed by expression and gesture. The important point here is that unlike bird-song, which is almost purely vocal-auditory and very stereotyped, variation is possible in the intensity of each mode of the primate signalling system. The result is a complex and graded system of communication with a very much higher information content than is found elsewhere in the animal kingdom.[1]

What do primates communicate about? Hediger (1961) finds that most groups of social animals are concerned with five main types of event, and primates are no exception:

1. warning of predators
2. courtship and territory
3. mother-child contact
4. social structure and cohesion
5. announcement of food.

The emphasis may vary among different species. For example, the chimpanzee (*Pan troglodytes*) has next to no predators and little territorial sense: their chattering is mainly concerned with mother-child contacts, food and social structure. Small monkeys which live in the open savannah or at the edge of the forest like the vervets (*Cercopithecus aethiops*) have serious predator problems, and alarm calls are well evolved (Struhsaker, 1967). Howlers (*Alouatta villosa*) which live high in dense canopy, seem to be mainly concerned with

11

social cohesion and troop spacing, and depend to a great extent on vocalisation.

Like gesture and expression, vocal-auditory signalling has traditionally been interpreted as an aspect of emotional response, or motivation, which is probably fairly closely defined by genetic programming, and informs other members of the troop of the subject's state of excitement or fear. No reference to the environment needs to be implied. This seems to be acceptable in the face of our general knowledge of animal behaviour and primate social life, but there are some important instances where the distinction between subjective response and environmental reference seems to be slight. The vervet monkeys, mentioned above, have 36 recorded and distinct calls, of which 3 are alarm calls: one for hawks, one for snakes and one for other terrestrial predators. The snake warning call, described as a chutter, presumably, according to the traditional theory, indicates a state of snake-fear, as distinct from hawk-fear (the rraup) or carnivore-fear (the chirp). Yet these sounds could equally well be treated as environmental reference to three classes of animals. Even if this interpretation is not accepted, the data do suggest how object-naming and classifying may have arisen in human evolution. Admittedly, this kind of predator differentiation has been found in other groups from birds to small rodents, but this does not lower its interest to us as an accomplishment of primates.

The recording and analysis of primate call-systems is in its infancy and studies have only been carried out on 3 or 4 of the 50 odd species known. Struhsaker (1967), who has made this important study of vervet monkeys, reports that some may intergrade, and Rowell has clearly shown this to be the case for the rhesus monkey (Rowell, 1962). In this species, Rowell has been able to show that nine recognisable and distinct agonistic calls actually constitute one system, linked by a continuous series of intermediates. Within the system we also find alternative variations are possible where certain calls can grade into any one of three others. This intergrading makes possible a vast number of possible calls with intermediate meanings over and above the nine basic types, and constitutes the most complex system of vocal communication known in any primate. As an example of this in man, the common alarm call 'ow' may grade into a shriek or even into a scream, depending on the level of stimulation.

The differences between the primate call-system and human language may be summarised as follows (Hockett, 1960; Reynolds, 1968):

1. A call system does not show temporal or spatial displacement: as far as we know, a call is emitted only in the presence of an appropriate stimulus. This can be summarised as 'out of sight, out of mind' and constitutes Hockett's 10th feature of language design. It is this feature of displacement which makes possible in man environmental reference or object naming (Geshwind, 1965; Lancaster, 1968). It is this which stands out so clearly as the most striking feature of man's culture, the feature which makes man the 'symbolic animal' and according to most anthropologists and philosophers (eg Cassirer, 1944) separates him most clearly from the rest of the animal kingdom.

2. A call system is closed, a language open. In general it seems that calls are mutually exclusive, though it may be too soon to be dogmatic about this. (Hockett's 11th feature—productivity.) The call system could break down into some kind of pre-language by the blending of calls signifying different situations. The mechanisms and possibilities involved here have been discussed by Hockett and Asher (1964). Because the rhesus calls described by Rowell (1962) arc all agonistic, they do not perhaps qualify.

3. Duality of patterning (Hockett's 12th feature), which is absent in non-human primates, necessitated in human evolution the production and detection, not of a suitable call, however complex, so long as it was a total acoustic *gestalt*, but of the precise component features, the morphemes, which make up words (Hockett and Asher, 1964; 144).

4. Finally, of course, a call system probably carries quite detailed genetic programming of the actual sounds, while a language is learned, though it depends on a unique and highly evolved genetic potential (Lenneberg, 1967, 1969).

To summarise, it seems clear that the primate call-system is as complex as is necessary in the primate environment. There appears to be no great selection pressure for a system of signals for environmental reference. Primates evidently need only express their emotions and motivations by means of gesture and the call system to maintain their social relationships. These conditions are satisfied by a finely graded multimodal system of signalling which is the most complex and delicate in the animal kingdom.

Man has evidently moved significantly forward in evolution in this respect, and has produced an entrely new cultural tool. However, the new means of communication that he has evolved has not replaced but been superimposed upon the primate call-system which has survived more or less intact. This multimodal call-system still stands supreme in the expression of subjective emotion. In contrast, language seems to be concerned primarily with technology and ideas.

B. The anatomy of language

The differences between apes and men in this respect lie not so much in the larynx as in the brain, but it does appear that differences have evolved in the throat which may make vowel sounds a simpler proposition for man. The thicker tongue and the lengthened pharynx (the space between the epiglottis and the soft palate) form an effective pipe of variable cross-section, and this makes possible resonant human phonation. The chimpanzee so carefully and with such difficulty trained to speak three or four words by the Hayes (1951) was unable to utter more than one hoarse vowel sound—a whispered 'ah'. As Lieberman (1968) has shown, and as others have argued (eg DuBrul, 1958; Campbell, 1966) there appears to be a real difference here between human and non-human primates which has been overlooked by some recent authors (eg Lancaster, 1968; p. 453).

Having produced a range of vowel sounds, we must also have learned to interrupt them with the consonants of speech. Just as the sucking reflex concerns the lips and tongue, so the consonants are formed at the lips, tip and base of the tongue. The large mobile tongue allows the formation of gutturals and clicks in some languages. On the whole, the act of speaking uses body parts of quite diverse primary function, with only limited modification. The jaw, tongue, larynx and lips are supplied by motor nerve supplies (V, XII, X and XI respectively) of very different origin in the brain. At the same time, as Spuhler (1959) has pointed out, while such co-ordinated muscular movement usually requires adjustments from proprioceptors, they are absent from the important laryngeal muscles, and feedback control comes by way of the ear (VIII). (Hence speech-problems of the congenitally deaf.) The only place where the different motor organs and steering apparatus of speech could be connected is in the cerebral cortex.

But this is not the only reason to emphasise the importance of cortico-cortical connections in the brain. The most obvious distinction between human and other primate brains, beside their size and degree of convolutedness, has been identified as an increase in the association areas. As is well known, the association areas border the so-called 'primordial' areas of the limbic cortex on the one hand (which is on

14

the medial surface of the temporal lobe and is concerned with sensations and activities involved with emotional states) and the visual,
auditory and somesthetic areas of the cortex on the other. The late
appearance of the association areas in evolution is reflected in the late
appearance and late myelination of these areas in ontogeny (Vogt,
1906; Flechsig, 1920). In this sense the association areas are described
as 'intermediate'. In primates, cortico-cortical connections do not arise
from the primordial areas, but from their respective association areas.
However, by no means all possible connections exist in non-human
primates. According to Geschwind (1965), the association area for
vision has major connections with only three other areas of the cortex:
the limbic system, the classic motor cortex, and the opposite side of
the brain via the corpus callosum. The only wiring between the visual,
auditory and somesthetic areas are via the limbic system; that is,
indirect and with emotional connotation. This was demonstrated by
Ettlinger (1960) who showed it to be a relatively simple matter to train
a monkey to form an association between a non-limbic stimulus (visual,
auditory or somesthetic) and a limbic stimulus (for example, an electric
shock), but very difficult for a monkey to form an association between
two non-limbic stimuli (say, visual and auditory).

In man, the neuroanatomy is different. Between the 'intermediate'
association areas of Flechsig, we find new, very late maturing areas
which he calls 'terminal', and these are found on the frontal lobe
(middle frontal gyrus), on the inferior and middle gyri of the temporal
lobe, and on the inferior parietal lobule in the region of the angular
gyrus. (Maturation is not completed until the 18th year or even later.)
This last is of importance here: it lies between the visual, auditory
and somesthetic areas, and has been described by Geschwind as the
'association area of association areas'. Although he has no good proof
of it, he suggests that the intermodal association involved in learning
names is possibly accomplished through the cortico-cortical connections in this area: that is, between visual and auditory stimuli. This is
an area with few vertical connections to the thalamus. There are also
auditory-somesthetic connections and these can be established without
reference to the limbic system with its ever-present emotional conno-
tations. Here indeed we seem to have a plausible anatomical correlate
of man's much-vaunted detachment—his supposedly rational thought.
Although this particular hypothesis may in time prove to have been
naïve, it does show us the kind of correlate which we may hope in the
future to uncover, between neuroanatomy and behaviour.

From this particular point in the twentieth century, we can of course recognise that the purely rational man was a figment of our eighteenth century imagination (not of our dreams), and that the limbic associations are still present to weight and prejudice the workings of pure reason. This is not so much a human defect as a biological need: by weighting association the limbic system controls its importance and retrievability in the memory bank. Natural selection has adapted the limbic system to select experience on the basis of biological requirements.

C. Words and things

Having discussed a site for the visual-auditory association, we must turn to the site of the auditory-motor association for word production. In the frontal lobe we find Broca's famous speech area alongside the motor association cortex. Here and in the motor association cortex, the complex motor programming for word production is, we suppose, carried out, and then finally put into effect by the classic motor cortex of the precentral gyrus, where movements of the diaphragm, larynx, pharynx, tongue and lips are initiated.

We find some confirmation of this scheme in the reports of cortical excision and electrical stimulation experiments carried out by Penfield and Roberts (1959). These not only confirm that the three areas concerned are indeed the centres of speech production (in the dominant hemisphere), but indicate their relative importance. The parietal area is evidently the most vital, and the motor cortex, which is in any case duplicated in both hemispheres, the least essential. It is also clear that speech and writing (an alternative and very recent motor form of word expression which requires no novel evolutionary developments) are correlates of the dominant hemisphere.

The whole process of word formation is of course far more complex than I have implied, but the point that I want to make is that there may be fairly clear-cut anatomical correlates of language which are absent in non-human primates. At a microscopic level, correlates of language may also be detected: on the motor (output) side we find the highly evolved pyramidal tracts with their direct links to the motor neurons. On the sensory (input) side we may expect similar developments. Although the auditory capacity of man may not surpass that of other primates, there is little doubt that species-specific and highly complex decoding mechanisms must have evolved in the auditory cortex in response to language evolution.

D. The evolution of language

Having reduced language to anatomy it is appropriate to look for it in the fossil record but, as I have already said, we only have evidence of cranial capacity as our guide, and cranial capacity alone is no real guide to linguistic ability.[2] The elephant and the whale, with brains vastly bigger than our own (5000 cc and 6700 cc respectively), do not have language, while human so-called 'bird-headed' dwarfs whose brains are no bigger than those of chimpanzees or early hominids (varying from 400-600 cc) can talk like a 5 year old child (Seckel, 1960). Evidently they carry the anatomical correlates of language. On the other hand, devoted teaching by the Hayes parents could not induce their chimpanzee baby to learn more than three or four words (Hayes, 1951), though chimpanzees (eg Washoe) can be taught an extensive vocabulary of gestures (Gardner and Gardner, 1969), which now extends to over 90 gestures of the American Sign Language. Therefore we are entitled, I think, to assume that the roots of language in the form of new cortico-cortical connections may have appeared well before the brain expanded, but that the immense memory bank which language requires, and the extensive ability to associate between modalities, necessitated an increased brain size. This increase represents the flowering of the specifically human adaptation—not its inception.

The facts, for what they are worth, are that at a date of about 1·75 to 1·0 millions years BP (before present) we have a skull with a cranial capacity of around 680 cc (Tobias, 1964) and individuals about 1·20-1·35 m tall with cranial capacities averaging 500 cc: brain size was already big in relation to body size. Then at 400,000 years BP we have skull remains from Hungary which indicate a full-sized human brain of at least 1400 cc (Thoma, 1966), and this is fully confirmed by fossils of a somewhat later date. The size increase was very sudden in evolutionary terms and relatively late, and it was certainly well after the appearance of stone implements, which are now dated back to about 2·5 million years in East Africa.

The increase in brain size is not therefore correlated with the beginnings of stone tools, but it came later and does seem to correlate with the beginnings of well organised social hunting, which we can identify by the regular appearance of the remains of large mammals on living floors in the Middle Pleistocene. Such socially organised hunting would have required shared concepts of aims and methods, of animal species, plants, tools, geography and time. A more complex environment came with more complex perception. The men would have probably returned from the hunt to rejoin the women who remained to gather plant food near the base camp. Language was perhaps stimulated by

B

17

the need for intercourse as a result of the division of labour, as Roe (1963) suggested. Language made possible the organising of experience and of the environment, the necessary technology involved in all these activities would have stimulated object-naming and classification of features of the environment *in absentia*: 'displacement' would by now have entered language. Typically independent primate troops must have evolved a between-troop structure: to put it into human terms, bands may have become organised into clans. Here was a further need for abstract concepts with words to represent them. Language capitalises thought, and in human evolution, it must have stabilised ideas which were necessary for social development. In all modern hunting-gathering people (such as the Bushmen and Australians) we find an important part played by myth. In these groups, as in our own recent history, myth and ritual formalise social affairs; they are the means by which social structure and behaviour are stabilised. Since myth depends for its existence on words and language, we can say that language is man's unique means of coding social affairs and technological knowledge.

Having said this, it must be recalled that evolution is a slow, steady process, and that language undoubtedly developed over a long period. Though we are closely related to the chimpanzee and gorilla, the hominids may have been an independent line for as much as 20 million years, and there was ample time for the evolution of the specialised brain structures which make language possible. At an early point in hominid evolution, primate cells may have reached a dangerously high level of ambiguity: at this point no unusual evolutionary phenomenon need be invoked. Object naming would have been slowly added to the existing call system. The advantages to the early hominids of language would have led naturally to its steady selection as a behaviour pattern of great value. We can suppose that speech perception evolved step by step with speech production.

E. Discussion and summary

The origin of language is one of science's most difficult problems. Lancaster (1968) has recently reviewed some of the material discussed here and we must agree with her, with Reynolds (1968) and Hockett and Ascher (1964), that there is a very clear gap between primate communication and human language. Both levels of communication are clearly seen in child development. Children rely solely on primate signals for the first 1½ to 2 years. For the first 6 weeks of life children do not use their tongues to modify the vocal tract. Later, when words

18

appear, they do not replace the call system but introduce in addition the new factor of object-naming by means of speech. It has been shown that object words are the first to be used, followed by so-called operator or pivot words. These latter are the action words, equivalent to verbs, but not necessarily verbs (Braine, 1963). Object words do not directly relate to emotions and moods. 'Mama', 'Dada', 'bottle' and 'cup' are the kind of words which are important to a baby. The expression of mood or emotion follows later. The cry, the smile, the giggle, the laugh and the temper still survive: and they survive into adult life.

And not only are these expressions surprisingly stereotyped, but so are the more complex adult behaviour patterns such as greeting, flirting and praying (Bastian, 1965; Eibl-Eibesfeldt, 1968). It seems to me that in order to understand the evolution of language and its use today, we shall also need to study these non-linguistic means of communication available to us.

I have reviewed the evidence that language is a slowly evolved behaviour pattern depending on the evolution of novel structures in the brain for both input and output. These structures could not have evolved suddenly. The evolution of the vocal tract would follow the need for improved phonation, and again would have taken time. This view is not widely different from Darwin's discussion of the subject (1871), but is in direct contrast to the more widely held views more recently put forward by biologists and anthropologists such as Paget (1951), Pumphrey (1951), Haldane (1952, 1955) and Dart (1959) who for different but related reasons believe that language did not predate the late Palaeolithic. Their views were based on deductions made on the basis of the sudden flowering of material culture and art during Aurignacian times (35,000-20,000 BP). However, in a recent article, Hockett and Ascher (1964) come to a more or less similar conclusion as myself, on linguistic grounds.

Finally, it seems important to repeat that language does not replace the primate call system, but is superimposed upon it. While the primate call system still holds pride of place in the most profound aspects of human relationships, words have evolved to capitalise environmental processes and the abstract concepts arising from new complexities of social structure. Language has ushered in the consciousness of self, of I and thou. But the older system of communication profoundly influences our behaviour, including our use of language. The primate call-system is a substrate in which language is rooted and from which it has grown. Language has conferred humanity upon a primate species; myth and technology are its fruits.

Footnotes

[1] A good case can be made for the claim that dogs, which are social carnivores (like early man), have a more highly evolved social behaviour and more complex multimodal call system than any primate. Being primarily herbivorous, primates do not require the degree of social discipline found among hunting dogs and wolves.

[2] Reconstruction of the vocal tracts of fossil hominids such as we find in Negus (1949, 200 fig. 191) and Lieberman (1968, 1581), I consider to be an exercise with no valid basis in fact.

References

BASTIAN, J. R. (1965), Primate Signalling Systems and Human Languages. In I. DeVore (ed.), *Primate Behaviour; Field Studies of Monkeys and Apes*. New York: Holt, Reinhart and Winston, pp. 585-606.

BRAINE, M. D. S. (1963), The Ontogeny of English Phrase Structure: The First Phase, *Language* **39**, 1-13.

CAMPBELL, B. G. (1966), *Human Evolution, an Introduction to Man's Adaptations*. Chicago: Aldine.

CASSIRER, E. (1944), *An Essay on Man*. Newhaven: Yale University Press.

DART, R. (1959), On the Evolution of Language and Articulate Speech, *Homo* **10**, 154-65.

DARWIN, C. (1871), *The Descent of Man.* London: John Murray.

DARWIN, C. (1872), *The Expression of the Emotions in Man and Animals.* London: John Murray.

DUBRUL, E. L. (1958), *Evolution of the Speech Apparatus.* Springfield: Charles C. Thomas.

DUBRUL, E. L. and REED, C. A. (1960), Skeletal evidence of Speech? *Amer. J. Phys. Anthrop.* **18**, 153-156.

EIBL-EIBESFELDT, I. (1968), Ethological Perspectives on Primate Studies. In P. C. Jay (ed.). *Primates; Studies in Adaptation and Variability.* New York: Holt, Reinhart and Winston, pp. 479-486.

ETTLINGER, G. (1960), Cross-modal Transfer of Training in Monkeys, *Behaviour* **16**, 56-64.

FLECHZIG, P. (1920), *Anatomie des Menschlichen Gehirns und Rückenmarks auf Myelogenetischer Grundlage.* Leipsig: Vert Comp.

GARDNER, R. A. and GARDNER, B. T. (1969), Teaching sign language to a chimpanzee. *Science* **165**, 664-672.

GESCHWIND, N. (1964), The Development of the Brain and the Evolution of Language, *Monogr. Ser. on Language and Linguistics* **17**, 155-69.

HALDANE, J. B. S. (1952), The origin of language, *Rationalist Annual,* 38-45.

HALDANE, J. B. S. (1955), Animal Communication and the Origin of Human Language, *Sci. Progr.* **43**, 385-40.

HAYES, C. (1951), *The Ape in Our House.* London: Victor Gollancz.

HEDIGER, H. (1961), The evolution of Territorial Behavior. In S. L. Washburn (ed.), *The Social Life of Early Man.* Chicago: Aldine, pp. 34-37.

HOCKETT, C. F. (1960), Logical Considerations in the Study of Animal Communication, *Animal Sounds and Communication.* American Inst. of Biological Sciences Publ. No. 7, 392-430.

HOCKETT, C. F. and ASHER, R. (1964), The Human Revolution, *Curren Anthrop.* **5**, 135-168.

KOHTS, N. (1935), Infant Ape and Human Child, *Sci. Mem. Mus. Darwinianum,* Moscow 3.

21

LANCASTER, JANE B. (1968), Primate Communication Systems and the Emergence of Human Language. In P. C. Jay (ed.), *Primates; Studies in Adaptation and Variability*. New York: Holt, Reinhart and Winston, pp. 439-457.

LENNEBERG, E. H. (1967), *The Biological Foundations of Language*. New York: Wiley.

LENNEBERG, E. H. (1969), On Explaining Language, *Science* **164**, 635-643.

LIEBERMAN, P. (1968), Primate Vocalizations and Human Linguistic Ability, *J. Acoust. Soc. America* **44**, 1574-1584.

LIEBERMAN, P., KLATT, D. H. and WILSON, W. H. (1969), Vocal Tract Limitations on the Vowel Repertoires of Rhesus Monkey and other Nonhuman Primates, *Science, N.Y.* **164**, 1185-1187.

MARLER, P. (1965), Communication in Monkeys and Apes. In I. DeVore (ed.) *Primate Behavior; Field Studies of Monkeys and Apes*. New York: Holt, Reinhart and Winston, 544-584.

NEGUS (1949), *The comparative anatomy and physiology of the larynx*. New York: Hefner.

PAGET, R. A. S. (1951), The origin of language, *Sci. News* **20**, 82-94.

PENFIELD, W. and ROBERTS, L. (1959), *Speech and Brain Mechanisms*. Princeton University Press.

PUMPHREY, R. J. (1951), *The Origin of Language: an Inaugural Lecture*. Liverpool University Press, 39 pp.

REYNOLDS, P. C. (1968), Evolution of Primate Vocal-Auditory Communication Systems. *Amer. Anthrop.* **70**, 300-308.

REVESZ, G. (1956), *The Origins and Prehistory of Language*. London and New York: Longmans Green.

ROE, A. (1963), Psychological definitions of man. In S. L. Washburn (ed.), *Classification and Human Evolution*. Chicago: Aldine, pp. 320-31.

ROWELL, T. E. (1962), Agonistic Noises of the Rhesus Monkey (Macaca mulatta), *Symp. Zool. Soc. Lond.* **8**, 91-96.

SECKEL, H. P. G. (1960), *Bird-Headed Dwarfs*. Basel: Karger.

SPUHLER, J. N. (1959), Somatic Paths to Culture, *Hum. Biol.* **31**, 1-13.

STRUHSAKER, T. (1967), Auditory Communication among Vervet Monkeys (*Cercopitheous aethiops*). In S. A. Altmann (ed.), *Social Communication among Primates.* Chicago: University Press, 281-324.

THOMA, A. (1966), L'Occipital de l'Homme Mindélien de Vertesszöllös, *Anthropologie, Paris* **70**, 495-534.

TOBIAS, P. V. (1964), The Olduvai Bed I Hominine with Special Reference to its Cranial Capacity, *Nature, Lond.,* **202**, 3-4.

VALLOIS, H. (1961), The Social Life of Early Man: The Evidence of Skeletons. In S. L. Washburn (ed.), *The Social Life of Early Man.* Chicago: Aldine, pp. 214-235.

VOGT, O. (1906), Der Wert der Myelogenetischen Felder der Grosshirnrinde (Cortex palii), *Anat. Anz.* **29**, 273.

2

Can Humans Talk?[1]

John C. Marshall

2

Can Humans Talk?[1]

John C. Marshall

MRC Speech and Communication Research Unit,
University of Edinburgh,
Scotland

A. Introduction

B. Language as representation
C. The 'Classical' Approach
D. A Neo-classical approach
E. Coda

A. Introduction

If one asked a behaviourist whether he thought animals had a language, the reply might take the following course:

1. The social behaviour of many animal species is (partially) regulated by the interchange of 'communicative signs'.

2. Many aspects of human life are regulated by the interchange of signs drawn from a peculiarly human communication-system, normally referred to as 'Language' . . . with a capital 'L'.

3. Human Languages are undoubtedly more 'complex' than any other known communication system; they have a larger vocabulary and a more elaborate syntax.

4. However 'complexity' is, in one sense, a matter of degree not kind. Accordingly, it would be impossible, or pointless, to attempt to state necessary and sufficient conditions for regarding a 'communication-system' as a 'Language'.

5. Therefore, the question of whether animals have a language is a pseudo-issue, discussion of which can safely be left to philosophers, linguists, theoretical psychologists and other mystics who have failed to appreciate that psychology is the science of behaviour.

The authors of the most interesting and revealing attempt (so far

24

and by far) to teach language to a chimpanzee (an intelligent young female, by name, Washoe) appear to subscribe to the above argument, at least as a useful working hypothesis: "From time to time we have been asked questions such as 'Do you think that Washoe has language?' or 'At what point will you be able to say that Washoe has language?' We find it very difficult to respond to these questions because they are altogether foreign to the spirit of our research. They imply a distinction between one class of communicative behaviour that can be called language and another class that cannot.' (Gardner and Gardner, 1969, p. 671).

The antiquity of the Gardners' approach to language and communication is (at least) co-extensive with the antiquity of radical behaviourism as a general philosophy of psychology. We might characterise that approach in the following terms: One of the most important overt aims of behaviourist psycholinguistics is to rid theoretical accounts of 'meaning' and 'communication' of two ontological monsters: *ideational* descriptions of the content of speech-acts, and *intentional* descriptions of the 'events' behind speech-acts. These aims are well-known, having been stated, more or less explicitly, by a long line of, more or less radical, behaviourists from Meyer (1921) to Skinner (1957) and Quine (1960). It think it therefore unnecessary to justify, at length, the historical accuracy of the above characterisation. The flavour of the approach is captured, however, by the following quotations from Meyer (1921, p. 195): "Animals respond to certain stimuli, sometimes internal, sometimes external stimuli, by the contraction of certain muscles whose function is of no direct consequence to the animal itself, but affects other animals by stimulating them to act . . . " Meyer calls the class of responses described above "signaling reflexes", and he regards these inherited behaviour patterns as the basis for the acquisition of more complex 'learned' signals: "Altho speech is nothing but a development into complicated habits of the original signaling reflex acting on the other animal's auditory organ, it assumes a new role in the Other-One's life through being used by him in order to signal to himself . . . "[2]

Similarly, I think it unnecessary here to inquire deeply into the reasons which lay behind the behaviourists' attempts to purge traditional mentalistic terms from theories of language and language-use. Suffice it to say that certain doctrines of logical positivism combined with over-generous use of Lloyd Morgan's canon led quite naturally to the view that the sole objects of psychological investigation were observable behavioural regularities. It follows from this position that the basic status of 'verbal responses' is no different from that of any other observable behaviour. We end up, then, with the position, neatly summarised by Morganbesser (1969), that "it is unscientific to be anthropomorphic about human beings".

Since it is not at issue that human beings can produce and respond to verbal stimuli (in some sense, however vague, of that term), behaviourists must provide a vocabulary in which one can describe speech-episodes and they must provide an account of the acquisition and maintenance of the verbal behaviour in which speech-episodes are manifested. Consider how a behaviourist might define a 'communicative-episode': We take an initial stimulus-situation (ISS) and two 'linked' organisms (O_1 and O_2). 'Communication' consists of an ordered sequence of behaviours in which the ISS provokes the response R_1 from O_1 and this response in turn acts as a stimulus which provokes the response R_2 from O_2. What might appeal to a behaviourist about this definition is its generality. Thus, imagine that O_1 and O_2 are vervet monkeys: the following behaviour sequence might occur (cf Altmann, 1968):—

Initial stimulus situation: initial perception of major avian predator.

O_1: "Rraup, rraup".
O_2: runs away from open areas.

Now imagine that O_1 and O_2 are human beings: the following behaviour sequence might occur:—
Initial stimulus situation: initial perception of rampaging elephant.

O_1: "Theresarampagingelephant".
O_2: runs away from open areas.

In order to avoid certain rather obvious objections to the definition, it is customary to restrict instances of communication to cases where the relationship between stimulus and response are examples of information-transfer, not solely energy-transfer. This restriction has been observed in the above examples. Biologists would add a further important qualification. Marler (1967) considers the question 'Is the mouse rustling in the grass communicating with the owl that hunts for it?' Mentalists might wish to answer 'No' on the grounds that there was no 'intention' to communicate. This description is, however, ruled out by behaviourist metatheory. Marler's answer is therefore "Clearly not, for mice have undoubtedly been selected for avoidance of emission of stimuli that a predator might detect". In other words, the notion of 'adaptation to the environment' replaces the appeal to 'intentional' monsters. (See Marshall, 1970, for further discussion of this point.) We thus find ourselves with a definition of a 'communicative-episode' as a stimulus-correlated act by one organism which 'triggers' a further act by another organism, such that the probability of the species' survival is augmented rather than diminished by the occurrence of the first act. (There is some similarity between such a method of preserving the notion of 'communication' without appeals to 'intentions to inform' and the strategies whereby behaviourists are permitted to describe behaviour as 'goal-directed' without crediting animals with knowledge of 'goals'.)[3] There are admittedly certain problems in generalising the biological utility criterion to human linguistic episodes. Appearances could be saved by postulating that children who say 'Please give me my cornflakes' are permitted to starve to death less frequently than those children who merely scream loudly.[4]

It should now be obvious that there is one sense in which the plausibility of behaviourist approaches to language is quite independent of one's beliefs concerning two currently fashionable topics; the extent of pre-programmed principles of organisation which (partially) determine the course of grammar-acquisition; the complexity (as formal, uninterpreted calculi) of the grammatical theories which (partially) describe the end result of language-learning. Quine's *Word and Object* (1960) contains the most cogently argued statement of behaviourist psycholinguistics, and it is Quine (1968)—replying to criticisms of that work—who provides "an explicit word of welcome toward any innate mechanisms of language aptitudes, however elaborate, that Chomsky can make intelligible and plausible" and notes that "Innate mechanism, after all, is the heart and sinew of behaviour" (Quine, 1968). The question of whether or not well-informed linguistic 'responses' are sufficiently complex to necessitate describing their *form* by production-systems which are as powerful as transformational grammar is likewise irrelevant. It is sometimes necessary to state the obvious: what leads us to describe certain human behavioural repertoires (irrespective of complexity, sensory modality and mechanism of acquisition) as 'Languages' is that they function semantically as 'systems of representation'. Let us now consider how this obvious, but far from trivial, fact is manifested in behaviourist writings.

B. Language as representation

If, by operant conditioning techniques, a behaviourist trains an organism, such as a rat, to lift its left front leg if and only if a red stimulus is visible, then left leg-lifting is described as a discriminative

27

conditioned response (or, in 'Skinnerian' terminology, a discriminated operant). But what happens when the organism is a child and the response is vocal? Allport (1924) describes how to condition the response 'dolly' to the presentation of a dolly. Success is achieved which Allport describes as follows: "The object itself thus becomes a stimulus adequate for evoking the response of speaking its *name*." (My italics: J.C.M.) Thirty-three years later, Skinner (1957, p. 84) writes: "A child is taught *the names* of objects, colours, and so on when some generalised reinforcement (for example, the approval carried by the verbal stimulus 'Right!') is made contingent upon a response which bears an appropriate relation to a current stimulus." (My italics: J.C.M.) It seems to me that the following question is in order: what is this mysterious theoretical transfiguration whereby a rat which wiggles its left front leg shows evidence of conditioned *responding* but a child which wiggles its vocal chords shows evidence of conditioned *naming*?[5]

It was, of course, by meditating upon the semantic-functions of *naming, predicating, asserting* and so forth that speculative philosophers formulated the notion that abstract entities, termed 'propositions', are the bearers of truth-values and that the ability to conceive of propositions, true and false, is what most clearly distinguishes man from animal. It is this tradition that is reflected in pre- and early anti-behaviourist psycholinguistics. Thus we find Hughlings Jackson (1893) remarking that "to speak is to propositionalise". Likewise, Lloyd Morgan (1909) notes that the proposition is "the primary unit of language, expressive of a judgement as the primary unit of thought" The importance of these notions is also stressed by early developmental psycholinguists. We find Stern (1914, p. 109) writing as follows: "The understanding of the relation between sign and meaning that dawns on the child . . . is something different in principle from the simple use of sound images, object images and their associations. And the requirement that *each* object of whatever kind has its name may be considered a true generalisation made by the child—possibly his first". Similarly, Buhler (1918), considering the notion of a declarative sentence, writes: "We discover the real function of this sentence when we state its truth or falsity . . . ". That function, says Buhler, is 'representation' ("Darstellung"). In the classic (ie unread) writings of both Buhler (1930) and Vygotsky (1934) we find the truly amazing suggestion that it might be possible to produce *evidence* that the child, at a certain age but not before, manifests these semantic-functions in his verbal behaviour.

A consistent behaviourist would, of course, reply that all this talk of 'naming', 'describing', 'asserting', 'referring', etc was empty mentalist verbiage. If caught saying that a child had learned how to name objects, the expression would be disclaimed as a slip of the tongue or a bad habit picked up by talking to too many mentalists. Skinner (1957; *Verbal Behaviour,* Chapters 5 and 12) is quite clear on this issue. His book contains a lucid exposition of his belief that the use of these terms does not result in a more adequate description of language-behaviour than can be obtained simply by describing stimuli, responses and reinforcement contingencies; that is, statements of the relevant inter- and extra-verbal associations plus the conditions of their acquisition and maintenance are descriptively sufficient and the basic vocabulary in which these factors can be expressed need not be extended beyond *stimulus, response* and *reinforcement-schedule.* Thus Skinner defines a *tact* as simply a three-term contingency between, for instance, a doll, saying 'Doll' and the generalised reinforcement for saying 'Doll'. Skinner concedes that "It may be tempting to say that in a tact the response 'refers to', 'mentions', 'announces', 'talks about', 'names', 'denotes', or 'describes' its stimulus." However, the fact remains that "It serves no useful purpose, and may be misleading, to call a tact an 'announcement', 'declaration', or 'proposition', or to say that it 'states', 'asserts', or 'denotes' something, or that it 'makes known' or 'communicates' a condition of the stimulus" (Skinner, 1957, p. 82). Just how tempting these terms are may be gauged from the fact that the above-quoted passages occur approximately a page and a half prior to the description of how a "child is taught the names of objects, colours, and so on . . . ". If temptation is resisted, however, behaviourism provides a useful antidote to over-enthusiasm in crediting complex 'symbolic' functions to young children and chimpanzees.

It is this vocabulary-purging aspect of behaviourist metatheory that has, I believe, received less attention than it deserves. The larger part of critical discussion has been concerned with such issues as the vagueness of the notion of stimulus (a famous example of Skinner's is that 'This is war' is a response to a 'confusing international situation') and the factual falseness of the claim that the verbal behaviours of adults in normal situations are stimulus-occasioned acts. Chomsky (1959) and Fodor (1965) do mention that they believe behaviourist vocabulary to be a "misleading paraphrase" (Chomsky) for more traditional terms. Both papers contain some discussion of the problems that arise when the notion of *true* is eliminated from the theoretical vocabulary of psycholinguistics. Fodor (1965) asks the question: How can we translate the fact that " 'Tom is a thief' claims that someone named Tom is a thief" into the vocabulary of the conditioning model. I have already quoted Skinner's position on this question; the reply is 'You don't', because describing 'Tom' as a *name* and 'thief' as a general term predicted of Tom is unnecessary. The description goes beyond the observable data in an unprincipled fashion.

If we return to the Gardners' chimpanzee, it seems to me that any cognitive psychologist who believes that it is, in principle, possible to give a sensible answer—yes or no—to the question 'Does Washoe have a language?' must meet Skinner — as vocabulary purgative — on his own ground. That is, anyone who wishes to describe Washoe's performance as 'naming', 'asking', 'indicating', etc must state the evidence which prompts these descriptions rather than descriptions in terms of Skinner's reduced vocabulary of mands. tacts and autoclitics. (By 'evidence', I mean 'grounds' not 'criteria'; that is, I agree with Fodor (1968) in believing that 'mental' terms cannot be logically entailed by behavioural descriptions.) Exactly the same request can, of course, be asked of any investigator who believes that children can name objects, ask questions and assert or deny the truth of propositions;[6] in other words, child-psychologists must learn to treat their children like animals. My point is this: early developmental psycholinguists were convinced that children could 'use' words appropriately (in one sense) well before it becomes necessary to credit them with the ability to 'name', 'describe', 'ask', etc. Many of the traditional observations and theories are beautifully described in Vygotsky's *Thought and Language*. Vygotsky summarises his own position in the following terms:

> "1. In their ontogenetic development, thought and speech have different roots. 2. In the speech development of the child, we can with certainty establish a preintellectual stage, and in his thought development, a prelinguistic stage. 3. Up to a certain point in time, the two follow different lines, independently of each other. 4. At a certain point these lines meet, whereupon thought becomes verbal and speech rational."
>
> (Vygotsky, 1934; English Translation 1962, p. 44).

If we can give real substance to Vygotsky's theory, then it would seem plausible to regard the point at which the 'lines meet' as the beginning of true language. How difficult it would be to persuade psychologists that 'languages' are just those behavioural repertoires to which the traditional vocabulary for 'symbolic' processes may plausibly be applied, I do not know. I suspect, however, that philosophers who have been influenced by behaviourism would not find the idea too uncongenial. We find Wittgenstein (1953, p. 187) writing: "If you trained someone to emit a particular sound at the sight of something red, another at the sight of something yellow and so on for other colours, still he would not yet be describing objects by their colours. Though he might be a help to us in giving a description." We might also consider the following, very carefully worded, passage from Quine (1960, p. 81): "The operant act may be the random babbling of something like 'Mama' at some moment when, by coincidence, the mother's face is looming. The mother, pleased at being named, rewards this random act, and so in the future the approach of the mother's face succeeds as a stimulus to further utterances of 'Mama'." What one notices from this passage is that 'being named' is the interpretation that the mother imposes upon her child's behaviour, not a description of the child's performance *per se*. Quine gives a child's eye view of the matter in the next line: "The child has learned an occasion sentence."

The problem, then, is simple: a basic theoretical prerequisite of a mature psycholinguistics is to provide an account of how the child moves from the ability to utter appropriate occasion sentences to real language-behaviour. A central descriptive issue is specifying the kinds of evidence that permit us to claim that the child has made the transition and to see whether chimpanzees are capable of making it. The evidence must, of course, be *behavioural* evidence . . . but no sane mentalist has ever denied this. (Chomsky (1959) states that " . . . anyone who sets himself the problem of analyzing the causation of behaviour will (in the absence of independent neurophysiological evidence) concern himself with the only data available, namely the record of inputs to the organism and the organism's present response, and will try to describe the function specifying the response in terms of the history of inputs. This is nothing more than the definition of his problem.")

C. The 'classical' approach

Hard-nosed readers will by this time be complaining that it is one thing to praise traditional terminology and quite another to justify its use. Let us see, then, just what a 'classical' approach can achieve. The account I intend to build on is Buhler's theory of the three functions of language, with modifications culled from Vygotsky (and Skinner). Briefly, Buhler's doctrine is that three states can be distinguished in the process of language-acquisition; 1. The stage where language has

31

an indicative (or expressive or symptomatic) function. 2. The stage where language has a stimulative (or 'release' or 'communicative') function. 3. The stage where language has a representational (or descriptive) function. The stages form a hierarchy "in the sense that each of the higher ones *cannot* be present without all those which are lower, whilst the lower ones *may* be present without the higher ones" (Popper, 1953). It is Buhler's (1930, p. 56) claim that the transition to the third stage marks a boundary in conceptual ability between man and the animals: "The functions of indication and release are common to human language and the cries and calls of animals." The representational function, however, "has not as yet been demonstrated in any animal". Transposing the argument into Vygotsky's terms the representational stage is the point where "thought becomes verbal and speech rational".

The account of linguistic stages does owe a considerable debt to Buhler (and the tradition in which he worked) but I am not here concerned with historical exegesis. Rather, I wish to explore appropriate conceptual frameworks within which language-learning may be interpreted. Accordingly, I shall modify the classical story whenever it seems (to me) desirable to do so.

Stage 1. Indicative utterances

If we are to have grounds for classifying certain vocalisations as the first 'words' (rather than the last babbles), it is necessary that these vocalisations be responses in the behaviourists' technical sense (ie stimulus-occasioned acts). The observation of significant correlations between 'states of the world' (both internal and external) and responses constitutes the evidence that something more than random babbling is going on. We can conceptualise this stage in fairly straight stimulus-response terms. The child has learned (acquired) a mapping of a 'perceptual' space into an articulatory space by If/Then connections. Let us represent 'points' in the perceptual space by integers between *1* and *n,* and 'points' in the articulatory space by letters (and letter-sequences). The general theory simply states that instances of 'If *integer,* then *letter'* correlations have been acquired. The process of determining *which* instances have been acquired proceeds exactly as the behaviourists would have us believe. We need to know how the perceptual space is organised into stimulus classes; the familiar techniques of generalisation and transfer trials provide the relevant information. The experience of every scholar who has studied language-acquisition counsels against crediting the young child with the adult's stimulus classes. Kirkpatrick (1904, p. 229), for instance, writes: "The child is always liable to associate a word with a different characteristic from the one intended. To one little girl, 'chair' meant not so much the article of furniture as the act of sitting, and to another, 'quack' meant not only a duck, but the water in which it was seen." The problem is to specify what counts as another instance of a particular stimulus class *for the child*.

Likewise, we need to know how the articulatory space is partitioned into response classes; that is, an estimate of the range of response-tokens which are elicited by an individual stimulus-token is required. No doubt there are strong innate constraints upon membership of both stimulus and response classes. With respect to stimuli, we are not surprised to learn (Kirkpatrick, 1904) that " 'Kitty' meant to M not only the animal, but anything that was soft to the touch . . . " We would, however, be surprised if told that 'Kitty' meant 'the head and the tail' of any animal. With respect to response-classes, we already know a little about constraints upon the system of (universal) phonemic oppositions and their order of acquisition (cf Chomsky and Halle, 1968; Jakobson, 1941, 1960).[7] Finally, we require an account of the mechanisms responsible for observed stimulus-response pairings. Some, no doubt, are 'built in'—cries of pain and coos of pleasure seem obvious candidates. Other pairings are clearly learned. I shall assume for the moment (more out of convenience than conviction) that the operant conditioning story is the correct one That is, given schema of the type: —

If 5 then $((z)$ (at $p=0/1$ as a function of R))

where p is a probability measure which varies between 0 and 1 and R is an appropriate reinforcer, I assume that letters initially enter the response-space at random, and that 'training' consists of occurrences of (innately-given) positive reinforcers increasing the probability values attached to particular stimulus-response pairings (and conversely for negative reinforcers).

If no relevant information is obtainable other than the existence of stable, statistically-significant stimulus-response pairings of the nature described above, then the appropriate terminology for describing 'what is learned' is Skinnerian tacts or Quinian 'occasion utterances'. Under these circumstances, the temptation to impute 'higher' processes because, for example, the stimulus-space looks 'abstract' (whatever that means) or the response-space looks 'complex' (whatever that means) must be resisted. The occurrence of a particular vocalisation (within the domain of an If/Then rule) is 'indicative' of the prior

C

occurrence of a particular value in the perceptual-space. No more need be said—no higher 'ontology' can be justified without further data.

Stage 2. Stimulative utterances

Interestingly enough, Buhler gives an anti-mentalist account of the stimulative (or 'release' or 'communicative') stage. The relevant passage (Buhler, 1930; p. 55) reads as follows: "When a sound exists or is suitable for releasing in the audience a certain attitude, we shall call this the function of release. The clucking of the hen, for example, obviously fulfils the natural purpose of making the chicks run to the mother, or at least of keeping them together. The so-called warning cry of many gregarious animals that place 'sentinels' like the chamois, belongs to this category. When the particularly observant 'sentinel' notices something suspicious, he emits a cry and the whole herd take to flight. That is release. Whether the animal itself knows anything about the objectively purposive connection or not, is for the time being, irrelevant to our concept."

The last line reveals Buhler's account as 'Skinnerian' (with due allowance for the anachronism of this description). The logic of Skinner's 'mands' would likewise regard as an irrelevance remarks about any 'purposive' connection between mand and consequence. Skinner would presumably despair of a scholar who 'thought' that certain utterances of 'Please pass the salt' indicated that the speaker 'wanted' to be given the salt. In the absence of further evidence, he would, of course, be quite right to despair. Skinner (1957, p. 35) describes mands as follows: "In a given verbal community, certain responses are characteristically followed by certain consequences. *Wait!* is followed by someone's waiting and *Sh-h!* by silence. Much of the verbal behaviour of young children is of this sort. *Candy!* is characteristically followed by the receipt of candy and *Out!* by the opening of a door." 'Purposes' and 'intentions' are characteristically absent from this description.

Buhler's account of the release function fails to capture any interesting conception of 'communicative' stimuli; in particular, it fails to specify a system that could be developmentally progressive. For Buhler, it just so happens that certain indicative expressions are regularly followed by (biologically-useful) responses performed by another organism. The indicative expressions which do have this consequence are called 'stimulative'. It is here that Skinner's account is superior to Buhler's. If, as before, we represent tacts according to the schema:

If 5 then $(\,(z)\,(\text{at } p=0/1 \text{ as a function of } R)\,)$,
then we might try to represent mands as

(If 5 and $7_{+Animate}$) then $(\,(z_b)\,(\text{at } p=0/1 \text{ as a function of } R_b)\,)$.
That is, the 'simplex' stimulus for a tact (5) is developed into the complex stimulus (5 and $7_{+Animate}$) to represent the fact that (Skinner, 1957) "The speaker does not ordinarily emit the response when no one is present." Furthermore, the generalised (positive) reinforcement which increases the probability of emitting a tact is developed into a specific reinforcement $(\,(z_b) \text{ at } p=0/1 \text{ as a function } R_b)$ which is appropriate to the particular response. I have represented this as subscript congruence between z and R. As Skinner (1957, p. 57) puts it, a mand "may be defined as a verbal operant in which the response is reinforced by a characteristic consequence . . . ".

The above schema for mands is, however, manifestly inadequate as it stands. The most natural 'empiricist' interpretation of stimulus-terms in the tact schema is to regard them as applying to "medium-sized lovable or edible physical objects in the foreground of sense and interest" (Davidson, 1965). But it is precisely these terms that cannot (without further elaboration) plausibly figure as stimuli in a natural interpretation of stimulus position in mands. In 'mentalist' terminology, mands are commands that the *present* state of the world be changed, or requests for something which is *not* present here and now. It sounds a little peculiar to say that the *stimulus* for saying *Out!* is that the child is currently in, or that the stimulus for saying *Ball!* is the presence of an Alice-like noball. 'Mentalists' have typically avoided this problem (or pseudo-problem) by postulating that 'mand-like' utterances are holophrastic sentences in which only the predicate term is actually verbalised. Accordingly, they would interpret *Out!* as a reduced version of, for example, 'Take me out!'; likewise, *Ball!* becomes a variant of, for example, 'I want the ball', 'Give me the ball!', etc. (cf de Laguna, 1927.) This strategy, however, raises problems of its own, as McNeill (1969) points out: "In what sense do children have in mind the content of a full sentence while uttering a single word? No one believes that children have detailed and differentiated ideas in the adult manner. On the contrary, everyone who has written on the earliest stages of language acquisition agrees that the conceptual side of holophrastic speech is undifferentiated and global."

It is obvious, however, that there is a behaviourist solution to this complex of issues, a solution which does not necessitate semantic ascent in describing 'what is learned'. So far, I have assumed that the stimulus-space consists of discrete, unconnected points. This ignores

35

the fact that the child can learn 'associative' connections between points in the stimulus-space and events, other than its own responses, that have followed them. Some of these following events will have been verbal stimuli. Thus the child will have entered into memory correlations between 'internal' states (eg hunger, thirst, etc) and utterances such as 'Drink your *milk*', 'Here's your *milk*' etc. Likewise, external stimuli (eg chairs) will be 'associated' with utterances such as '*Up* you go'. We can now embed these correlations into the triggering term of If/Then connections. An example of a full schema for mands will now read:

$$((\text{If } 7_{+Animate} \text{ and } 5_a (5 \rightarrow 6_b)) \text{ then } Z_b) \text{ (at } p=0/1 \text{ as a function of } R_{ba}).$$

Essentially, what is being claimed is that the triggering conditions for evoking the mand 'Milk!' are (1) the perceived presence of a person $(7_{+Animate})$; (2) food-deprivation (5); (3) the existence of an association in memory between 5 and 'Milk'. The rule simply says 'Under these circumstances, move 6_b from the store attached to the stimulus-space into the response-space'. Appropriate reinforcement (reinforcement, that is, which cancels the second term in the stimulus-space, in this case a drink of milk) increases the probability of the final transition in the schema.

An organism which performs according to this schema may be regarded as having the capacity to 'communicate' (not merely to 'indicate'), albeit in a strictly behaviourist (non-purposive) sense. That is, if the entirety of the organism's 'communicative' responses are appropriately described in terms of the schema, there is, *pace* Skinner, no justification for crediting the animal with 'purposes' (or the ability to name, predicate, describe, ask, command, etc). I see no reason to doubt that higher primates other than man should be capable of reaching this stage. The observations of the Gardners *seem* consistent with this level of responding (see p. 24). Nonetheless, the stage is still 'primitive' in the sense that such responses are no more than complex forms of Quinian occasion-utterances. However, whilst it may be necessary to credit chimpanzees with this ability, there is every reason to doubt that many of the 'natural' signals of birds, insects, lower primates, etc, customarily called 'communicative' in textbooks (eg Sebeok, 1968), manifest this level of performance. My doubts are not so much concerned with the inappropriateness of invoking learning-theories to describe the acquisition of 'natural' signals, but rather with the fact that the evocation of these signals does not, in general, appear to depend upon the perceived presence of a putative message-recipient.

No doubt there are good biological reasons why this should be so, especially for animals whose habitat is densely foliated. Alarm cries are too important to be triggered by the conjoint perception of a predator *and* a co-species animal. Predators suffice.

Stage 3. Representational utterances

The first stage of utterance-learning which some writers have claimed is truly language-like (in the sense that it manifests the beginning of 'symbolisation') is the point where the child 'realises' that anything can be talked about appropriately. That is, there is a general rule that in such and such a situation it is appropriate to say so and so, even if, as a young child, you do not know what the so and so is. There is an apparent conflict in the mentalist literature concerning the question of whether this stage initially takes the form of 'realising' that everything has a 'name' or that expressions may be 'predicated' of anything. Stern (1914) exemplifies the 'naming' account, and he reports two "symptoms" of the realisation: (1) "the suddenly awakened enquiry as to the names of things"; (2) "the increase—often proceeding by leaps and bounds—of vocabulary . . . " Buhler (1930, p. 57) develops a similar position: "On the basis of already existing reproductive associations it pronounces the word 'dada' when it sees the father and the corresponding associated words for other objects; it is only when an object is met with that has not as yet been associated with anything, that the child stops and calls for the help of the adults by means of unequivocal gestures. This shows that the situation calls up a 'problem' in the child's mind, a problem for which it has the general source of solution —enunciating a word—but not always the particular means—a definite word."

Contrasting with this position, Sully (1885), de Laguna (1927) and McNeill (1969) argue that 'signifying' expressions are first acquired as predicates, or, more accurately perhaps, as 'comments' upon the extra-linguistic 'topics' provided by the non-verbal environment. Their views are thus closely similar to Vygotsky's (1934) interpretation of 'inner speech': "Inner speech is almost entirely predicative because the situation, the subject of thought, is always known to the thinker." Whilst de Laguna and McNeill do not discuss their predicative hypothesis with reference to Stern's observations, it would be consistent with their general position for them to re-interpret Stern's "symptoms" as indicating that the child was not asking 'What is so-and-so called?' but rather was inquiring 'Given such-and-such a situation, what is it appropriate to say about it?'

Both sets of authors are agreed that the child's one-word utterances are holophrastic sentences; the conflict is over the 'translation' of these sentences and hence over what the child 'means' by his gestures and 'interrogative' utterances when the stage of inquiry is reached. Some sample 'translations' demonstrate this point quite clearly. Stern (English translation, 1924, p. 148) writes: "It is not enough to translate the child's *mama* into adult speech by the one word 'mother', but sentences must be used, as: *'Mother, come here', 'Mother, give me', 'Mother, set me on the chair', 'Mother, help me'*, etc". For Stern, then, the utterance of 'Mama' is vocative, with the propositional content unexpressed. Sully (1885, p. 435), however, 'translates' as follows: "When a child of eighteen months on seeing a dog exclaims 'Bow-wow', or on tasting his food exclaims 'Ot' (hot), or on letting fall his toys says 'Dou' (down), he may be said to be implicitly framing a judgement: 'That is a dog', 'This milk is hot', 'My plaything is down'." For Sully, these utterances are 'comments' with an unexpressed 'topic'. Once again, Vygotsky (1934) puts the issue in a nutshell: "One might say without exaggeration that the whole structure of a theory is determined by the translation of the first words of the child." It is apparent that assumptions about the vocative/predicate controversy will interact quite strongly with related arguments about the 'parts-of-speech' which are represented in the child's early verbalisations (cf Dewey, 1894). Scholars who are prepared to credit the young child with 'verbs', 'adjectives' and 'prepositions' will obviously gravitate towards supporting the predicate hypothesis, although the converse implication need not hold. The apparent predominance of nouns (ie words which are nouns for adults) in the early speech of some children is probably to be explained in terms of the biases of *adults*. For example, the child sees (and points to) a rabbit running quickly across an open space. One suspects that, in this situation, adults are more likely to say 'That's a *rabbit*' than, for example, 'That's *running*', 'That was *fast*', 'It ran *across*', etc. Some further problems in assuming that adult-language nouns are also child-language nouns are noted by Kirk-patrick (1904): "In reality, however, the noun idea is not so prominent . . . for words that in adult language are nouns are to the child verbs, or else the distinction is not yet made. For instance, *M* used 'bed' in the sense of lie down, just as we use 'dress' to mean the act as well as the object. Prepositions also are at first for the child nearly always verbs, 'up' or 'down' signifying the act rather than the position." The assumption in almost all the writings of this period is that the child's language cannot be interpreted without reference to his ontology. 'Notional' definitions of the parts-of-speech fit neatly into this schema (cf Lyons, 1966).

Whilst Buhler and Vygotsky criticise what they take to be Stern's overly 'intellectual' account of what the child has learned upon reaching the stage of inquiry, they are both convinced that the stage constitutes a "decisive turning point in the child's linguistic, cultural, and intellectual development . . . " (Vygotsky, 1934). Vygotsky furthermore claims that the capacity for this type of inquiry is not to be found in animals other than man. It will therefore be of considerable interest to see if Washoe confirms or refutes his conjecture. Vygotsky's argument against Stern's interpretation of the stage of inquiry is that the realisation by the child of a general *link* between situations and vocalisations is not, in itself, sufficient evidence for claiming that the link is conceived of as *symbolic*. Rather, Vygotsky believes, the child thinks of the tie as one in which the word is a 'property' or 'attribute' of a perceived object or situation. Vygotsky's account of the child's 'pre-symbolic' knowledge of words is not too easy to understand. I find it helpful to interpret his remarks as follows: the child acquires cross-modal knowledge of objects. He learns to associate a particular *visual* representation X (a cat, for adults) with a particular *acoustic* representation (a 'mew'). Similarly, he associates X with the acoustic representation 'cat'. In other words, a correlation is a correlation is a correlation. Buhler (1930, p. 131) is equally convinced that Stern's interpretation is misleading: "We have already noticed that the child behaves as though it had discovered the general truth that every object has a name. I hope no one will venture to make the trivial remark that a child one year of age cannot be credited with such profound philosophical penetration! Naturally not in the way we have formulated it."

We might accordingly try to capture a 'behaviourist' account of the stage of inquiry in the following manner. Assume that some situation (n) which can enter the stimulus-space has not been associated with a situation-specific verbalisation in the memory-space; ie n ($n \rightarrow \emptyset$), where $\emptyset$ is a null symbol. Such situations may originally be accompanied by non-verbal indication of excitement and interest and by pointing. The child may also have a cover term for use in this situation, eg 'Dat' (acquired from observation of utterances such as 'That's a cat', 'That's Daddy', 'That's hot', etc?). It is furthermore possible that the child has noticed that utterances which frequently evoke a verbal response from adults have a characteristic intonation contour (cf Meumann, 1903). What seems to be required, then, is a rule whereby the child can produce (perhaps iteratively) one of these non-situation-specific responses (or indeed run through a set of them) until an adult responds verbally. That response (or part thereof) is then entered into the memory-space as a replacement for the first occurrence of $\emptyset$. An account of this nature could cover the relevant observations and still permit us to agree with Buhler and Vygotsky that the child had not yet realised the 'symbolic' nature of the tie between word and object. It also permits us to sidestep the argument over the vocative/predicative nature of holophrastic utterances until a more detailed account of the opposing theories is available. McNeill (1969) presents what is, so far, the most cogently argued case for the predicative hypothesis.

D. A neo-classical approach

We seem, then, to be back to Buhler's original claim—the ability to perform an act of judgement and to express that judgement by means of a proposition is what constitutes being a language-user.[8] Buhler is well aware of the difficulty of obtaining evidence which would support crediting an organism with this ability. He is, however, equally aware of the necessity of obtaining such evidence. For example, Buhler (1930) discusses some observations of Preyer's in which it is argued that appropriate generalisation of the response 'hot' indicates that the child can express judgements. Concerning these observations, Buhler (1930, p. 128) writes: "Preyer claims that these are the first judgements which his child formulated in language, and I do not doubt that they were real judgements. But if science is to advance, it must look for objective criteria." Buhler's (1918) remarks on the truth-functional aspects of sentence-use point to the type of evidence that we need.

Imagine an organism which is capable of perceiving forms and colours. We can test the animal's powers of learning and discrimination by 'conditioning' discrete responses to instances of shape-and colour-stimuli. Assume that we can train the animal to lift its left leg as a response to *all* and *only* circles (irrespective of colour) and to lift its right leg to *all* and *only* squares (irrespective of colour); viz,

Circle $\rightarrow$ Left
Square $\rightarrow$ Right

We next train the animal to nod once to *all* and *only* blue objects, irrespective of their shape. For green objects, the animal is trained to nod twice, for yellow objects, three times, and so on for a reasonably sized ensemble of colours, viz, —

Blue $\rightarrow$ Nod
Green $\rightarrow$ Nod, nod
Yellow $\rightarrow$ Nod, nod, nod
etc.

The next stage is to discover the animal's combinatorial ability. We present the complex stimulus CB (a blue circle) and reward the complex response LN (raise left leg and nod). Similarly, when the animal is presented with SG (a green square), we reward RNN (raise right leg and nod twice). If the animal is capable of 'generalising' from rewarded training-trials to other correct responses to complex stimuli which have not been individually trained, we can credit the animal with minimal combinatorial abilities. We now reverse the stimulus and response orderings. The experimenter shrugs his shoulders, lifts his left leg and nods; the animal is rewarded if it selects (eg 'points to') the blue circle from a stimulus-array consisting of a large number of colour/shape pairings, viz:

Shrug: Raise left leg; Nod $\rightarrow$ Select Blue Circle.

If responses of this nature generalise to other correct complex stimuli without further training, eg:

Shrug: Raise right leg; Nod $\rightarrow$ Select Blue Square,

we might venture a guess that the animal recognises some kind of isomorphism between (formally-identical) putative 'referring' expressions which can occur both in the stimulus-space and in its own response-space. The final stage is a little more complex: the experimenter presents a complex stimulus, performs a complex response, and rewards two *new* responses (raising the head, U, and lowering the head, D) elicited from the animal, according to the following schema:

(CB) : (LN) $\rightarrow$ U
(CB) : (RN) $\rightarrow$ D

If responses of this nature generalise correctly to other stimuli, eg $(SG) : (RNN) \rightarrow U$; $(SG) : (RN) \rightarrow D$, we have the beginnings of evidence that the animal can 'use' responses and 'interpret' stimuli 'representationally'. That is, the logical form of what has been learned is consistent with (although it does not entail) interpreting U and D as 'Yes' and 'No', or 'True' and 'False'. To put it slightly more neutrally, the complex pairings which are being presented in the stimulus-space are permissible/impermissible, according to the rules which the animal has previously acquired, under an interpretation in which LN,

41

for example, 'refers' to a blue circle. (For an excellent discussion of successive stages in the child's learning of the semantic representation of 'No', see McNeill and McNeill, 1968; for discussion in the context of 'the language of bees' see also Collins, 1968.) The above description of a 'symbol-using' organism should be regarded as an absolutely *minimal* characterisation of the abilities which must be possessed before it makes sense to credit a child or a chimpanzee with language-skills. It is obviously a far cry from the ability I have described to the full range of representational and communicative skills that every normal adult possesses.

However, I suspect (although I cannot show) that the type of 'formalist' approach to symbolisation that I have been pursuing here cannot be pushed much further. In particular, it seems necessary that adequate characterisations of a language-using organism (or automaton) should incorporate accounts of basic speech-acts (Austin, 1962). In order to describe the relevant 'communicative' relationships involved in referring, describing, stating, etc, a tri-partite internal organisation must be imputed to the language-user. I claim, then, that 'symbol-using' animals are characterised by the inter-relationships between three (functionally-distinct) components of language ability within an individual animal. These components are: (1) An internal model of the animal's world; (2) a grammar; (3) a model of *appropriate* internal state-changes (contingent upon the reception of structures generated by the grammar) in *another* organism. The relationships between these components are shown (in an overly schematic fashion) in Figure 1.

Briefly, I intend Figure 1 to represent the following facts: 'States of the world' are associated with sets of linguistic descriptions which are evaluated as true or false of those states; the (covert) utterance of particular (truth-conditionally evaluated) linguistic objects is evaluated with respect to appropriate state-changes in (the model of) another organism. I submit that nothing *less* than this degree of internal organisation is required if we are to credit an animal with language-skills. Theories of language-users which would, in principle, disallow this do not merit serious consideration. (It should be noted that, in Figure 1, I am using the notion 'grammar' in a sense which is widely extended from the customary use. I mean here by 'grammar', a production-reception mechanism for linguistic objects. This mechanism undoubtedly 'contains' a grammar in *some* sense, but probably not in a manner which is functionally distinct from the 'strategies' by which linguistic knowledge is realised.)

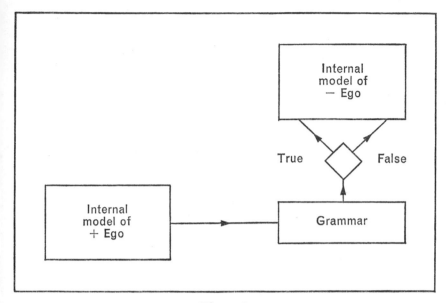

Figure 1

I shall now give some (very simple) examples of everyday situations which will, I hope, show why we need to consider theories of the language-user within the framework I have outlined. Consider a situation characterised by my conjoint perception of a red cup on a table and a person who, I believe, speaks English. The covert utterance 'There's a red cup on the table' is tagged 'true' and the semantic representation of the utterance is entered into my internal model of —Ego. We now subdivide the model of —Ego into two components— comprehension (into which we have entered the semantics of the utterance) and appropriate response (both verbal and non-verbal). In the case where there is no connection between the utterance and the preceding 'context of situation' we might expect that the entry in the appropriate-response sub-component would be zero (or a representation of the class of 'puzzlement' responses. Raised eyebrows, shrugs, 'So what?' are some of the more common manifestations in our culture). When made overt, such an exchange can be considered as the minimal 'degenerate' case of communication. Whilst degenerate, however, the case is not pathological. It would only be so if a cat or a (known) monolingual speaker of Mandarin were substituted for the English-speaker in the stimulus-conditions. The suggestion that I am making here seems capable of capturing at least one philosophical

43

answer to the question 'What does referring consist of?' MacKay (1968) claims that "referring is making *knowable* (not known) to our audience what we are talking about". The organisation of linguistic knowledge that I propose is at least consistent with MacKay's definition of referring.

Consider now a slightly more interesting case involving, for instance, myself and my wife. The stimulus-conditions are as follows: a representation in the internal model for +Ego of

1. My knowledge that there is only one piece of cake left in the refrigerator.
2. My desire to eat that last piece of cake.
3. The utterance (by my wife who, I know, knows where our cake is kept, and 'directed' to me) 'I want a piece of cake'.

The implicit utterance (by me) 'There is no cake left' is tagged as 'false'. The semantic interpretation of my utterance is entered into my internal model of —Ego. I also enter into the response section of the —Ego model a negative non-verbal specification (that my wife will not open the refrigerator) and a positive verbal specification (that the class of 'annoyance' responses is appropriate). I claim that any overt realisation of such an exchange is not truly 'communicative' unless it is backed by, at least, this degree of internal organisation. Any stimulus-response model of communication which does not characterise the fact that people can lie (appropriately) and know that they are so doing does not, to my mind, count as a model of communication. The fact that only humans talk *and* only humans indulge in the scientific enterprise is due to the fact that both skills presuppose the ability to lie (as a special case of the ability to entertain counterfactual conditionals). (See also Morton, *this volume,* p. 94.)

Simple-minded versions of stimulus-response theory, as applied to language, have been misleading because of the stress they have placed upon the *prediction* of actual responses and the consequent neglect of the 'logical backing' of those responses. A more plausible aim for the psychology of language is the delineation of classes of *appropriate* responses. Such a delineation will clearly include a specification of the "happiness" conditions (the term is Austin's) for the performance of speech-acts. (Some of the most interesting observations which are relevant to psycholinguistics will be found in Searle, 1969 and Rescher, 1966.) What must be characterised is the shared knowledge which makes possible the 'happy' performance of speech-acts. We must distinguish, then, between models of linguistic competence and what might be called models of language-competence. Cohen (1968) notes that the traditional characterisations of linguistic competence by generative grammars "completely ignore a normal speaker's ability to render his utterances appropriate to their socio-physical setting . . . ". He claims, correctly I feel, that "A machine that was able only to utter grammatical sentences, and paraphrase those it heard, independently of their socio-physical context of utterance, would not constitute a model for a normal speaker-hearer . . . ". One can, I think, agree with these sentiments without regarding them as a *criticism* of generative linguistics. That is, no useful purpose would be served by blurring the distinction between linguistic competence and language competence, although the extent to which the two develop separately has always been regarded as a vital empirical issue. Chomsky (1967, p. 84) has taken an extreme stand on this point: " . . . I think one could design an automaton which never thinks but which has the capacity of acquiring any specific human language in a rather short time from a small amount of data." It would be most interesting if this conjecture turned out to be true. A related, although somewhat less extreme, claim was made by Vygotsky (1934; English translation, 1962, p. 46) when he argued that the child "masters syntax of speech before syntax of thought". Whilst one can see a certain plausibility in both of these assertions, it is far from clear to me how either author could state the *syntax* of the child's utterances without knowing which propositions the child wished to convey (cf the previous discussion of 'holophrastic' sentences). Be that as it may, a healthy *general* theory of developmental psycholinguistics must provide an account both of the acquisition of linguistic structures and of the speech-acts that the child can perform by using them.

It would, of course, be ridiculous to suggest that the child's increasing mastery of the 'appropriateness' conditions for producing certain types of utterance has not been studied. Ever since the publication of Piaget's *Language and Thought of the Child* in 1926, arguments concerning the nature and significance of 'egocentric' speech have centred around precisely this topic. The only drawback (with respect to the problems discussed here) to such studies of 'role-taking' (Flavell, 1966) and 'communicative competence' (Glucksberg and Krauss, 1967; Krauss and Glucksberg, 1969) is that the particular tasks used are very difficult. Thus failures to demonstrate communicatively-adequate performance in, for example, five-year-olds do not necessarily indicate that the child has no concept of, for example, referring, naming, predicating, describing, etc. Rather, such failures *may* simply show that the child's performance is restricted. (After all,

45

no one would claim that a lecturer who loses his audience does not know the rules of the teaching-game.) It should also be noted that, whilst there is no argument about the occurrence of 'egocentric' speech in young children, recent experimental work strongly suggests that Vygotsky's interpretation of it is correct—that is, private speech plays a vital role in cognitive self-guidance (cf Kohlberg, Yaeger and Hjertholm, 1968). It is difficult to see how language could have this function unless the child had a basic grasp of how language 'represents' reality. Thus, it would appear that whilst some of the child's monologues express hypotheses concerning the syntactic structure of his language (Weir, 1962), others are representations of operations on internal world-models.[9] For communication to take place in adults, it is obviously necessary that the production and reception of linguistic utterances should result in semantic congruence between the contents of two minds. It is consistent with this end point that parents correct the factually misleading utterances of their children but do not bother to correct immature grammatical forms when the meaning seems clear (Brown, Cazden and Bellugi, 1969; Brown and Hanlon, 1970).

E. Coda

I have devoted much time and space to discussing classic writings that the cognescenti might consider interesting but outmoded. My excuse (or reason, depending on one's point of view) is this: I firmly believe that the central problem for psychological theories of language-acquisition is precisely what traditional mentalists thought it was—namely, explaining the development of 'symbolisation'. Radical behaviourists have always dismissed this as a pseudo-problem; for them, there are no such beasts as symbols. This position is patently false; yet the generative-grammar approach has been equally misleading. Scholars working in this tradition have paid lip-service to the creativity of language-use (a combination of freedom from stimulus-control *and* appropriateness to the situation). In their substantive writings, however, they have concentrated upon the *formal* structure of the child's successive grammars. This has diverted attention from the 'interpretation' of these structures and the role that they play in our thought and behaviour. The 'competence' problem for developmental psycholinguists could usefully be set by theories of (formal) universal grammar *and* of speech-acts *and* of symbolisation. That this is easier said than done should not cause us to lose sight of the goal. I would not wish, however, to have my emphasis upon the latter two problems construed as an implicit attack upon the importance of

46

generative grammars in describing the stages of language-acquisition.

Of course, anyone who is interested in language-acquisition will want to know what type of grammar underlies the child's output at different ages. It is similarly of interest to know what type of grammar underlies the behavioural repertoires of other species (cf Pribram and Tubbs, 1967; Tubbs, 1969). Suppes (1969) has argued that one might manage to train monkeys to perform as "reasonably complex one-sided grammars". Such a demonstration would be profoundly fascinating. But even if a chimpanzee, eg Washoe, could be trained to produce sequences of gestures which necessitate description in terms of the mathematics of *Aspects of the Theory of Syntax* (Chomsky, 1965), this, in itself, would not constitute grounds for crediting it with a language. Extrapolating back to the child, writing grammars that contain the rule *Sentence → Subject + Predicate* does not guarantee that the child knows how to predicate.

Footnotes

[1] I apologise to Professor Roland Puccetti for, partial, 'plagiarism' in my choice of title. See Puccetti, 1966.

[2] Esper (1968) provides an excellent summary of the behaviourist tradition with respect to language-studies.

[3] I am grateful to R. C. Oldfield for bringing this point to my attention.

[4] I propose that this postulate should be christened *Skinner's Last Stand*. That is, if one regards the species as a single unit, extinction can be interpreted as a particularly extreme value of negative reinforcement.

[5] Some behaviourist writers refer to *names* as *labelling responses* but this merely adds to the terminological obfuscation.

[6] For those philosophers who distrust propositions as abstract entities, I am quite happy to reconstrue truth "as a relation between a sentence, a person and a time" (Davidson, 1967).

[7] Similarly, it is known that there are species-specific constraints upon acoustic response-spaces in non-human primates. Cf Lieberman, Klatt and Wilson, 1969.

8 This insight did not originate with Buhler, although he was perhaps the first psychologist to realise the *full* import of this position for theories of language-acquisition. An early, and most interesting, debate on the topic is contained in the Webbe-Brookes manuscripts, c. 1630. "As in doggs, that once hearinge the bell and presently feeling the lash, will never after heare the bell, but will runne away barking or crying . . . God forbidd we should call this judgement or understandinge" (Webbe, c. 1630; cf Salmon, 1969, for discussion).

9 One might note that whilst 'egocentric' speech may decline with age, 'egocentric' writing clearly does not (in academic households, at least).

References

ALLPORT, F. H. (1924), *Social Psychology*. Boston: Houghton Mifflin.

ALTMANN, S. A. (1968), Primates. In T. A. Sebeok (ed.), *Animal Communication*. Bloomington: Indiana University Press.

AUSTIN, J. L. (1962), *How to do things with words*. London: Oxford University Press.

BROOKES, W. (c. 1630), British Museum Sloane MS. 1466.

BROWN, R., CAZDEN, C. B., and BELLUGI, U. (1969), The child's grammar from I to III. In J. P. Hill (ed.), *1967 Minnesota Symposium on child psychology*. Minneapolis: Minnesota University Press.

BROWN, R. and HANLON, C. (1970), Derivational complexity and order of acquisition in child speech. In J. Hayes (ed.), *Carnegie-Mellon Symposium on Cognitive Psychology*. New York: Prentice Hall.

BUHLER, K. (1918), Kritische Musterung der neuern Theorien des Satzes. *Indogermanisches Jahrbuch*, **6**, 1-20.

BUHLER, K. (1930), *The mental development of the child*. London: Kegan Paul (1st German Edition 1918).

CHOMSKY, N. (1959), Review of *Verbal Behavior* by B. F. Skinner. *Language* 35, 26-58.

CHOMSKY, N. (1965), *Aspects of the Theory of Syntax*. Cambridge, Mass.: M.I.T. Press.

CHOMSKY, N. (1967), The general properties of language. In C. H. Millikan and F. L. Darley (eds.), *Brain mechanisms underlying speech and language*. New York: Grune and Stratton.

CHOMSKY, N. and HALLE, M. (1968), *The Sound Pattern of English*. New York: Harper and Row.

COHEN, L. J. (1968), What is the ability to refer to things, as a constituent of a language-speaker's competence? Paper read at the Olivetti Symposium on Language: Milan.

COLLINS, A. W. (1968), How one could tell were a bee to guide his behaviour by a rule. *Mind* 77, 556-560.

DAVIDSON, D. (1965), Theories of meaning and learnable languages. In *Proceedings of the 1964 International Congress for Logic, Methodology and Philosophy of Science*. Amsterdam: North-Holland Publishing Co.

DAVIDSON, D. (1967), Truth and meaning. *Synthese* 17, 304-323.

DEWEY, J. (1894), The psychology of infant language. *Psychological Review* 1, 63-66.

ESPER, E. A. (1968), *Mentalism and Objectivism in Linguistics*. New York: Elsevier.

FLAVELL, J. H. (1966), Role-taking and communication skills in children. *Young Children* 21, 164-177.

FODOR, J. A. (1965), Could meaning be an r_m? *J. verb. Learn. verb. Behav.* 4, 73-81.

FODOR, J. A. (1968), *Psychological Explanation*. New York: Random House.

GARDNER, R. A. and GARDNER, B. T. (1969), Teaching sign language to a chimpanzee. *Science* 165, 664-672.

GLUCKSBERG, S. and KRAUSS, R. M. (1967), What do people say after they have learned how to talk? Studies in the development of referential communication. *Merrill-Palmer Quarterly* 13, 309-316.

D

JACKSON, J. HUGHLINGS (1893), Words and other symbols in mentation. *Medical Press and Circular* **2**, 205-214.

JAKOBSON, R. (1941), *Kindersprache, Aphasie und allgemeine Lautgesetze.* Uppsala: Almquist and Wiksell.

JAKOBSON, R. (1960), Why 'Mama' and 'Papa'? In B. Kaplan and S. Wapner (eds.) *Perspectives in Psychological Theory.* New York: International Universities Press.

KIRKPATRICK, E. A. (1904), *Fundamentals of Child Study.* New York: MacMillan.

KOHLBERG, L., YAEGER, J. and HJERTHOLM, E. (1968), Private Speech: Four studies and a review of theories. *Child Development* **39**, 691-736.

KRAUSS, R. M. and GLUCKSBERG, S. (1969), The development of communication: Competence as a function of age. *Child Development* **40**, 255-266.

DE LAGUNA, G. A. (1927), *Speech: its function and development.* New Haven: Yale University Press.

LIEBERMAN, P. H., KLATT, D. H. and WILSON, W. H. (1969), Vocal tract limitations on the vowel repertoires of Rhesus monkey and other non-human primates. *Science* **164**, 1185-1187.

LYONS, J. (1966), Towards a 'notional' theory of the 'parts of speech'. *Journal of Linguistics* **2**, 209-236.

LLOYD MORGAN, C. (1909), *Psychology for teachers.* London: Edward Arnold.

MCNEILL, D. (1969), The development of language. In P. A. Mussen (ed.) *Carmichael's Manual of Child Psychology.* New York: Wiley.

MCNEILL, D. and MCNEILL, N. B. (1968), A question in semantic development: What does a child mean when he says "No"? In E. M. Zalc (ed.) *Proceedings of the Conference on Language and Language Behavior: University of Michigan.* New York: Appleton-Century Crofts.

MACKAY, A. F. (1968), Mr Donnellan and Humpty Dumpty on referring. *Philosophical Review* **77**, 197-202.

MARLER, P. (1967), Animal Communication Signals. *Science* **157**, 769-774.

MARSHALL, J. C. (1970), The biology of communication in man and animals. In J. Lyons (ed.) *New Horizons in Linguistics*. London: Penguin Books.

MEUMANN, E. (1903), *Die Sprache des Kindes*. Zurich: Zürcher and Furrer.

MEYER, M. (1921), *Psychology of the other-one*. Columbia, Missouri: Missouri Book Co.

MORGENBESSER, S. (1969), Fodor on Ryle and rules. *Journal of Philosophy* **66**, 458-469.

PIAGET, J. (1926), *Language and Thought of the Child*. English Trans. 1959. London: Routledge and Kegan Paul.

POPPER, K. R. (1953), Language and the Body-Mind Problem. In *Proceedings of the 11th International Congress of Philosophy*. Reprinted in *Conjectures and Refutations* (1963). London: Routledge and Kegan Paul.

PRIBRAM, K. H. and TUBBS, W. E. (1967), Short-term memory, parsing and the primate frontal cortex. *Science* **156**, 1765-1767.

PUCCETTI, R. (1966), Can humans think? *Analysis* **26**, 198-202.

QUINE, W. V. O. (1960), *Word and Object*. New York: Technology Press and Wiley.

QUINE, W. V. O. (1968). To Chomsky. *Synthese* **19**, 274-283.

RESCHER, N. (1966), *The Logic of Commands*. London: Routledge and Kegan Paul.

SALMON, V. (1969), Review of *Cartesian Linguistics* by N. Chomsky. *Journal of Linguistics* **5**, 165-187.

SEARLE, J. R. (1969), *Speech Acts*. Cambridge: Cambridge University Press.

SEBEOK, T. A. (1968), *Animal Communication*. Bloomington: Indiana University Press.

SKINNER, B. F. (1957), *Verbal Behavior*. London: Methuen.

STERN, W (1914), *Psychologie der fruehen Kindheit*. Leipzig: Quelle and Meyer.

51

SULLY, J. (1885), *Outlines of Psychology*. London: Longmans, Green and Co.

SUPPES, P. (1969), Stimulus-response theory of finite automata. *Journal of Mathematical Psychology* **6**, 327-355.

TUBBS, W. E. (1969), Primate frontal lesions and the temporal structure of behavior. *Behavioral Science* **14**, 347-356.

VYGOTSKY, L. S. (1934), *Thought and Language*. English Translation, 1962. Cambridge, Mass.: M.I.T. Press.

WEBBE, J. (c.1630), British Museum Sloane MS. 1466.

WEIR, R. H. (1962), *Language in the Crib*. The Hague: Mouton

WITTGENSTEIN, L. (1953), *Philosophical Investigations*. Oxford: Blackwell.

3

Explaining Linguistic Universals

David McNeill

Department of Psychology,
University of Chicago,
USA

A. Introduction

B. Strong and weak universals

C. Methods of classifying linguistic universals

A. Introduction

Even the simplest of child utterances includes relations that are universal in language. Previously (McNeill, 1966) I have pointed out that the combinations of grammatical classes in the speech of one of R. Brown's subjects perfectly corresponded at 26 months to the abstract definitions of the basic grammatical relations contained in linguistic theory. This was the case even though such definitions are abstract (eg, Subject and Predicate) and hold for the underlying structure of sentences but are often violated by the surface structure. There cannot be a grammatical relation between two verbs, for example, and double verb sentences did not appear in the child's speech. However, such surface structures are fairly common in adult speech: eg, *come and play, sit and eat, run and look,* etc.

More recently Bloom (1968) has shown conclusively that the grammatical relations are incorporated into the speech of young children. Bloom's data include detailed descriptions of the context in which the children's speech was uttered and she thereby was able to ascertain meaning with a high degree of accuracy. Essentially nothing failed to be meaningful and in accord with the basic grammatical relations.

These observations are of children who already have begun to combine words into phrases and short sentences. This kind of speech is fairly familiar and I will not present examples of it (cf Braine, 1963; Brown and Fraser, 1964). What is much less well known is that different grammatical relations are involved in child speech one or two months *before* words are first combined. The incorporation of grammatical relations in combinatorial speech is merely a continuation of developments that occurred some months earlier. So far as I know Dr Patricia Greenfield was the first to notice this remarkable phenomenon. The following examples are from a diary she kept of her own child's speech (personal communication). The first relation was the assertion of properties. At 12 months and 20 days (12;20) the child said *hi* when something hot was presented to her, and at 13;20 she said *ha* to an *empty* coffee cup—clearly a statement of a property since the appropriate thermal stimulus was absent. At 14;28 the child first used words to refer to the location of things as well as to their properties. She pointed to the top of a refrigerator, the accustomed place for finding bananas, and said *nana*. The utterance was locative, not a label or an assertion of a property, since there were no bananas on the refrigerator at the time. It was not the label for the refrigerator since bananas in other places were also called *nana*. A short while later a number of other grammatical relations appeared in the child's speech. At 15;21 she used *door* as the object of a 'verb' (meaning 'close the door'), *eye* as the object of a 'preposition' (after some water had been squirted in her eye), and *baby* as the subject of a 'sentence' (after the baby had fallen down). By the time words were finally combined, these several grammatical relations had been available for several months. Greenfield's daughter first combined words productively at 17 months but at 15 months had expressed such relational concepts as attribution, location, subject, and object. Combining words was a new method for expressing these same relations. The form of a sentence changes while the concept of a sentence does not.

The notion of a sentence apparently arises at the beginning of linguistic development. It is not the result of an extended period of learning, but is a condition for learning the structure of sentences in a language, in so far as these structures invariably express the basic grammatical relations. To understand the acquisition of language therefore requires an explanation of the concept of a sentence. From what developmental processes does it arise? Is it the outcome of a homogeneous force, or does it represent a convergence of different effects? These questions bring us to a fundamental distinction between types of linguistic universals. The remainder of the chapter will be devoted to the discussion of this distinction.

B. Strong and weak linguistic universals

The concept of a sentence cannot be given an absolutely precise definition at present. It amounts roughly to the underlying structure of sentences, minus the lexicon and minus probably many syntactical markers that control the application of transformations. It thus includes the basic grammatical relations and such universal categories as noun, verb, modifier, and sentence itself. Later I discuss the verb *promise*. It is a convenient illustration of a weak linguistic universal, and few clear-cut examples yet exist, but I doubt that the effect of *promise* belongs to the concept of a sentence (eg, one can imagine a language that has sentences but lacks the idea of promising).

To explain the concept of a sentence, and more generally to explain the existence of any linguistic universal (for not all universals belong to the concept of a sentence), two theories must be borne in mind. One is stated by Schlesinger (in press), who writes that the underlying structures of sentences " . . . are determined by the innate *cognitive* capacity of the child" and that "There is nothing specifically linguistic about this capacity". Sinclair-de-Zwart (1970) states the same theory when she writes, "Linguistic universals exist precisely because thought structures are universal", and Morton (this volume) agrees in writing, "What I am questioning is . . . that perhaps the innate component is not specific to language". I could have cited others, especially Slobin (1966) and Lenneberg (1967), as proposing the same theory.

I will call this the theory that linguistic universals are 'weak', and contrast it with another theory, that linguistic universals are 'strong'.

1. *Weak linguistic universals* have as a necessary and sufficient cause one or more universals of cognition or perception.

2. *Strong linguistic universals* may or may not have such universals as necessary causes, but they do have strictly linguistic abilities as necessary causes, so cognition and perception are never sufficient.

The advocates of the theory that linguistic universals are weak typically argue that all linguistic universals are weak. However, there is no necessity in this implication. The question of whether a given linguistic universal is weak or strong is entirely empirical. It is by no means beyond imagination that the general form of language results from the convergence of strong and weak universals. The first step toward explaining the concept of a sentence must therefore be this empirical classification. By what methods can it be done? A few preliminary suggestions are made below.

C. Methods of classifying linguistic universals

I will first mention two methods that will *not* serve to classify universals

55

as weak or strong. I mention them only because they have inappropriately been used by others to identify certain universals as weak. One is to seek parallels of form or function between cognition and language. When parallels exist the linguistic universal is explained as a reflection of the cognitive one. An example of this line of reasoning is the parallel between the object-action and subject-predicate relations, the first being cognitive and the second linguistic. However, this method is inconclusive because strong linguistic universals also can be parallel to cognitive universals. In fact, parallel form is to be expected for strong universals insofar as a capacity for language evolved to express thought. The difference between a weak universal and a strong universal that parallels a cognitive one lies in the existence, within the strong universal, of a strictly linguistic ability, whose ontogenesis (and phylogenesis) is separate from that of its associated cognitive ability. So the striking similarity between the structure of thought at the end of the sensory-motor period and the structure of child sentences at the same time is inconclusive. The linguistic forms can equally reflect weak or strong universals.

I just alluded to the second inconclusive method. It is to show a synchronisation in the development of parallel linguistic and cognitive forms. Not only does the relation of subject and predicate parallel that of object and action, but the resolution of the one accompanies the resolution of the other in development. The sensory-motor period closes at roughly 18 months with the distinction between object and action clearly drawn. At the same time words are first combined to express grammatical relations between actions and objects. Again, however, the method does not achieve a separation of weak and strong universals. For the only way a strong linguistic universal could fail to be in synchrony with a parallel cognitive universal is when the necessary linguistic ability develops *after* the associated cognitive one. In fact, as we see from Greenfield's observations, the reverse order holds in development. Some kind of linguistic ability appears before the conclusion of the sensory-motor period.

If parallels in form or function and synchrony of development will not distinguish strong and weak linguistic universals, how then can the classification be made? I have no doubt that several methods could be found. I will mention two and give an example of each.

1. *A constant cognitive effect achieved through inconstant linguistic means*

Linguistic universals corresponding to this rule probably are weak. An example is the effect of *promise,* which is the same in Japanese and English (and presumably all languages with the verb) but the linguistic means of achieving it are different. *Promise* reverses the normal actor and action relationships in sentences with complements. It does so in English by undoing the so-called Minimum Distance Principle, as in the word-order contrast between *John told* **Bill** *to come* and **John** *promised Bill to come* (Rosenbaum, 1967; Chomsky, 1969). The actor in each case is in bold face. Japanese accomplishes this effect by changing the postposition attached to the actor, as between *John-wa* **Bill**-*ni come told* ('John told Bill to come') and **John**-*wa Bill-ni come promised* ('John promised Bill to come'). The Minimum Distance Principle does not exist in Japanese, as *Bill-ni* **John**-*wa come promised* ('John promised Bill to come') and **Bill**-ni John-wa come told ('John told Bill to come') present the same contrast of meaning.

The effect of *promise,* the reversing of actor-action relations, presumably has a necessary and sufficient cause in the way the concept of promising is understood. It does not depend on any particular linguistic device since in English the means of expression is a reversal of word order whereas in Japanese it is an exchange of postpositions. Whatever method a language uses in general for indicating actor-action relations, the effect of *promise* is to reverse it.

Before the concept of promising has been grasped Japanese speaking and English speaking children make identical cognitive errors while differing linguistically. This is in accordance with the classification of *promise* as a weak universal. English speaking children think that Bill will be the one to come in *John promised Bill to come*; in this, they incorrectly follow the Minimum Distance Principle (Chomsky, 1968). Japanese children incorrectly follow the postposition *ni,* which usually indicates the receiver of an action, and thus they also think that Bill will be the one to come in *Bill-ni John-wa come promise.*[1] In both languages children follow the general rule for determining the actor in complement constructions and do not reverse this rule before the concept of promising has been grasped.

2. *A constant linguistic means is used to express an inconstant cognitive effect*

Universals that fit this rule are probably strong. Braine (1970) taught his young daughter two invented words, one the name of a kitchen utensil (*niss*) and the other the name of walking with the fingers (*seb*). The child had no word for either the object or the action before she was taught *niss* and *seb*. Neither word was used in a gram-

57

matical context by an adult but the child used both in the appropriate places. There were sentences with *niss* as a noun, such as *that niss* and *more niss,* and sentences with *seb* as a verb, such as *seb again* and *seb Teddy.* More crucially, there were sentences with *seb* as a noun, *that seb* and *more seb,* but none with *niss* as a verb. Braine noted the same asymmetry with actual nouns and verbs. It suggests that verbs are weak universals and nouns strong. Association with an action is necessary and sufficient to make a word into a verb but some strictly linguistic property makes a word into a noun (one is suggested below). Association with an object is not necessary for a word to be a noun and association with an action does not prevent it.

We cannot tell from Braine's observations if the association of a word with an object is sufficient for it to become a noun. If it is we should further subdivide linguistic universals into weak (cognition is necessary and sufficient), strong (cognition is necessary but not sufficient), and 'erratic' types. An erratic universal is one in which the linguistic universal has two sufficient causes and therefore no necessary ones. We cannot be certain at this point if such universals exist.

The division of nouns and verbs into the respective categories of strong and weak linguistic universals coincides with the relations of concord between nouns and verbs. Verbs are typically inflected to agree with nouns (eg, for number or gender), whereas nouns are rarely (or never) inflected to agree with verbs (eg, for tense or aspect). Concord depends on the strictly linguistic effects of nouns in an asymmetry that is the same as the asymmetry noted by Braine. In both, verbs assume noun characteristics but nouns remain uninfluenced by verbs. The properties of nouns responsible for concord can be represented as syntactic features. If there is a specific linguistic ability to organise words in terms of the features that appear with nouns, an ability which is quite distinct from the conceiving of objects, the asymmetry noted by Braine would be explained. Any word can be assigned these noun features, thereby becoming a noun, whereas the opposite process cannot take place since a roster of verb features does not exist. It is completely consistent with this theory that word formation by adults goes more naturally from verbs to nouns than from nouns to verbs. Noun features are available to be assigned to verbs, creating new nouns, but verb features are not available to be assigned to nouns.

The distinction between strong and weak linguistic universals must be respected if the concept of a sentence is to be explained. I have illustrated a methodology for making a classification into these two categories and have tried to show that plausible results can be obtained by employing it. I can only hope that others will contribute further methods. It will serve no useful purpose to assert, as many have done, that linguistic universals have a homogeneous cause. Such sweeping remarks cross the line between science and dogma.

Footnote

[1] This confusion appeared consistently in an experiment with 20 Japanese children, 4 and 5 years old, conducted at the Himawari School of Kyoto, Japan. I am most grateful to Nobuko B. McNeill, who conducted the experiment. Mr and Mrs M. Fujiki, the Headmaster and Headmistress of Himawari School, were generous in making available their students and facilities. The experiment was made possible by a grant (MH 17272-01) from the US National Institute of Health to Harvard University and by a travel and foreign expense award from the University of Chicago.

References

BLOOM, LOIS M. (1968), Language development: form and function in emerging grammars. Doctoral dissertation, Joint Comm. Grad. Instr., Columbia Univ.

BRAINE, M. D. S. (1963), The ontogeny of English phrase structure: the first phase. *Language* **39**, 1-13.

BRAINE, M. D. S. (1970), The acquisition of language in infant and child. In C. Reed (ed.), *The Learning of Language*. New York: Appleton-Century-Crofts.

BROWN, R. and FRASER, C. (1964), The acquisition of syntax. In Ursula Bellugi and R. Brown (eds.), *The Acquisition of Language*. Monogr. Soc. Res. Child. Develop, **29**, No. 1.

CHOMSKY, C. S. (1969), *The acquisition of syntax in children from 5 to 10.* Cambridge, Mass.: MIT Press.

GREENFIELD, PATRICIA (1970), Development of the holophrase (personal communication).

LENNEBERG, E. H. (1967), *The Biological Foundations of Language.* New York: Wiley.

MCNEILL, D. (1966), Development psycholinguistics. In F. Smith and G. A. Miller (eds.), *The Genesis of Language.* Cambridge, Mass.: MIT Press.

ROSENBAUM, P. S. (1967), *The Grammar of English Predicate Complement Structures.* Cambridge, Mass.: MIT Press.

SCHLESINGER, I. M., Production of utterances and language acquisition. In D. I. Slobin (ed.), *The Ontogenesis of Grammar.* New York and London: Academic Press (in press).

SINCLAIR-DE-ZWART, H. (1970), Sensorimotor action schemes as a condition of the acquisition of syntax. In R. Huxley and E. Ingram (eds.), *Mechanisms of Language Development.* New York and London: Academic Press.

SLOBIN, D. I. (1966), Comments on 'Developmental psycholinguistics.' In F. Smith and G. A. Miller (eds.), *The Genesis of Language.* Cambridge, Mass.: MIT Press.

4

Comparing and Contrasting

Roger Wales

Department of Psychology,
University of Edinburgh,
Scotland

A. Introduction

In commenting on a paper by Polanyi on *Beauty, elegance, and reality in Science,* Mackay observed (1962, p. 117) "I think he put his finger on something which one feels particularly with the behavioural sciences, where mathematical laws are often produced which do not give us any sensation of 'pleasant surprise'. Although they fit the facts perfectly, we have the unhappy feeling that their implications are all *summaries.*" It was perhaps just such a sensation of surprise which distinguished our reaction to Chomsky's theories of linguistics as compared, say, to our reaction to Zipf's Law. Similarly the early results of Miller and his colleagues seemed at the time pleasantly surprising. However, once Miller and then others had shown that fairly simple correlations wouldn't hold up between transformational complexity and measures involving the application of essentially old psychophysical methods, the formerly 'surprising' was now described as 'simpliste' and implausible. Since then it has sometimes been a little difficult to decide whose theories generate problems which challenge solution and whose generate problems which count as evidence against the theory, except perhaps in terms of the origin of the theory. The contemporary psycholinguistic scene is rather like the Scottish hills,

61

with beautiful vistas suddenly obliterated by mist, which the winds of change may just as suddenly disperse to allow further advance and wider views. (These hills are of course the only ones of any 'interest'!) With contemporary linguistics currently in ferment and the psychology of language in a somewhat infantile state, it seems best at present to try to grasp what sorts of variables and which sorts of questions are significant in this area of psychology.

This chapter[1] is concerned with the biological characteristics of man which seem to make him unique in his possession of language and with the ways in which the structure of sentences affects the relative ease of processing them. The first is considered from the vantage point of a study of the acquisition of comparision; the second is considered in the light of studies of the relevance of definiteness, topicalisation and presupposition in processing sentences. In conclusion certain aspects of both these issues will be drawn out and discussed.

B. A possible relational primitive

The issue of the biological basis of language has become a very live one in the past few years by virtue of Chomsky's anti-behaviourism and his advocacy of the need to reconsider the rationalist view of 'innate ideas'. Chomsky's (1965, footnotes p. 30, 47 *et seq.*) arguments refer to the failure in principle to account for the 'facts' of language acquisition simply in analytic empirical terms, and the need to postulate a theoretical parallelism between an account of the child's structural prerequisites to acquire language and the essential features of his general theory of language. This position has gained some apparent support from Lenneberg's researches arguing not only for language being something which is specific to our species but also that this is due to the particular way in which our brain is organised to handle this kind of information; that is, that a radical evolutionary discontinuity in cerebral organisation is to be observed in the relevant comparative study of primates, etc.

Two of the several lines of argument which Lenneberg (1967) has advanced to support his discontinuity view of the biological basis of language are based first on its independence of general intelligence and secondly on evidence of a critical period for first language learning. The claim about the independence of language capacity and general IQ is based on findings such as those with children who are severely retarded as indicated by IQ measures, but still acquire language. This evidence, of course, leaves completely out of account possible prelinguistic capacities which may be necessary precursors of language, for example, the Piagitean object constancies (cf Piaget and Inhelder, 1969) and social factors as emphasised by Vygotsky (1962). If such structural general capacities are found to be necessary—and it's a little difficult to see how naming etc could develop without them[2]—then we would merely have one more instance where global IQ measures are not very revealing. Secondly, the critical period hypothesis is held to be supported by the following kinds of evidence: on several physical measures human brain maturation reaches an asymptote at around the age of puberty; it also happens that a child who has a brain injury on the left side and loses its language before this date may relearn the language, but a child who receives the injury after this date, and who doesn't recover in the next six months, is unlikely to be able to relearn the language. While the evidence here is in fact rather tenuous—which is of course no fault of Lenneberg—it is also unclear what is being claimed. Is it that no language may be acquired on the right side as it were, after the critical period? In which case, whether the younger child relearns the language as if it were his first or his second language might be held to be unimportant. However, if the day comes when we can actually say whether first and second language learning are in fact anything more than superficially different, and if so in what ways, we might want to say that the child relearning the language is either recovering his first language or else learning it again as if it were a second language. This kind of issue would surely carry implications about what we were prepared to claim for the nature of the critical period. At present it seems unnecessary to fixate on certain theoretical assumptions when we just don't know. The following study is intended merely to suggest that evidence can be obtained and interpreted supporting some kind of continuity.

First however, a necessary aside on the grammar of comparison. A number of generative grammarians, notably Lees (1961), Smith (1961) and Chomsky (1965), have espoused a position which might be roughly illustrated as follows: with a sentence such as *John is more clever than Bill*. This would have a base structure of, matrix, *John is more than . . . clever* with constituent, *Bill is clever*. In the derivation the T-rules apply first to the embedded phrase marker and then to the full configuration to produce *John is more than ⧣ Bill is clever ⧣ clever*. The comparative transformation then deletes the boundary markers, the adjective in the embedded sentence and permutes the segments —*than Bill is*— and —*clever*— to produce *John is more clever than Bill is*. There is then a final option of deleting the second copula. There are a number of differences in these analyses and in fact Chomsky only uses

63

them to discuss problems these constructions raise for the then-current deletion conventions. Other problems with the above characterisation of comparatives have been indicated in Campbell and Wales (1969).

In an attempt to produce an alternative account that would bring the syntax and semantics closer together we have proposed that it is unnecessary to have a separate comparative transformation and that comparatives should be considered as simply the *adjectival* equivalents of transitive *verbal* sentences. Much of the motivation for this analysis follows from elaborating a parallelism between verbal and adjectival structures noted by many linguists. For example, Lyons (1966) has suggested that there is a close relationship between simple adjectival sentences, eg *Mary is beautiful,* and simple intransitives, eg *Mary dances.* We have argued that this misses the important distinction between adjectival sentences which contain 'contrary', and those which contain 'contradictory' predicates, and suggest that those which contain contradictories, eg *Mary is dead,* are to be related to simple intransitives, whereas those containing contraries, eg *Mary is beautiful,* are to be related to short passives since in both cases some sort of deleted following nominal is involved, either a complement of comparison or an agent. Full comparatives are then considered to be the adjectival equivalents of full passives. Comparatives are then treated as a class of locative constructions (in a very general sense of locative).[3] The formal details of either sort of description need not concern us here. They are contrasted in that one requires a comparative trans-formation, while the other does not; one treats the base adjective as absolute, while the other treats it as relational or essentially compara-tive. For example, one requires that *the plank is long* may read, roughly, *the plank is (absolutely) long, long* in some absolute sense is grammatically prior to *longer than,* whereas in our view *the plank is long* would have to read even in this form *the plank is (implicitly) longer than (some standard).* If there is any correspondence between grammars and the structural properties of young children's speech we should be able to find out if they handle the superficially uncompared adjective as either absolute or relational. Now anyone in any way familiar with the discrimination learning literature will be wondering if we saw the obvious parallel in this question to those studied in the transposition literature. For psycholinguists not raised in classical psychology let me summarise the point. While a number of the ancients, such as Wundt, had recognised the relativity of judgement, and Hobhouse (1901) had tried experimentally to establish, over against Thorndike, the relativity of discrimination and problem solving, it was Köhler (1917-18) who first showed clearly that children, apes and chickens transpose a relation of size or brightness from one pair of stimuli to another; that is, they learn to choose the larger or the brighter of two objects without regard to absolute size or brightness. The challenge to S-R theory of these findings did not go unanswered and Spence (1937) postulated a model involving different excitatory and inhibitory generalisation gradients to handle these results within an absolutist framework, and at the same time to handle the so-called distance effect, that is, the fact that the further away the test stimuli were from the training stimuli, the lower the likelihood of a relational response. Since those days there has of course grown up a large literature on the topic but it is perhaps worth commenting that no clear evidence seems to have been obtained showing definite absolute responses, though many results with several species do show, especially with the distance effect, a decrement of the relational response. There is some—controverted—evidence which suggests that the distance effect is overcome by the child of six or seven who can verbalise the relevant relation.

What we did was to take a number of series of six cylindrical blocks in ascending height or width or both, and present the first four in the series, then tell the child to 'give me the big one' (or wee, thick, thin, tall or short one). Then we would take away two blocks—in the case of 'big', the two smallest—and add two more—in the case of 'big', two larger ones—thereby continuing the series in the relevant direction. An 'absolute' judgement would be revealed by selecting the same block twice, a 'comparative' judgement by selecting the largest (or smallest) block on both occasions. The blocks were differently coloured, and the directionality or non-directionality of the series was manipulated to control for position effects in favour of comparative or absolute judgements. (This in fact made no great difference to the results.) Orders of presentation were counterbalanced. There were three groups of children of mean ages: Group 1: 5·6; Group 2: 4·6; Group 3: 3·6. The range of each group was less than one year. There was a total number of 36. The basic results are given in Table 1. We subsequently ran essentially the same experiment, this time using subseries which were five times the diameter (or height) of the original series—this was used rather than the more conventional five times the overall size, to try and ensure we obtained the distance effect if there was one. Some of the data are presented in Table 2. For 'big' and 'wee' the results are quite clear for all groups, with 'comparative' responses never dropping below 80% (most are above 90%) and 'absolute' responses never rising

E

Table 1

Results of choices across groups where the second sub-series (2) was ordered in the same direction as the first (positional) or where the position of the blocks in the two sub-series was randomised (non-positional)

Group	% correct on series (1)	Positional % correct on series (2)	Comparative*	Absolute†
1 (Mean age 5·6)	81·0	83·5	79·5	1·5
2 (Mean age 4·6)	74·0	69·0	64·0	9·0
3 (Mean age 3·6)	81·0	66·0	64·0	7·5
		Non-positional		
1	85·0	83·0	78·0	5·0
2	79·0	60·0	60·0	15·0
3	81·0	70·0	62·5	14·0

Table 2

Percentage selection of 'comparative' and 'absolute' responses—means of positional and non-positional groups

Group (double responses)	Big (Totalled) (72)	Wee (Totalled) (72)	Thick (24)	Thin (24)	Tall (24)	Short (24)
			Regularly graded series			
1 *	96	92	13	38	63	32
†	0	0	38	25	7	0
2 *	82	79	13	38	50	26
†	6	11	19	13	13	26
3 *	82	78	44	26	38	38
†	7	9	19	19	19	7

'Distance-effect' series (figures in parenthesis indicate scores where choices of either two relevant blocks of the extremal sub-series are pooled)

1 *	73(90)	56(90)	7(7)	32(50)	63(69)	32(38)
†	2(2)	2(2)	19(19)	13(13)	0(0)	19(19)
2 *	65(90)	57(76)	19(19)	7(32)	63(69)	19(19)
†	8(8)	4(4)	7(7)	7(7)	0(0)	26(26)
3 *	54(88)	42(77)	38(38)	19(44)	44(51)	32(38)
†	9(9)	9(9)	25(25)	13(13)	19(19)	26(26)

* Indicates the percentage of children making correct responses on both of series (1) and (2).
† Indicates the percentage of children making the correct response on series (1) and selecting the same block on series (2).

above 10%. With 'thick' and 'thin' neither the 'comparative' nor 'absolute' responses differ from a chance level. These findings are true for all series. With 'tall' from age 5·6 to 3·6 there is a decline in 'comparative' responding from 60% to 40%, while 'short' produces about 35% throughout. 'Absolute' responses increase insignificantly. Exactly the same tendency is true for the 'distance-effect' series except for a slight increase in 'comparative' responses throughout. This is the case when the choices for 'correct 1 and 2' are scored by pooling the choice for 'big' of either of the two largest blocks as 'correct'. This is plausible since operating on differences of, for example, 0·5 cm diameter, it is not easy to discriminate between them for size.

What this means is, I think, that when the children know the adjective they respond comparatively even to the so-called 'absolute' form of it. We also know from other studies that 'big' is the dominant spatial adjective for this age group and is almost always used correctly except when dimensions are in conflict, for example, with a series where the longest block has the smallest total area (cf Wales and Campbell, 1970). If the child does not understand the adjective then responses merely approach randomness. The important point is that there is no evidence for any intermediate stage of absolute responses between random response and comparative response. An interesting result is that the distance effect was not reflected in the children's choices, but in the youngest group there were some verbal indications of recognising a subjective discontinuity in the series, one child being particularly explicit and throughout commenting, 'that's the wee-wee one, that's the wee-big one', etc. Apart from this evidence of children seeing the relation between the first and second trials in each case, there is also evidence from asking (separate groups) 'which block did you choose before?' and the children usually give the right answer. Someone might truly observe that an instruction 'give me the big one' suggests a superlative rather than a comparative reading (in the restricted sense of 'comparative'). This is not particularly relevant to the argument at this point, since either reading is in our view a comparative one in the sense of reflecting a simple two-place relation. This is in contrast to the absolutist attempt to reduce comparative relations to one-place predicates (which is impossible without the psychologically implausible use of an infinite number of predicates). Now what I want to suggest is that the structural capacity that is required to learn simple forms of relational language, such as comparatives and transitive verbs, is no different from what is required to perform relationally in a discrimination learning task. That is, it would come as no surprise to us if there were formal continuities in the capacity to perform these two kinds of tasks appropriately. It is worth noting that Hobhouse made much the same point though in more general terms. Of course ours is only suggestive evidence since the issue will only be resolved when we know more about the psychological variables controlling the responses. More recently Harlow (1958) has argued that he expects to see the psychological evidence on the evolution of learning come more into line with the continuity evident in the neuroanatomical evidence. Perhaps the best expression of support for reconsidering the continuity issue is Lashley's (1951, p. 197) conclusion to his paper on the *Problem of serial order in behavior.* He asserted: "I am coming more and more to the conviction that the rudiments of every human behavioural mechanism will be found far down in the evolutionary scale and also represented even in primitive activities of the nervous system. If there exist, in human cerebral action, processes which seem fundamentally different or inexplicable in terms of our present construct of the elementary physiology of integration, then it is probable that that construct is incomplete or mistaken, even for the levels of behaviour to which it is applied." What seems to have bedevilled discussion of this kind of issue is not taking seriously the simple distinction between the formal properties of certain structures, and what we do with those structures: in this instance the distinction between properties of the language user as distinct from language use.

C. Structure and function

This raises the deep and complex issue of the functional relevance of the formal structures. It has been suggested that continuity might be claimed, on the basis of the similarity between the structures of walking and talking, and that this could lead to a *reductio ad absurdum* argument against the suggestion made here. In fact it does not seem a necessarily misleading view to consider the possibility that language is not a cognitively and biologically independent system. Rather it may have to be defined by the different structural systems which are brought to language and which are defined as the system of language by virtue of their functional co-ordination in that system of communication (cf Morton, this volume). We shall return to consider some implications of such a view of language in our conclusion. For the present we are particularly concerned with the biological problem and two points can be made. Some ethologists have felt it necessary to postulate that behaviour, like morphological characters (biological!), can change function in the course of evolution, that is, that behavioural characters can often be shown to have been 'derived' from movements which had a different function in the ancestor. However, before the flood gates are opened and every application of a theory of formal systems is used to support evolutionary continuity, we can point out the otherwise trite fact that functionally-similar judgements are required of the subjects both in transposition experiments and in our study here of the use of linguistic comparison. It therefore seems plausible to hold open the possibility that the child brings to the task of language acquisition structures already fundamental to the organisation of its visual perceptions.

D. Context and performance

Not only has the distinction been blurred between properties of the language user and language use, but also a great deal of confusion has resulted from the difficulty of distinguishing clearly between language and language use— or to put the point another way, idealisation has been confused with abstracting language from its communicative function. This point has been argued in some detail by Campbell and Wales (1970) with special reference to studies of child language. The second half of this chapter is concerned with sketching some experimental approaches to the problem of studying language use. In particular we will be trying to illustrate the point that, since subjects presented with sentences construct contexts for them if they are not supplied, it is both necessary and illuminating to study the variables involved in this kind of language use.

In the first study definiteness is used to predict the selection by adult subjects of topics of active and passive sentences. The second study is concerned with predicting the use of definiteness as a function of the systematic variation of the context. The importance of definiteness and topicalisation in these studies of the comprehension and production of sentences was assumed because of their relation to the presuppositions controlling the interpretation of the sentences and their contexts.

Some recent pioneer studies in this area have been conducted by Wason and Johnson-Laird. Wason (1965) showed that the relative difficulty of processing negative statements disappeared if contexts were found in which it was just as plausible to deny something as assert something else. Johnson-Laird (1968a, b) obtained findings with passive and active sentences which might be interpreted as indicating that the function of the passive is to emphasise the logical subject by placing it in the position of the surface subject. The importance of word order in handling sentences has been re-emphasised in Johnson-

Laird (1969) with experiments on multiply-quantified sentences. Now, Clark (1965) using a substitution-in-frames technique had found that there were clear differences in the kind of terms which were likely to be used as subjects or objects in active and passive sentences; for example, the surface subject of passives was more likely to be animate. This result made us wonder whether Johnson-Laird's kind of result was perhaps reflecting some other linguistic aspect than just word position. In particular we hypothesised that the relevant variable might not typically be word position but rather definiteness, which seemed to mark what the sentence was primarily about (ie its topic). We first of all used different sets of active and passive sentences with reversibility, definiteness, order of presentation, etc, all counterbalanced, and varying instructions the while, asked 120 subjects to indicate by underlining what they considered the sentence to be primarily about. With sentences in which one noun phrase was definitely marked and the other indefinitely, the one that was definitely marked was almost invariably underlined. In sentences of the form *the N V the N* there was some tendency, though a relatively small one, for the first NP to be underlined. In sentences of the form *a N V a N* the verb was as likely to be underlined as either noun phrase. It seemed that word position played some part but if there was any conflict with definiteness then the latter won hands down. An illustrative sample of the data is presented in Table 3. Note that where ambiguous quantifiers such as 'some' are concerned, they are ambiguous with respect to definiteness.

Table 3

Frequencies of selections of first or second nominal or verb
(n=40, with four instances of each sentence type)

		Selections		
	Example of sentence type	N_1	V	N_2
1.	the boy hit the girl	89	50	21
2.	the boy hit a girl	110	26	24
3.	a boy hit the girl	34	13	113
4.	a boy hit a girl	67	73	20
5.	the girl was hit by the boy	91	44	25
6.	the girl was hit by a boy	126	16	18
7.	a girl was hit by the boy	36	17	107
8.	a girl was hit by a boy	73	66	21

We next presented these sentences to subjects and asked them to write questions to which the supplied sentences could count as answers. We analysed the responses in terms of lexical constants (though a small percentage were uninterpretable in this way): that is, those elements which were referred to in the questions which were supplied in the answers. Again we found that word position interacted with definiteness but that when in conflict definiteness was clearly selected for cross-mention between question and answer. This was particularly clear in the case of passives. With 105 subjects we conducted a follow-up study on short and long passives, using not only the definite article but also pronouns and proper names. As is now well known, pronouns and proper names are as definite linguistically as *the nom*.[4] The same kind of increased probability of mention of all of these occurred as compared to use of the indefinite article. With short passives an indefinite subject would be more likely to have the question refer to the action. Full details of these experiments are given in Grieve and Wales (forthcoming). These indicate that such linguistic features as definiteness (as well as animacy, word order, stress, etc) might carry information about what could be assumed by the hearer regarding the topic of discourse.

We then noticed that Harris (1751, p. 215) had expressed a related intuition: "A certain Object occurs . . . What is it? . . . An Individual —Of what kind? *Known* or *unknown*? Seen now *for the first time*, or *seen before* and now remembered? — 'Tis here we shall discover the use of the two Articles *A* and *THE*. *A* respects our *primary* Perception, and denotes Individuals as *unknown*; *THE* respects our *secondary* Perception, and denotes Individuals as *known*. To explain by an example—I see an object pass by, which I never saw till then. What do I say? *There goes A Beggar with A long Beard*. The man departs and returns a week after. What do I say then? *There goes THE Beggar with THE long Beard*. The Article only is changed, the rest remains unaltered. Yet mark the force of this apparently minute Change. The Individual, *once vague*, is now recognised as *something known*, and that merely by the efficacy of this latter Article, which tacitly insinuates a kind of *previous* acquaintance, by referring the present Perception to a like Perception already past." We tested this in the following way. Two film clips were made and shown to student subjects who might be presumed to know the individual in clip *A*, but not the individual in clip *B*. The subjects were told the experiment was one on testimony. Each clip showed the individual appearing and introducing an object, an envelope in *A*, a book in *B*. Both men then departed and returned to work with the object, stamping the envelope in *A*, taking notes from the book in *B*. From a separate check the protocols were withdrawn of those who didn't know the individual in *A*, or did know the one in *B*, or failed to mention the envelope/book in the second half of the

71

clips. The order of presentation was counterbalanced. The descriptive responses were classified as follows: for *Definitely marked* (DM) persons: proper name, the + nominal, pronoun; *Objects*: the + nominal. For *Indefinitely marked* (IDM) persons: Someone, a + nominal; *Objects*: a + nominal. Total $n = 75$. The hypotheses and results are given in Table 4. It is clear that all the hypotheses are convincingly

Table 4

			Prediction	DM	IDM
Clip A	object	1st mention	indefinitely marked	1	74
		2nd mention	definitely marked	75	0
Clip B	object	1st mention	IDM	1	74
		2nd mention	DM	75	0
Clip A	person, known	1st mention	DM	44	31
		2nd mention	DM	75	0
Clip B	person, unknown	1st mention	IDM	5	70
		2nd mention	DM (since now known)	75	0

supported with the exception of the first mention of the known person. We suspected this might be because the experiment was ostensibly one on testimony and this might be causing some subjects to mark the known person indefinitely on the assumption that the reader of the testimony would not know him. We took a further group of subjects ($n = 15$) and we told them their accounts would be read by someone who had not previously seen the clips and who would not be familiar with the people or events involved. This then changes the hypothesis relating to the *first* mention of the known individual to IDM. All other results were as before. For this hypothesis the results were DM: 4, IDM: 11. This is in the predicted direction. Whatever the long term status of the sorts of studies we have mentioned, it seems fairly clear that there is 'gold in them thar hills'—even if contrary results occasionally mist things up. In fact, it seems one of the more hopeful aspects of this approach that such contrary results suggest interesting further experiments rather than leaving one saddled with rather unrevealing null hypotheses and sterile arguments about plausibility.

E. Presuppositions and child language

A remark is perhaps in order here about the relevance of considering presuppositions in child language.[5] It is frequently the case that the kind of young child's utterance that elicits a wry smile in the adult is a function of the operation of different kinds of presupposition—from the deviant use of such basically linguistic constraints as anaphora to the misperception of the relevant cultural constraints operating in a given utterance context. The following illustrates the latter aspect. A boy of four is asked how many legs a horse has, and he refuses to answer. Margaret Donaldson,[2] knowing that the boy knew the correct answer asked him afterwards why he had not given it—'If that big man didn't know, then I wasn't going to tell him!' It seems reasonable to hope that the study of the operation and development of presuppositions in children's language might contribute crucially to making sense of so-called egocentric speech as discussed particularly by Piaget (1926) and Vygotsky (1934). One demonstration of the relevance of linguistic pre-supposition is the following observation made on ten children, mean age four and a half years. Given a set of blocks which are gradable in size but placed in random order. Then the child is given one of the following instructions (followed by the other).

(A) 'Put the blocks in a row so that the biggest is at one end and the wee-est at the other end.'

(B) 'Put the blocks in a row and have the biggest at one end, then the next biggest and so on.'

Instruction (A) was obeyed by placing the biggest block at one end and the smallest at the other, but with the blocks ungraded in the row linking the two. However with instruction (B) the same children constructed a perfectly graded series of blocks. There did not seem to be any order effect in the instructions. No doubt we were rather fortunate in hitting on some children exhibiting this phenomenon, and its true significance can only be assessed by placing it in its appropriate developmental context. However it does strongly suggest that with these children (B) can be appropriately interpreted (in the normal adult sense) since the gradable nature of the instruction is conveyed by the conjunction of simple comparative relations; whereas the apparent 'failure' with (A) is because of the failure to operate in terms of the implication of grading of the conjunction of the polar adjectives and/or the failure to interpret the 'so that' clause as a type of phrasal modification (= 'such that') restricting the type of 'row' required, instead of as a type of sentential modification (= 'in order that'). This observation does suggest the general possibility that pre-supposition may in fact be studied in child language.

F. Locative and innateness

It must be fairly obvious to anyone acquainted with linguistics that all of the above results can be tied down to the notion of deixis—that is, the categories which handle the orientational features of language which are relative to the spatio-temporal features of the utterances. Perhaps it is the child's ability to construct and articulate such relations which partially accounts for the distinctiveness of human language: it can't be simply analysed as a Chimpsky language.[6] This would lend support to the postulated importance of Hockett's 'duality of patterning' and illuminate the obviously incorrect but entrenched notion that children start language learning by learning to name objects (cf Lyons, 1966). Note also as suggestive lines of thought, the following diverse proposals which can be found in the linguistic literature—all related to deixis: that existential and possessive sentences are derived from locative sentences. That comparatives are forms of locative sentences. That 'that' is the stressed form of the. That verbs like come are deictic. That negation is tied to locative or existential statements . . . and so on. Why this seems particularly suggestive is because it lends credibility to the notion that 'locative' is a universal feature of language and indicates the possibility that it is innate. What is attractive about this possibility is that such notions as 'locative' can be unpacked and cashed in terms of spatio temporal co-ordinates, extralinguistic cognitive characteristics such as agency, animacy and dependency, etc which might reasonably be described in a psychological theory which is related to what we already know about the human organism and hope yet to find out. This would not only justify the view of language indicated above as one of what the organism brings to his unique communicative function but also justify the theoretical status of some linguistic primes such as 'locative' being based on biologically determined cognitive universals. This proposal has some formal interest in the light of recent trends in 'generative' semantics inveighing against the use of mnemonic labelling such as 'noun-phrase', 'verb-phrase', etc.

As argued by Lakoff (1970) the move to semantics is a move away from 'arbitrary' (Chomskyan) syntax to a 'natural syntax' position, and that this, concomitantly with a greater degree of theoretical abstractness of the underlying structures involved, supports his contention that syntax and semantic representations are essentially the same. However, the question arises as to how to justify what is 'natural', and it is at this point that his plea for abstractness works against him unless certain 'naturalness conditions' can be set up on the basis of the relatively concrete cognitive structures that are typically recruited by human language.[7] It would therefore seem to be in precisely this area that the justification Lakoff correctly sees to be lacking for motivating a decision regarding the true nature of syntactic representations is to be sought. The possibility that what one wants to set up as a linguistic universal—locative—is in reality a complex of cognitive structures which can be independently justified would lead one to expect—what is apparently already the case—that the notion 'locative' is currently being used in a number of rather different senses. A general implication of this position is that the Chomskyan requirement that the study of performance requires a (logically) prior prototheory of competence is misplaced. However I have no wish to extrapolate further since the theme of this chapter is that there is a serious possibility that we may be able to find answers to psychologically interesting questions with the aid of formal linguistics and experimental study, and not just argue about speculations. Not least of the spinoffs of this line of attack is the possibility of forgetting the notion of psycholinguistics and being just psychologists (or linguists) again!

In commenting on the Psalmist's claim *I am wonderfully made,* Dickson, an old Scottish divine, noted (1655): "As the Lord's rare works, without considerance, look to a man very common-like; so his common works, being well considered, become very wonderful." It was Chomsky's achievement that he indicated that man's creative use of language might be precisely characterised. It seems reasonable to hope that the psychology of language may yet, if unrushed, achieve results which give one the same sensation of pleasant surprise.

Footnotes

[1]   Most of this work has been conducted in close collaboration with Robin Campbell and Bob Grieve—the latter being particularly involved also in the running of the experiments reported here. Margaret Donaldson undoubtedly earned the reader's gratitude. Michael Garman has been a discerning aide in the production of the final draft. Obviously all these

persons are conventionally irresponsible, but I am nevertheless very grateful to them.

² The reference to the Piagetian notion of object constancy as being a necessary (though obviously not sufficient) ground for 'naming', is that it would seem necessary for the child to be able to symbolise the continued existence of the objects being 'named' when not perceptually present. If out of sight was literally out of mind and 'naming' was still said to occur, we would lay ourselves open to the banalities of behaviourist 'accounts' with any stimulus-response connection a candidate for the status of 'naming'. It seems to be that traditional accounts of the 'linguistic' status of the child's early utterances—in their attempt to find when the child first 'has' language—ran into trouble more because of the prevailing background definitions of 'propositions' and 'sentence' than because of not spelling out clearly what 'naming' was all about. First, the insistence on the importance of the truth or falsity of propositions to the evaluation of the child's early utterances (eg Bühler, 1930) is liable to miss the point neatly put by Geach (1962, p. 26) that "a name may be used outside the context of a sentence simply to name something . . . such an act of naming is of course no proposition, and, while we may call it correct or incorrect, we cannot properly call it true or false. It does however, as grammarians say concerning sentences; express a complete thought; it is not like the use of 'Napoleon' to answer the question: 'who won the battle of Hastings?' where we have to take the single word as short for the complete sentence." Geach's reference to the western grammatical tradition indicates a related problem area: the nature of the 'sentence', whether sentences need always to be true or false was questioned long ago by Aristotle (*De Interpretatione*) where he claimed, in distinguishing sentences from statements, that a prayer, for instance, is a sentence but neither true nor false. (Perhaps he was here anticipating Austin's arguments about 'speech acts'!) The separation of cognitive accounts of the sentence (ie expresses a complete thought) and formal accounts (ie expressing conditions on well-formedness) seems to have led to the implications of the former for the latter being largely ignored—this tendency having been aggravated perhaps by an overconcern with the 'word'. The Indian linguistic tradition as discussed by Matilal (1966) seems to have been more helpful in its attempt to come to grips with this problem, indicating a need to qualify its attempts to account for the wellformedness of sentences (accepted intuitively as both grammatical and meaningful) by introducing such notions as competency, expectancy and contiguity. While these general problems are interesting and important in the continuing evaluation of empirical claims about child language, it seems to me a misguidedly idealistic and prescriptivist view of the scientific enterprise to assert that their theoretical solution is a prerequisite to serious empirical study. Such a position is a bit like making the clarification of the grounds

for claiming something as having 'life' a prerequisite to serious study on the border between organic chemistry and biology. Within the Christian tradition God's truth came by progressive revelation. It seems even more reasonable here to expect that we will have to develop and change our interpretations as our descriptive knowledge progresses!

[3] Note that the suggested shift from a *categorial* (adjective-verb) to a *sub-categorial* (stative verb-action verb) distinction in terms of a 'notional' theory of the parts of speech (Lyons, 1966; p. 221) involves a rejection of 'linguistic-isolationist' analysis in favour of a more cognitively based approach. Current linguistic research is typically concerned with complex interactions of contrasts of the type 'static'-'dynamic', 'effective'-'affective', 'imperfective'-'perfective', etc. One could suggest, for example, that *Mary is beautiful* and *Mary is seen* are only aspectually distinct, and that 'perfective aspect' rather than 'past tense' (cf the traditional term past participle) is crucial to the passive construction. While this research does not by itself support the continuity hypothesis, it clearly opens the way for psychological structures to be related to linguistic ones (cf also Bever's (1970; p. 1) concern to approach language as "a conceptual and communicative system which recruits various kinds of human behaviours" rather than as uniquely 'grammatical').

[4] It is interesting, however, to note that they are rather peculiar types of *the nom*—for example, with respect to restrictive relativisation. Thus, there is *The man I* $\begin{smallmatrix}(met)\\(like)\end{smallmatrix}$ *left* but neither of the following—**The man I met I like left, *John I like left*. Note that, if *John* here is taken as a surface realisation of a restrictive relative embedding, of the type 'the one who is John', then a very general restriction on nesting of restrictive relatives accounts for both of the asterisked examples above. Note also that, in view of the possibility of *The John I like left,* one could argue that the traditional characterisation of proper names as 'particulars' is misleading insofar as it is *the John* (rather than *John*) which refers to a particularised individual; and it is *the John* again which presupposes that the assumed hearer in the situation of utterance is familiar with the person talked about. It may be suggested, in view of this, and what was noted above with respect to quantifiers, that 'definiteness' is only a first approximation to an appropriate analysis for tying down presuppositions of this sort; and that *John,* while in one sense being a type of *the nom,* is also, like the quantifier *some,* a variable ranging over a relatively undefined set—as opposed to *the John*—with concomitant distinctions in the types of presuppositions that are set up in each case. However, at this stage of the game, we have to make do with the notion of 'definiteness'.

* This symbol indicates that the sentence following is not an acceptable English sentence.

[5] John Marshall pointed out to me that there is a 'paradox' involving the hypothesis of Harris above, and the experiment in the first part of this chapter. That is, what 'previously known' object is presupposed in the first response to the instruction 'give me *the* big one'? This paradox is more apparent than real, since the blocks previously placed on the table may now be 'presumed known'. Secondly, the particular force of Harris is the contrastive use of *a* and *the*, ie 'the apparently minute change'.

[6] With the incidence of discussions of the relation between sign languages and spoken human languages the following speculation may be relevant here. Gesture languages seem to differ from what has been claimed for human language by apparently being relatively unstructured syntactically. Could this be because of the available mechanisms of short-term memory (STM)? The 'acoustic confusion' literature (which indicates that with visually presented orthographic material confusions in STM are determined by acoustic rather than visual similarities) suggests the possibility that there are special auditory rehearsal mechanisms in STM (cf Sperling, 1967). Analogously, it might be that there are particular mechanisms for dealing with, for example, nested dependencies in language which is basically spoken. If these mechanisms of storage did not operate in visual modality it might follow that gesture languages are likely to reduce to simple 'propositionalised' forms of communication where there is not the same need for structural constraints, such as ordering, to operate. This would suggest a likely direction of change for any gesture language modelled on 'natural' language (cf, Schlesinger, this volume).

[7] As a case in point, with reference to the naturalness conditions between cognitive primes and linguistic units, take the vexed question of gender. First, note that the assertion of a diachronic development in Indo-European from a primitive animate-inanimate contrast into a later, sex-differentiated, three-term system, holds implications for the investigation of ontogenetic development. Secondly, note that where there is contrast between 'natural' and 'grammatical' gender, the latter is typically argued to be derivative with respect to the former diachronically, and this process leads to the sort of situation which Kuroda (1969) attends to in French. He correctly has to argue for a syntactic as well as a semantic account of gender precisely because, in terms of what is suggested above, certain naturalness conditions on gender have been violated. It is important that the particular form of the violation is language-specific; involving for French the 'dominance' of (grammatical) masculine gender over (grammatical) feminine gender, in the sense that, where the principal noun is masculine the concordial marking is with reference to the natural gender system (male vs female) but that where it is feminine, it is with reference to *either* the natural *or* the grammatical system, but that neither alternative makes for a wholly acceptable utterance. The resulting anomaly, Kuroda points out, does not reside in the peculiarity of the (semantic) idea

being expressed, but in the fact that neither (syntactic) construction expresses very well the desired meaning. This sort of situation, it should be noted, is not an argument against naturalness conditions—since its idiosyncracy is to be characterised precisely in terms of their being violated—which, if this were never the case, would simply mean that they hold trivially.

References

BEVER, T. G. (1970), The cognitive basis for linguistic structures. In J. R. Hayes (ed.), *Cognition and Language Learning*. New York: Wiley.

BÜHLER, K. (1930), *The Mental Development of the Child*. London: Kegan-Paul.

CAMPBELL, R. N. and WALES, R. J. (1969), Comparative structures in English. *J. L.* **5**, 215-252.

CAMPBELL, R. N. and WALES, R. J. (1970), On the study of language acquisition. In J. Lyons (ed.), *New Horizons in Linguistics*. London: Penguin Books.

CHOMSKY, N. (1965), *Aspects of the Theory of Syntax*. Cambridge, Mass.: M.I.T. Press.

CLARK, H. H. (1965), Some structural properties of simple active and passive sentences. *J. Verbal Learning and Verbal Behavior* **4**, 365-370.

GEACH, P. (1962), *Reference and Generality*. Ithaca: Cornell University Press.

GRIEVE, R. and WALES, R. J. Passives and topicalisation (forthcoming).

HARLOW, H. (1958), The evolution of learning. In A. Roe and G. Simpson (eds.), *Evolution and Behavior*. New York: McGraw-Hill.

HARRIS, J. (1751), *Hermes*. (reprinted Menston: Scolar Press, 1968).

79

HOBHOUSE, L. T. (1901), *Mind in Evolution*. London: MacMillan.

JOHNSON-LAIRD, P. N (1968a), The choice of the passive voice in a communicative task. *Br. J. Psychol.* **59**, 7-15.

JOHNSON-LAIRD, P. N. (1968b), The interpretation of the passive voice. *Quart. J. Exp. Psychol.* **20**, 69-73.

JOHNSON-LAIRD, P. N. (1969), On understanding logically complex sentences. *Quart. J. Exp. Psychol.* **21**, 1-13.

KURODA, S.-Y. (1969), Remarks on selectional restrictions and presuppositions. In F. Keifer (ed.), *Studies in Syntax and Semantics, Foundations of Language, Supp. Series,* **10**.

KÖHLER, W. (1918), Simple structural functions in the chimpanzee and in the chicken. (Eng. trans., 1935). In W. Ellis (ed.), *A Sourcebook of Gestalt Psychology*. New York: Humanities Press.

LAKOFF, G. (1970), On generative semantics. In D. Steinberg and L. Jakobovits (eds.), *Semantics—An Interdisciplinary Reader*. London: Cambridge University Press.

LASHLEY, K. (1951), The problem of serial order in behavior. In L. Jeffress (ed.), *Cerebral Mechanisms in Behaviour*. New York: Wiley.

LEES, R. B. (1961), Grammatical analysis of the English comparative construction. *Word* **17**, 171-185.

LENNEBERG, E. H. (1967), *Biological Foundations of Language*, New York: Wiley.

LYONS, J. (1966), Towards a 'notional' theory of the 'parts of speech'. *J. Linguistics* **2**, 209-236.

MACKAY, D. M. (1962), a discussion in S. Korner (ed.), *Observation and Interpretation in the Philosophy of Physics*. New York: Dover.

MATILAL, B. K. (1966), Indian theorists on the nature of the sentence (*vākya*). *Foundations of Language* **4**, 377, 393.

PIAGET, J. and INHELDER, B. (1969), *The Psychology of the Child*. London: Routledge and Kegan Paul.

PIAGET, J. (1926), *Language and Thought of the Child*. English translation 1959. London: Routledge and Kegan Paul.

SMITH, C. S. (1961), A Class of complex modifiers in English. *Language* **41**, 37-58.

SPENCE, K. W. (1937), The differential response in animals to stimuli varying within a single dimension. *Psychol. Rev.* **44**, 430-444.

SPERLING, G. A. (1967), Successive approximations to a model for short-term memory. In A. Sanders (ed.), *Attention and Performance*. Amsterdam: North Holland. (Special edition of *Acta Psychologica* **27**.)

VYGOTSKY, L. S. (1934), *Thought and Language*. English translation 1962. Cambridge, Mass.: MIT.

WALES, R. J. and CAMPBELL, R. N. (1970), The development of comparison and the comparison of development. In G. D'Arcais and W. Levelt (eds.), *Proceedings of Psycholinguistics Conference at Bressanone*. Amsterdam: North Holland.

WASON, P. C. (1965), The contexts of plausible denial. *J. Verbal Learning and Verbal Behavior* **4**, 7-11.

F

5

What could possibly be innate?

John Morton

MRC Applied Psychology Unit,
Cambridge,
England

A. Introduction

The claims that language is innate in man seem to be based on a few facts, a number of suppositions and a great deal of faith. The facts are that it is possible to define 'language' such that: 1. All humans have language; 2. No animals have language; 3. Young humans can learn any language regardless of their racial origins; 4. Across languages and races the ontogeny of language acquisition appears to be equivalent.

It might be noted that such a definition of language is not straightforward and gets more difficult as more is known about the communicative behaviour of other species. It used to be thought possible to make the distinction on the basis of function (eg Hockett, 1960) but inasmuch as the distinction is attempted nowadays, it is based on the structural properties of language.

The simplest explanation of the facts listed above is that all languages are, in some sense, identical; that all young humans are in most senses identical; that one of the ways in which all babies are identical is a feature or set of features not shared by any other species; and that this species-specific attribute is one which enables the child to

82

apprehend the universal aspects of language in the one to which he is exposed, and then to determine the way in which the particular language manifests the universals in speech.

By suitable tailoring, the above explanation can be made to fit any of the currently proposed models for language behaviour as well as all the theoretical positions. The extreme empiricist would say that the equipment the child uses is quite general, for language acquisition is not different in principle from learning to press a lever to obtain food; merely more complicated. The extreme nativist would believe that very specific complex structures exist in the neonate which map exactly the universal features of the grammar of his choice. All that needs to be determined are the nature of the identities among languages and the specificity of the equipment the child uses in language acquisition.

B. Differences between humans and animals

Let us first briefly discuss the role of the physical make-up of man. One thing is quite clear; that the only crucial difference between man and other species must lie in the central nervous system. The higher apes have homologous articulatory structures (Lenneberg, 1967) but have little ability (or inclination) to mimic human sounds. It seems likely, from the work of Lieberman (1968), that what is missing is fine control over the movements of the articulators and an inability to sequence their operation precisely. The minah bird, on the other hand, has virtually no homologous structures and yet can mimic very well. The dolphin, according to some recent reports (and Aristotle) can produce speech-like sounds in the air but does so with a totally different phonatory system. (On the question as to whether or not dolphins have a language, I would like to comment paranthetically that from the evidence I have seen, if they do have a language they are going to extraordinary lengths to conceal the fact from us.) In addition both the congenitally dumb (Lenneberg, 1967) and deaf (Schlesinger, this volume) are capable of acquiring language.

I am taking as a premise that language is represented in the brain in a way that reflects different levels of abstraction. These different levels will resemble language as we observe it (for example, on the printed page) at the lower end, and will be more closely related to thought at the other end. Since it is obvious that languages differ widely in their overt form then we must look at the more abstract levels to find the identities between languages. This brings us to the notion of linguistic universals.

C. Language acquisition

Linguistic universals have been discussed most recently, at most length and with reference to language acquisition by users of transformational-generative grammars. The discussion that follows is then partially, though not completely, tied to such a grammatical theory.

Within such theories there are two main candidates for consideration; the base structure (or 'deep structure') and the abstract properties of the transformations which relate deep structures to surface structure. Let me quote from Chomsky on each of these:

"It seems to be true that the underlying deep structures vary very slightly, at most, from language to language. That is quite reasonable, because it seems impossible to learn them, since they are not signalled in the sentence and are not recoverable from the signal in any non-trivial way by any inductive or analytic operation, so far as I can see. Since it is hard to imagine how anyone could learn them, it is pleasant to discover that they do not vary very much from language to language. That fact enables us to postulate that they form part of the technic which a person uses for acquiring language: that is, they are part of the conceptual apparatus he uses to specify the form of the language to which he is exposed, and not something to be acquired.

Second, it seems to be true that the abstract properties of transformations are also universal. This is what one would expect, again for the same reason, since it is difficult to imagine how operations of this kind could be abstracted from data. There is certainly no process of generalisation or association of any kind known to psychology or philosophy, or any procedure of analysis that is known in linguistics that can come close to determining structures of this kind."

(Chomsky, 1967, pp. 80-81).

These statements of Chomsky remain neutral as to the form of the innate component with regard to two alternatives. The first of these is that the developing nervous system is structured in a way that permits the internal representation of the basic properties of grammars to be constructed from more general principles at the appropriate time in development. The second alternative is that the innate component is language specific, by which must be meant that in the nervous system of the infant there are circuits which are specifically designed to generate deep structure relationships and other circuits specifically designed to manipulate the outputs from the former circuits—the language specificity being manifested by such circuits being primarily connected to the auditory recognition system on one end and to that part of the motor cortex which deals with articulation on the other end. (cf Fodor's (1966) distinction between 'innate' and 'intrinsic').

In any event, following analyses such as that quoted above, nativists have often made an assertion which I would like to question. The statement usually takes the form 'Since language is so complex to learn and since the child learns it so quickly from a set of what are largely ungrammatical utterances, it must be given assistance in the form of pre-existing information concerning the nature of languages'. Such a statement is, of course, independent of any theoretical framework and, if thought to be valid, would remain so even if Chomsky's claims about the impossibility of determining the structure of a language from speech were not true. What I would like to question are the two assertions that language is complex and that the child learns it quickly. Complex compared to what? Quickly compared to learning what? The protagonists of such a viewpoint seem to argue from two sides. Firstly, anything else which is acquired in the same time or more quickly is automatically deemed to be simpler, and then, things which take the child longer to acquire are either said to be no more complex or imagined to be learned the hard way.

Let me take as a representative statement, one by Dave McNeill. This is by no means as extreme as some others but will serve the purpose. It comes from McNeill (1966, p. 15).

"The fundamental problem to which we address ourselves is the simple fact that language acquisition occurs in a surprisingly short time. Grammatical speech does not begin before one and a half years of age; yet, as far as we can tell, the basic process is complete by three and a half years. Thus a basis for the rich and intricate competence of adult grammar must emerge in the short span of twenty four months. To appreciate this achievement, we need only compare the child with himself in other departments of cognitive growth as outlined, say, in the work of Piaget. Add to rapid acquisition the further fact that what is acquired is knowledge of abstract linguistic structure, and the problem of accounting for language development can be seen to pose unusual difficulties for our collection of explanatory devices."

Here, the comment on 'other departments of cognitive growth' is implicit but unmistakable.

The reason for this curious state of affairs is that we have at least the beginnings of a full and systematic description of language from several linguists with different theoretical approaches and in all cases the result is indeed complex. Unfortunately, we do not have similar descriptions of other human activities and so, perhaps, assume they

85

are simple in structure. But, how complex a job, for example is it for a child to learn how to walk? This achievement involves not just muscular co-ordination but also requires the development of a body image, and co-ordination with visual and other information. Is this more or less complex than learning how to speak?

And what kind of learning is involved in the example cited by Mario Pei (1965), to the effect that Young American Males never rotate the axis of their eyeballs while their eyelids are closed. Young American (and British) females do this; and I am sure they are not taught in school.

More seriously, it seems clear that we cannot make a direct comparison of the complexity of language with that of other structures which have to be acquired. No-one has yet analysed pattern recognition or sensory-motor co-ordination in sufficient detail. We can, however, get some ideas as to the order of magnitude of the task of pattern recognition by considering the processes necessary for a computer to perform a task as seemingly simple as determining from a two-dimensional picture the three-dimensional objects present. No claim is being made as to the applicability of these routines to human pattern processing; that is just as questionable as the direct applicability of a grammar to the way in which we understand sentences. The analysis will, however, dispel any presuppositions that picture analysis is simple.

1. *Picture grammars*

The program I will summarise has been devised by Guzman (1968). The basic input is a picture such as that in Figure 1 which we instantly

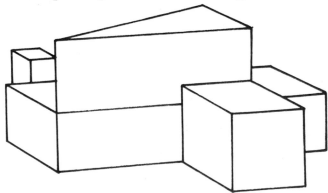

Figure 1. A line drawing of four solid objects: the type of picture analysed by Guzman's (1968) program described in the text.

interpret as comprising of four solid objects. This picture has to be broken down into a specification of all the lines, vertices and surfaces and the relationships between them. It is also necessary for the program to know what area of the picture constitutes the background.

The program then examines each vertex and classifies it. On the basis of the classification, links may be established between some of the surfaces meeting at the vertex. Some of the significant vertices are shown in Figure 2.

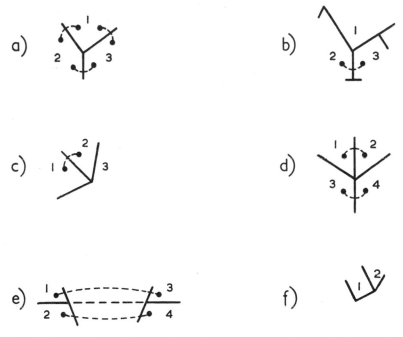

Figure 2. Types of vertex. The numbers refer to separate regions in the pictures; the dotted lines show the 'links' that are formed between the regions. The names of the vertices are (a) FORK, (c) ARROW, (d) X, (e) T—in which the bodies are colinear, (f) LEG—in this case only a 'weak' link is formed between the regions. (b) shows restrictions on the applicability of a FORK.

Fork — this is illustrated in Figure 2a. Links are established between the three regions unless one of them is part of the background. These links may be cancelled if one of the adjacent vertices is of a particular type. Thus in Figure 2b the link between regions 1 and 2 is not produced because of the 'L' vertex; the link between regions 1 and 3 is not produced because of the 'passing T' vertex. The link between 2 and 3 will be produced in this case.

Arrow — this is shown in Figure 2c. A link is established between regions 1 and 2. Nothing can be said about 3.

X — if the *X* is formed by the intersection of two lines it provides no evidence. If it is of the form shown in Figure 2d then links are established as indicated, but cancelled if there is a 'passing *T*' vertex on the continuous line.

T — When a *T*-vertex is found, a search is made for another *T*-vertex which has a body colinear and is facing, as in Figure 2e. Links are established between regions 1 and 3 and between 2 and 4. Links between the background and something which is not background are cancelled.

Leg — a combination of vertices such as that in 2f will cause a 'weak' link to be established between the two surfaces. A weak link does not carry the same weight as a normal (or strong) link.

There are other vertices and combinations possible which have not been illustrated, some of them quite complex in their definitions and implications.

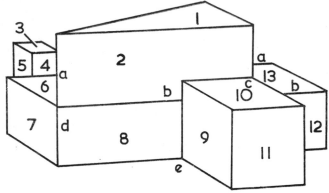

Figure 3. The picture of fig. 1 with the regions numbered and some of the vertices labelled for reference.

In Figure 3, our original picture has been reproduced with numbers on all the surfaces. The links which would be formed by the rules described above are shown in Figure 4. Some of the links are explained below.

6-13: this is formed from the pair of T-vertices labelled 'a' in Figure 3.

2-13: this (mistaken) link is formed by the pair of T-vertices labelled 'b' which also link (correctly) 8-12.

7-8: this is formed by the X-vertex labelled 'd'. But for 'a' 2 would be linked with 6.

2-10:   this is mistakenly formed by the fork vertex labelled 'c'. Note
        that 13 is linked neither to 2 nor 10 because of the adjacent
        vertices 'a' and 'b' (cf Figure 2b).

The vertex labelled 'e' does not create the link 8-9 because the third
surface at that vertex is the background.

6-7:   the dotted line refers to the weak link formed by the 'leg' (also
        12-13).

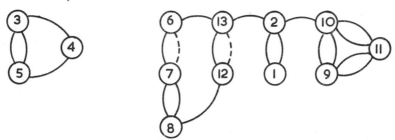

Figure 4. The links between the regions resulting from the application of the rules
concerning vertices. The dotted lines are weak links.

The program then operates to form nuclei. A nucleus is formed
by concatenating any two regions, or nuclei, which are connected by
two strong links. This leads in the first instance to the nuclei and links
shown in Figure 5. The nucleus 3-5 is then seen to be connected to
region 4 by two links and the three can be merged (Figure 6). A further
rule then allows a weak link to reinforce a strong link which leads to
the merging of 6-7-8 and 12-13, as in Figure 7. These two can then be

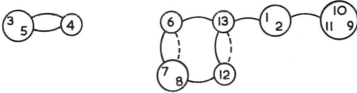

Figure 5. The nuclei resulting from the first application of a concatenation rule.

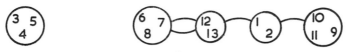

Figure 6. The nuclei formed when weak links reinforce strong links.

Figure 7. The objects finally identified by the program.

connected together as there are now two strong links between them. The nucleus 1-2 is only connected to other nuclei by one link which is insufficient. Thus the errors made in the first stage, in this case, have had no ultimate effect and the resulting analysis agrees with our own analysis of the picture.

Two things should be noted immediately. Firstly I have simplified the original program considerably in the telling. Secondly the program supposes that the bodies in the picture are solid objects formed by plane surfaces. If we were more naturalistic and allowed curved surfaces, the necessary operations would be much more complex. In addition Guzman's approach is somewhat empirical. A more abstract account of picture grammars may be found in Clowes (1968).

The point of going into even this amount of detail is to demonstrate that the identification of solid objects is not elementary. When the task is analysed in detail we are made aware of the complexity of the operations required. Furthermore we have no idea at present how a child learns to perform these, or other, equally complex operations. It has been argued that the identification task discussed above is artificial and that in reality there are lots of other cues available to a person while identifying a cluster of objects. Thus from the visual field we have information on texture and colour and we can obtain three dimensional information from the two eyes or by moving ourselves with respect to the objects. I feel this view is mistaken. These extra cues may prevent us from misidentifying objects but their use must made the processes more complicated not less. More rules and restrictions must be built in, and methods of combining different forms of information must be created. When someone has managed to formulate all these operations in a suitable symbolic form, it is at least possible that the resulting 'picture-grammar' will be indistinguishable from the grammar of a language and it is fairly probable that even if the grammars turn out to be very different in principle, it will not be possible to distinguish between them on any suitably abstract criteria of complexity.

2. *Some suggested innate properties*

It seems then that at the moment we should perhaps stifle our wonder at the growth of language in the child as it can get out of hand. Let me take a couple of examples.

Cushing (1968) showed that primary stress in American English is placed on a syllable by means of dropping the fundamental frequency on the following syllable. He makes much of the fact that we do not hear the shift in fundamental frequency as a change in pitch claiming that this observation "constitutes significant evidence for the hypothesis . . . that the language capacity is innate in man". When we are listening to a group of sounds we either classify them as linguistic or non-linguistic. Upon the classification depends our perceptual experience; in this case either a primary stress mark or a shift in pitch. Cushing continues "It is difficult to see how one might account for this phenomenon without assuming some sort of innate structure in the mind that classifies all heard sounds as either 'linguistic' or 'non-linguistic'. Without such a structure, there is no reason why a child learning English should ever start hearing the same frequency in different ways." It is the specificity of the postulated innate structure that I object to. In the first place it is easy to find similar examples of contingent classification; thus, when an ellipse is projected on our retina we interpret it in one way when we know that the object concerned is a rugby football, and in another way when we know it is a plate. The second objection is that it is often the case that when a higher level of organisation of a complex stimulus is possible, a lower level of description rarely reaches awareness—thus in reading a word we are usually not aware of the component letters. Thirdly it seems to be the case that persons uninstructed in phonology are capable of retrieving the information that a stress is signalled by a pitch change when questioned sufficiently deeply.

The second example of a specific claim is based on the fact that a particular phoneme, such as $/d/$, has a very different sound structure in different vowel contexts—as in the words 'did' and 'do' (Liberman, et al, 1967). That we hear the initial phonemes of these two words as being identical must be related to the well accepted supposition, with good experimental backing, that the instructions given to the muscles controlling the speech production mechanisms are identical when we are about to say the two words. Let us see what two authors have to say on this point. Firstly an 'innate' viewpoint:

"The simultaneous evolution of a mechanism for the production of speech and of man's mental ability would, for example, account for the close relationship that we find between speech production and speech perception. It would have been 'natural' and 'economical' for the constraints of speech production to be structured into the speech perception system if both of these abilities developed at the same pace. We would thus expect to find the speech recognition routines that involved a match with the constraints of speech production (the motor theory of speech perception) to be structured into a speech

91

perception centre that would be species specific, rather than in the peripheral or central auditory systems, which probably are similar for men and other animals."

(Lieberman 1968, p. 1584).

In paraphrase, Lieberman is suggesting that a model of the vocal tract is prewired into the auditory analysis system or at least that a part of this system is specially set aside for just this purpose. After considering virtually the same evidence another author concludes the "experience with the generation of speech movements and with simultaneous observation of the acoustic consequences of these movements plays an important role in shaping the process whereby speech is perceived." (Stevens, 1968, p. 102.)

I cite these examples, both in the area of speech recognition, as they are a good deal more specific than similar statements applied to syntax or semantics. There is no proof that either viewpoint is correct; at this stage in the growth of the science we are dealing largely with plausibility as the criterion.

D. The generality of the innate component

To return to the main theme—these comments should not be interpreted as implying that I think language is simple or that the child needs no innate mechanism to acquire it. What I am questioning is that the innate component is especially important for language learning compared with other learning and, further, that perhaps the innate component is not specific to language. This is by no means a completely novel suggestion.

Lenneberg's view was that the innate component that is universal is a 'mode of calculating with categories'—a capacity for extracting similarities from physical stimuli or from deeper classes of structural schemata. He goes further in saying (Lenneberg, 1967, p. 394) "No features that are characteristic of only certain natural languages, either particulars of syntax, or phonology, or semantics, are assumed here to be innate." To him it is the *processes* not the structures which are species specific. And these processes are not language specific.

Chomsky (1967), while leaning in that direction, hedges when he says "I have no doubt that other cognitive systems, other aspects of human behaviour, other aspects of animal behaviour, share many of these (basic) properties (of grammars)". The "many" is perhaps unnecessary.

Fodor, while allowing that it is likely that other behaviour can be represented by trees and with bracketing which is preserved under psychological operations that satisfy such formal descriptions as deletion, adjunction, permutation, etc, "ie that behaviour is transformational" (Fodor, 1966b), nevertheless equips his child with inference rules designed, so far as I can see, for language alone (Fodor, 1966a).

What I want to do is suggest that the difference between man and the other animals is, in principle, fairly simple. It seems to me that survival, of the species or of the individual, depends on the ability to model and manipulate the environment. To do this we must be able to extract the regularities and general laws which exist in the environment. This must apply to some extent to all organisms which need to generalise, discriminate, learn contingencies, impute causality, etc. The special thing about man might simply be the extent to which the internal representations of these regularities are connected together. It is possible that beyond a certain point the increase in complexity leads to a qualitative difference in cognitive ability with an abstract code as its basis. Speech then becomes possible as a manifestation of this abstract code which has the advantage that it is discrete and distinctive—it forces categorisation, makes possible a more efficient storage and retrieval system and simplifies the computations upon which behaviour must be based. On this line of reasoning we would expect language universals to reflect those features of the structure of the universe which it is biologically necessary for organisms to know.

Let me discuss very briefly one or two universals in the light of what has just been said. It should be apparent that the Noun is a form of generalisation the contingencies of which become more and more refined as we learn which of various discriminanda are relevant under what other conditions (define 'table' for example). The gradual focusing of 'Dada' onto one person seems identical to the gradual restriction of the baby's smile to the mother's face alone. These seem to be of the same type of operation, but more complex and multimodal, as generalisation and discrimination behaviour of lower species. The universal head noun-modifier relationship seems to be no more than an extension of this. The discriminanda becomes generalisable and the generalisations can be consistently discriminated among without loss of the category. The agentive relationship, another universal, is clearly related to the biologically essential ability of an organism to deal with causality.

An analysis of this kind must ultimately be presented more rigorously and some account must be given of the way in which a

93

system such as the one suggested can acquire language. The beginnings of such an account have been described by Schlesinger (1968, 1970) and some related suggestions as to the form of the language system in adults have been made by Morton (1968).

E. Time-Coding

There does appear to be one other feature of human behaviour which requires a further statement. I have suggested that the crucial innate feature in man is a richly interconnective system between functions which are universal for all organisms—and implied that one property of this net is the efficiency of its information storage. This is still not enough; one other thing must be included—the notion of time-coding in memory. It is this which makes possible the ability to talk about relationships between objects or attribution to one object or concept in the past in a way which contradicts the apparent relationship between the same objects in the present. Under most circumstances this can be done without affecting what is said about the present relationship. As examples, we say: 'The red tree in our garden has turned brown', 'The boy next door is grown up now and lives in London', 'The bus-stop at the corner has been moved down the street', 'She is better'. Thus the concept *the tree in our garden* is linked to the concept *brown* and the link is time-coded in the present. Simultaneously the first concept is linked to *red* with a time-coding which is interpreted as being 'past'; and these two links can co-exist without interference. It seems unlikely that any other species is capable of this feat. (The circumstances under which this dissociation breaks down with humans are interesting for slightly different reasons.) The implications for linguistic theory of sentences of this kind has been discussed by Bach (1968).

In addition, and more vital, is the point that it is such a time-coding — with a null or imaginary value of the variable — which makes possible planning, deceit and imagination.

It is also, I suspect, a biological *sine qua non*. Consider a hypothetical tribe of well developed apes which have, at the point of time at which we observe them, evolved the organs of speech and the interconnective system and accordingly have a fully fledged language *but* have not got an effective time-coding system. One alternative is that this tribe would just sit around chatting about the present—commenting on the trees and what others were doing. This would be very jolly and would no doubt take the place of a lot of other activities in consolidating the group. The other possibility is that our tribe would be

94

incapable of making distinctions between what was, what is, and more crucially, what might be. Meanwhile, however, nearby, a more primitive tribe is doing more useful things like play fighting or picking fleas out of each other. At the same time, a third group is busy making plans about where they are going to meet tomorrow after they have scattered in their foraging for food. I do not give much for the evolutionary chances of our hypothetical tribe.

So I am trying to answer the question in my title by suggesting that what is innate is not language specific and that the universals are universals of cognition. Neurologically the evidence is equivocal.[1] It used to be believed that cerebral dominance was related (ontogenetically and phylogenetically) primarily to language, and led only secondarily to preferred handedness. The reason for this belief was the widespread knowledge of the effects on language functions of damage to the (usually) left hemisphere and the corresponding lack of effects following damage to the right hemisphere. The relation of left hemisphere lesions to apraxia—that is the breakdown of skilled voluntary actions — was first noted somewhat later than the first systematic observations on aphasia and has been less fully studied. It remains possible that language is parasitical upon a dominant hemisphere which has developed in response to the need for the initiation and control of manipulative skills. The difference between the hemispheres is then primarily that the dominant hemisphere is responsible for initiation and the exercise of 'will'. Thus Oldfield (1969) found that left-handed musicians experienced no problems in playing their right-handed instruments. Only in conducting was it found difficult or impossible to transfer. Equally with language it is the intellectually expressive rather than the receptive functions which suffer more from lesions in, or removal of, the dominant hemisphere (see, for example, Smith, 1966).

F. Summary

The current suggestions are that language arises as a result of particularly rich interconnections among functions which are quite general biologically, together with an efficient storage and retrieval system which is mediated by a discrete and distinctive verbally based code and is capable of coding time relations among concepts. That language influences cognitive development is implicit in this picture; that it does not wholly influence cognition is shown by Schlesinger (this volume). In addition to these factors there has to be a language environment to potentiate development and additionally a conducive social environment as Leontiev (this volume) argues. In the latter respect it is interesting to note that attempts to teach mynah birds to speak using operant conditioning techniques have failed (Grosslight and Zaynor, 1967). Apparently social interaction with a human is required, in spite of the fact that imitation of speech is not language for the bird.

While the present chapter does little to clarify the issues raised in the introduction to this volume, it does seem clear that the intricacies of language development will only be unravelled when we avoid dogma and accept that the human brain is very complex indeed.

Footnote

[1] I am grateful to Professor O. L. Zangwill for discussing some of these issues and apologise especially to him for this somewhat sketchy account.

References

BACH, E. (1968), Nouns and noun phrases. In Bach E. and Harms, R. T. (eds.), *Universals in Linguistic Theory*. New York: Holt.

CHOMSKY, N. (1967), The general properties of language. In Millikan, C. H., and Darley, F. L. (eds.), *Brain Mechanisms underlying Speech and Language*. New York: Grune and Stratton.

CLOWES, M. B. (1968), Transformational grammars and the organisation of pictures. Seminar paper No. 11. CSIRO Division Computing Research, Canberra.

CUSHING, S. (1969), English as a tone language: the acoustics of primary stress. MIT Research Laboratory of Electronics, Quart. Progress Report No. 92.

FODOR, J. A. (1966), (a) How to learn to talk: some simple ways. (b) Discussion of Kalmus, pp. 288-294. In Smith, F., and Miller, G. A. (eds.), *The Genesis of Language*. MIT: Cambridge, Mass.

GROSSLIGHT, J. H. and ZAYNOR, W. C. (1967), Verbal behavior in the Mynah Bird. In Salzinger, K., and Salzinger, S. ((eds.), *Research in Verbal Behavior and some Neurophysiological Implications*. New York and London: Academic Press.

GUZMAN, A. (1968), Decomposition of a visual scene into three-dimensional bodies. *Proceedings of the Fall Joint Computer Conference* **29**, 291-304.

HOCKETT, C. F. (1960), The origin of speech, *Sci. Amer.* **203**, 88-96.

LENNEBERG, E. H. (1967), *The biological foundations of language*. New York: Wiley.

LIBERMAN, A. M., COOPER, F. S., SHANKWEILER, D. and STUDDERT-KENNEDY, M. (1967), Perception of the speech code. *Psychol. Rev.* **74**, 431-461.

LIEBERMAN, P. (1968), Primate vocalisations and human linguistic ability. *J. acoust. soc. Amer.* **44**, 1574-1584.

MCNEILL, D. (1966), Developmental psycholinguistics. In Smith, F. and Miller, G. A. (eds.), *The Genesis of Language*. MIT: Cambridge, Mass.

MORTON, J. (1968), Consideration of grammar and computation in language behavior. In Catford, J. C. (ed.), *Studies in Language and Language Behavior, Progress Report VI*; Ann Arbor.

OLDFIELD, R. C. (1969), Handedness in musicians. *Brit. J. Psychol.* **60**, 91-100.

PEI, M. (1965), *The Story of Language*. London: Unwin.

SCHLESINGER, I. M. (1968), Learning grammar: from pivot to realisation rule. Presented at the Center for Advanced Study in the Developmental Sciences—Ciba Foundation joint study group on *Mechanisms of Language Development*, May 1968.

SCHLESINGER, I. M. (1970), Production of utterances and language acquisition. In Slobin, D. I. (ed.), *The Ontogenesis of Grammar: Some Facts and Several Theories*. (in press.)

SMITH, A. (1966), Speech and other functions after left (dominant) hemispherectomy. *J. Neurol. Neurosurg. Psychiat.* **29**, 467-471.

STEVENS, K. N. (1968), On the relations between speech movements and speech perception. *Zeitschr. f. Phon.* **21**, 102-106.

G

6

The Grammar of Sign Language and the Problems of Language Universals

I. M. Schlesinger

Hebrew University of Jerusalem,
and the Israel Institute of Applied Social Research,
Jerusalem,
Israel

A. The problem

B. Preliminary findings

C. The experimental method

D. Results

E. Communication in *ISL*: an overview of the results

F. Implications for universals of language

An experimental study of the sign language of the deaf as used in Israel has yielded some results which seem to have important implications for the theory of language.[1] Specifically, these findings raise some questions concerning the hypothesis of universality of the base component of language. Various versions of this hypothesis are possible (cf Bach, 1968), and I shall try to examine these in the light of our findings.

A. The problem

The claim has been made by some writers that the sign language of the deaf has no syntax. This is obviously a very unsophisticated statement. It is based on the observation that sign language has no inflexions and that, furthermore, it does not appear to adhere to strict rules governing the sequence of signs in the sentence.

If these observations were substantiated, they would throw an important light on the question of the universality of language. One way of dealing with the situation would be to dismiss the relevance of sign language to linguistic theory on the grounds that, so one might claim, sign language is not a 'real' language, but merely a makeshift one like the trade jargons described by Jespersen (1922), and by Reinecke (1938). But such an argument seems quite unconvincing to me. I see no reason to accord to sign language, or to other makeshift languages for that matter, a special status as far as the problem of universality of language is concerned. We are dealing here not with finger spelling (in which every letter of the language spoken by the environment is represented by a constellation of fingers), but with an independent language in which every gesture or position of the hand stands for a concept. To show why sign language is to be regarded as a language in every respect, a short description of its uses will be given here.

Sign language is spontaneously acquired, as far as we know, in every community of deaf persons who lack spoken language. It serves adequately all normal purposes of communication between them, as one can easily confirm by observing a group of deaf people in contact with one another. At the centre for the deaf in Jerusalem we have had ample opportunity to do this. The young people who attend this centre are a mixed lot. Some of them have completed their elementary education at an oral school for the deaf, and therefore know some Hebrew; others have only a partial education, and a few have never attended school. The language common to all is sign language, which they use in conducting their affairs. This is not a derived language (unlike Creole languages): although there seems to be a large amount of interference from the spoken language of the environment, sign language is not modelled on the latter, and in translating from sign language to the spoken language one does not get a one-to-one translation.

It should be made clear that sign language is not a pantomime enacting situations referred to, but a regular language with fixed, conventional signs. Thus it is possible to compile a dictionary of the various sign languages; such dictionaries have already been compiled for the American, Russian, English and different Scandinavian sign languages, and we are currently engaged on the completion of such a dictionary for the Israeli sign language (over 1,400 signs have already been collected).

The use of sign language ranges over a wide gamut of topics, from playing checkers and arranging trips, to personal intrigues, election of the chairman of the centre, and determining matters of policy. We note in passing that a year or so ago the chairman was a young man completely ignorant of Hebrew or any other spoken language. He was elected by the deaf after a vigorous campaign held by him entirely in sign language, and has been filmed by our research team using this language — the only one at his disposal — to address the group on matters of common interest. Talks on current affairs are at present being given in sign language by a speaking person of deaf parentage who is a native signer. Indeed, the limit of applicability of sign language seems to be set by the level of education of its users. Those of the deaf who have high school education typically do not participate in the activities of the Jerusalem centre. When among themselves, these youngsters speak Hebrew, employing lip-reading, occasionally in combination with sign language.

The sign language used in Israel differs considerably from that used in other countries, but not so much as to bar communication between signers from different countries. The extent of these differences is presently under investigation.

In the following we shall speak, then, of the Israeli sign language (*ISL,* for short). Dialectical variations of this language exist, of which the signers themselves are aware. Frequently an informant has pointed out to us that a certain sign was in use in Tel Aviv only, while a different version was used, for instance, in Jerusalem. This too shows that there are conventional ways of signing which remain to some extent constant over time.

ISL, then, is an independent conventional means of communication, like any other language. It is different on many counts from spoken languages, but this does not render it a nonlanguage. To claim that sign language has no relevance to the problem of universality because it lacks a certain characteristic of syntax, or simply because it is 'primitive' (whatever that may mean) is to indulge in a circular argument, according to which those languages which fail to fit into a given scheme of universals of language are simply pronounced to be 'out of the game'.

What, then, is the basis for the impression of some writers that sign language lacks syntax or that sign order is highly variable? Word order may be variable even in languages which do not have inflections. In these languages, while there is usually a predominant word order, deviations from it may be possible whenever there is sufficient redundancy to make the message understood. The alternative word orders may either be accompanied by changes in prepositions, as in English: I sent the girl a present; I sent a present *to* the girl; or there may be no attendant change in morphemes, as in Hebrew, where both the above word orders may be employed with 'to' preceding 'the girl' in each case. One may argue, therefore, that this holds for sign languages as

100

well. In everyday give and take there will usually be enough linguistic context to make it obvious which sign stands, for example, for the object and which for the subject of the sentence, and hence there would be no need to indicate these by means of sign order. From this it does not follow that the order of signs is syntactically irrelevant. Rather, one may expect that when pragmatic cues are less abundant, as may happen when the subject matter is more difficult, or unusual, or abstract, order will serve as an indication of grammatical relationships.

It follows that in investigating the grammar of sign languages it may be insufficient to analyse a corpus of the language. Such a corpus may be replete with deviations from the rule by which signs are ordered. The investigator of sign language grammar should therefore create such a situation where the informant will be required to muster all the grammatical resources at his disposal in order to make himself understood. To this end an experiment was designed based on the method of Fraser, Bellugi and Brown (1963) in their study of grammatical competence in children, and subsequently employed by Cooper (1967) with deaf subjects.

Pairs of pictures, differing from one another in a single detail, were used. The difference between the pictures corresponded to a grammatical contrast. For example, one pair of pictures shows (a) a black dog biting a white dog, and (b) a white dog biting a black dog; the grammatical distinction required in order to distinguish between the two is that between subject and object. The experimenter points out one of these two pictures to a deaf subject. This subject then describes the picture in sign language to another deaf subject, who evidences his understanding of the message by indicating which picture has been described. If he fails, the sender is encouraged to describe the drawing once again. After a series of drawings has been treated in this manner, the two subjects interchange roles of sender and receiver.

In this experiment, which was exploratory and still rather informal, we tried to investigate among other things how *ISL* expresses the relations 'subject of' and 'object of'. For this purpose we used, in addition to the above drawings of a white (or black) dog biting a black (white) one, drawings of (1) a monkey biting a dog; (2) a dog chasing a woman; (3) a car crashing into a train; (4) a boy hitting a man, and their counterparts, in which the roles were reversed (ie, a dog biting a monkey, a woman chasing a dog, etc).

B. Preliminary findings

Our experiments were successful in general insofar as the co-operation of the subjects was concerned. They were all interested in the game and tried their best to fulfill the experimental task imposed on them. The results, however, were baffling. True, a certain sign order was dominant, namely, the one in which the agent precedes the object or the goal of the action. This parallels the word order of Hebrew. (The position of the verb was variable and will be discussed below.) But the strange thing was that about half the subjects were inconsistent in the use of this rule, and sometimes put the object before the agent. If the context had been unambiguous, such an inconsistency might have been dismissed as a stylistic variation, but this was not the case in our experiment, where any such variation was bound to lead to confusion.

What, then, could be the reason for our failure to find a consistent order? Could it be that *ISL* has no rule for expressing these very simple relations? Indeed, some of our subjects' comments seemed to suggest just this. One subject who failed to identify an indicated drawing correctly, started an argument with his partner as to whether his manner of signing had been correct (ie, whether one should sign 'black grab white' or 'white grab black'). Obviously this pair of subjects did not share a common rule of grammar here.

Such a conclusion, however, seemed contrary to all our preconceptions about what a language must be like. How can *ISL* function effectively if it has no means of expressing unequivocally such simple relations? Rather than accept the implications of our experiment, we started to struggle against them. Surely, we argued, if sign order is so variable, there must be something wrong with the experiment.

We therefore set out to devise an improved experiment. Cartoon-like drawings were prepared to describe situations in which the deaf signer would presumably have to use a subject, a direct, and an indirect object. A drawing of a woman throwing a banana to a monkey had to be distinguished from one showing a monkey throwing a banana to a woman, or a drawing of a boy giving an apple to a girl from that of a girl giving an apple to a boy. It was hoped that since the description was somewhat more complicated than in the previous experiment, the deaf subjects would be induced to stick to the rules of their grammar, if such should exist.

But this set-up had a number of drawbacks. First of all, there were only two drawings to choose from. It was sufficient to employ some grammatical means of indicating, for example, the agent of the drawing, alone; the object would then be automatically identified with no further grammatical indication. Two additional sets were therefore designed, each of which included four drawings. One set included the

102

following: (a) a man holding a monkey and handing it to a girl standing opposite him; (b) the same as (a) without the girl; (c) a man holding a girl and handing her to a monkey standing opposite; (d) a girl handing a monkey to a man. To describe (a), the indirect object 'the girl' had to be mentioned, otherwise the drawing was liable to be confused with (b). Further, to distinguish between (a) and (c), it was not enough to indicate which was the agent, but either the direct or the indirect object had to be indicated by signing. An additional set of four drawings was similarly designed.

The results with these materials were again disappointing. We could find no rule which was consistently followed by all subjects. Most of them did not even follow an idiosyncratic rule of their own; instead, they changed from one sign order to another within the experimental session.

On the other hand, there were five deaf subjects who used one and the same sign order almost consistently. This order was the same as the Hebrew word order, namely, subject-verb-direct object-indirect object, except that the sign for the verb would more often than not be placed after that standing for the direct object. While it was not quite clear why just these subjects followed a rule consistently, the impression was that this might have something to do with their greater knowledge of Hebrew. Our deaf subjects varied widely in their degree of mastery of this language. Some had attended an oral school for the deaf and spoke Hebrew fairly well; others had a much poorer knowledge of the language, usually knowing no spoken language at all, while still others had picked up only a few isolated words at the most. Hence, interference from the Hebrew was to be expected in differing degrees.[2]

In studying the syntax of the *ISL* we are thus faced with the problem of bilingual interference. Since the word order imported from the Hebrew by the above subjects will presumably contaminate the manner of signing of other deaf people with whom they have contact, it will be difficult to isolate the contribution of Hebrew. What is of interest here is the substratum of the spontaneous language of the deaf which has not yet been influenced by the language spoken in the environment. If the 'original' *ISL* has no way of expressing the very common grammatical relations involved in our experiment, this would indeed have far-reaching theoretical implications for the problem of universals of language.

Could those subjects who did not follow any sign order consistently be typical of the users of 'original' sign language? This supposition certainly occurred to us, but we were not yet ready to accept it. The lack of any transformation rule to express relations like 'subject of', 'object of' was so implausible that we decided to devise yet another experiment with more rigidly controlled experimental conditions.

There was also the suspicion that the experiments carried out so far did not eliminate alternative explanations. For instance, instead of relying on sign order to convey the content of the drawing, the sender might have preferred to use some other cues such as the spatial location of the figures in the drawing. The next experiment tried to unconfound the possible effects of such spatial cues and sign order. It was also decided to make the experimental task still more difficult, in the hope that the subject might fall back on the use of syntactical rules (provided, that is, that they know such rules). In this experiment six drawings, instead of two or four, were presented to the sender, who had to describe one of these six.

C. The experimental method

The materials of the final experiment consisted of sets of six drawings. Each drawing showed a man, a monkey and a bear, all approximately the same size. In one drawing the man was handing the bear to the monkey, who faced him with hands outstretched. In another, it was the monkey who was holding the man while the bear was the recipient, and so on, using all six possible combinations. The situations in the drawings had to be unusual as it was necessary that each of the figures should appear as agent as well as recipient in different drawings; ie, they had to be animate. An inanimate noun would normally be used as direct object and its position in the sentence would thus not be crucial. At any rate, the fairy-tale-like quality of the situations described did not seem to disturb our subjects.

For any combination there were two possible spatial arrangements: the agent of the action could appear at the right side of the drawing with the recipient at the left, or vice-versa (agent at the left, and recipient at the right). Each of the above two arrangements was used in three of the six drawings of the set. Two sets of drawings, A and B, were used. These are described in Table 1.

Subjects participated in this experiment in pairs. One of them served as 'sender' and the other as 'receiver'. The sender and receiver were seated opposite one another. The experimenter placed in front of the sender the six drawings of either set A or B, and in front of the receiver, in a different order, copies of the same set of drawings. Two systematic arrangements were used for set A (and two others for set B),

Table 1

Comparison of the two sets of drawings

Serial number	Agent	hands over	to	Location of agent in drawing in set A	in set B
1	man	monkey	bear	right	left
2	man	bear	monkey	left	right
3	bear	man	monkey	right	left
4	bear	monkey	man	left	right
5	monkey	bear	man	right	left
6	monkey	man	bear	left	right

such that no one drawing appeared in the same place for the sender and for the receiver. A wooden screen obstructed the receiver's view of the drawings used by the sender. The sender described in *ISL* the drawing pointed out to him by one of the experimenters and the receiver indicated from the set in front of him which he thought was the intended drawing. If he was correct, the next drawing was treated in the same manner; if not, the sender was encouraged to try again to explain the content of the same drawing. After the six drawings had been thus described, one after another, the sender and receiver reversed roles, employing the second set of drawings.

Two experimenters conducted the experiment; one of them had been conversant with *ISL* from childhood, and the other had acquired a good working knowledge of it. 'Verbatim' protocols of subjects' descriptions were made, and comments made by subjects were recorded. Experimenters also noted which drawing was selected by the receiver, when this was incorrect.

The experiment was conducted at centres for the deaf in Tel Aviv and Haifa. Twenty deaf persons in Tel Aviv and 10 in Haifa served as subjects.

D. Results

1. The position of verbs and modifiers

Analysis of the results showed that our subjects used a great variety of sentence structures to describe these simple drawings. One grammatical rule, however, was clearly apparent; this concerned the position of the verb[3] in the sentence.

105

Although the verb frequently appeared after the first noun, as it does in Hebrew, English and many other languages in declarative sentences, it was more often found to appear following the second noun (eg, 'bear monkey give man'), with the latter sequence (noun-noun-verb) outnumbering the former (noun-verb-noun) by about two to one. Occasionally, the verb appeared only at the end of the utterance, following the third noun (eg, 'bear monkey man give'). The verb was found in these positions regardless of the inner sequence of nouns, that is, whatever the position occupied by the subject, direct object and indirect object. There was only one position in which the verb never appeared: at the beginning of the utterance, before the first noun. Referring back to the protocols of the previous experiments, the same regularity was found. A post-hoc explanation of this fact which suggests itself is that the sign denoting 'give', 'hand over' or 'receive' conveys no clearly visualisable picture when standing in isolation. The sign denoting the action becomes 'meaningful' only in connection with a sign standing for the agent, the object of the action or its recipient, and since its interpretation thus depends on the noun, the noun will be found to precede it in the sequence of signs.

A similar explanation may apply to another finding from one of the previous experiments: that the adjective always follows the noun modified by it. Thus: 'dog white'; 'dog black'; 'man big'. The adjectives white, big, etc, seem to be indeterminate in meaning unless they occur with the noun they modify. It so happens that in Hebrew the same order is obligatory, but the sign language used by the deaf in Germany is also reported to observe this order (Wundt, 1921), whereas in the German spoken language the modifier must precede the noun.[4]

Wundt (1921) has explained the above regularities along similar lines. Such a psychological explanation, however, leaves open the question as to why these are not universal rules of the surface structure of languages. A recent experiment by Dolinsky and Michael (1969) seems to be relevant here: it was shown that a noun can have what these authors call an "integrating" function when it comes at the end of a phrase. Conceivably such a 'post-integrating mechanism' may turn out to be less powerful than a 'pre-integrating mechanism' which may be assumed to operate when the noun comes first. Clearly such a conjecture must await experimental verification.

At any rate, one important conclusion may already be made on the basis of the above finding. The claim that the Israeli sign language has no syntax can now safely be dismissed. There are transformations which prescribe that the verb may not appear in an initial position (at least in the sentences of the type elicited in our experiment) and that the adjective follows the noun it modifies.[5]

The question of whether there are additional rules regulating the sequence of nouns will be examined further on. Before discussing this problem it must be observed that *not* all utterances contain a verb. A few subjects just signed three nouns denoting the 'dramatis personae' in the drawing: bear, monkey, man. In four cases the sequence in which these were signed corresponded to their spatial location in the drawing and in two cases deviated from it. This tendency to 'introduce' the figures in the drawing may have been more widespread than the few cases just mentioned, which complicates the analysis of our experimental protocols. For instance, in the sequence: subject - indirect object-direct object - verb - subject, do we have a sentence structure in which the subject is repeated, or is this a case of the sender 'introducing' participants in the transaction described in the drawing (somewhat as follows: 'we have here X (the subject); Y (indirect object), Z (direct object), give X (the subject)'). It is even possible, though perhaps less likely, that both the subject and the indirect object are introduced? Pauses in signing may often serve as a clue, but it was not always easy to decide between alternative interpretations on this basis. Since many of the messages emitted by the sender contained a great deal of repetition, the interpretation as to which sentence structure had been used sometimes remained doubtful.

2. *The use of full sentences*

One might expect that any message which fully described any one of the six drawings used would consist of a sentence containing a subject, a direct and an indirect object and a verb. Such a sentence will be termed a *full sentence*. If the subjects had used full sentences throughout, it would have been a fairly straightforward task to describe how the above grammatical relations are expressed through the order of signs. As it is, the analysis was complicated by the fact that many messages comprised less than full sentences. This may be a perfectly sensible and efficient way to get the meaning across, as, for example, when a subject describes the bear handing the monkey to the man by:

bear stand; man stand: come.[6]

that is, the bear stands and the man stands and says: 'come'. Since in all drawings both the one who is handing over and the recipient are standing, while the third figure is not, such a description is unequivocal. But some other utterances were repetitive and complicated so that it was rather difficult to decide where a sentence ended and a new one began. The generally low rate of comprehension—which will be further discussed below—seems to indicate that this difficulty of the investigator tended to be shared by the receivers of the messages.

To what extent were full sentences used in signing? Ten of our thirty subjects did not use a full sentence even once.[7] Of the 20 subjects who did make use of full sentences, 12 did so only in some messages and only 8 used full sentences in every single message in the experiment. (A message, which was used as a unit of analysis in this paper, is defined as any attempt of the sender to communicate the content of a drawing. Many senders made more than one such attempt, and thus sent more than six messages for the six drawings.) The question arises as to why the full sentence should be so infrequently resorted to, considering that it appears to be the most economical and convenient way of describing the drawings. I suggest that the explanation is that full sentences are not indigenous to *ISL,* but rather imported into it from the Hebrew. Those of our subjects who knew Hebrew well would presumably tend to use its sentence structure when signing, while others, knowing it less well, would be less likely to use such a structure.

This can be put to the test by examining the relationship between degree of knowledge of Hebrew and the extent to which the full sentence form was used. One of the workers on our project was well acquainted with 17 of our Tel Aviv subjects, and without any knowledge of the experimental results, he rated their knowledge of Hebrew on a scale from zero (no knowledge) to 10 (perfect knowledge). As predicted, a relationship was found between the subject's rated knowledge of Hebrew and the number of messages in which full sentence form was used. (Only those utterances in which the subject was signed first were taken into account here; in Hebrew, as in English, the subject in declarative sentences comes first.) Only one of the 7 subjects whose knowledge of Hebrew was rated low (less than 6) twice used the full sentence form with Hebrew word order, with the remainder of subjects with low ratings using it once or not at all. On the other hand, all but two of the subjects with high ratings (6 or more) used such sentences in 3 or more messages. The means for these two groups of subjects were 0·57 and 4·40 respectively.[8]

Our data thus seem to indicate that *ISL* has begun to import from the Hebrew rules by which certain grammatical relations are expressed. The greater a deaf signer's knowledge of Hebrew, the more likely he is to adopt these ways of expression. These rules, however, are not part of the competence of all users of *ISL.* To the extent that it is still uncontaminated by Hebrew, *ISL* does not seem to express the grammatical relations under discussion by means of sign order in full sentences.

But how did subjects in our experiment make themselves understood if they did not use full sentences with a fixed word order? The answer is, in the first place, that in these cases they did not make themselves understood very well. Those who did *not* use full sentences were understood only in one-third of their messages; while this is above chance success (with six drawings to choose from), they were definitely less successful in communication than the subjects who did use a full form (more details on this point will be presented below). Thus, subjects certainly were not justified in rejecting the full form for a different way of communicating. This corroborates the above claim that failure to use the full form was due to lack of knowledge of this form.

3. *Other means of communication*

The full sentence form, then, appears to be acquired by users of *ISL* through bilingual contact. But does the original *ISL* put at the disposal of its users alternative ways of carrying out the experimental task?

When the full form is not used, the drawings can be described by two or more sentences, each of which contains only one or two nouns, for example, 'bear stand; monkey man get'. Such messages were frequent in our protocols for most of the subjects. Sentences which included both the agent and the object of the action were used once or more by 8 of the 10 subjects who never used the full form. The remaining 2 subjects only used sentences with one noun, such as in the following messages (with each message containing more than one such sentence):

bear stand; man hold; monkey get.
man stand; monkey give; bear give.

Note that in the latter message there are two noun-verb combinations, one of which consists of the action and its object (monkey give) and one of an agent and the action (bear give), and that this difference is not reflected in sign order. The first message shows a similar phenomenon.

To return to the more 'structured' sentences containing both agent and object, it should be noted that perfect comprehension can be obtained by using sentences of this kind, provided the same sequence of agent and object is used consistently. However, while the agent + object sequence was predominant, the reverse sequence was also

109

sometimes used. In this, the results of our previous experiments were replicated. Because of this lack of consistency, communication failed in about half the messages which contained an agent, an object and verb only.

Comprehension may have been hampered further by the fact that there were sentences containing two nouns which refer not to the agent and object but instead to the agent and recipient of the action. Our protocols contain the following utterances (for the bear handing the monkey to the man):

man bear give,
man I bear give present.

We even came across an utterance at the beginning of a message containing only the recipient and the object:

man; monkey give.

The last example but one illustrates an interesting feature found in many messages: the pronouns 'I' and 'you' were used to label figures in the drawing. Sometimes these would appear also in utterances containing no verb at all:

I bear; monkey; man.

Sometimes—though much less often—within a sentence:

bear give man you; bear give; bear man give monkey.
I man give monkey bear.

(Both the above mean that the bear gives the monkey to the man!) The sender, as it were, tries to help the receiver identify the figures in the drawing. This might be an efficient way of ensuring comprehension if a consistent rule were followed; as it is, personal pronouns, in particular 'I', were used to indicate the agent in some cases, the recipient of the action in others, and sometimes even the object of the action. Hence this expedient also failed to achieve its objective.

Another common ad hoc measure adopted by our subjects to cope with the experimental task was to indicate the location of the figures in the drawing. The signs for 'first' and 'second' were frequent in the experimental protocols. Other subjects used the terms 'here', 'there', or 'then'; for example:

bear; then monkey; then man gets.

Or, in conjunction with personal pronouns:

man I, bear here; monkey there.

Here, again, no consistency was found.

In some cases, the receiver of the message asked the sender who was 'first', but when the sender answered this query, the receiver still did not succeed in identifying the drawing correctly. It is interesting to note that in a previous experiment, a revealing linguistic discussion was observed to take place between two of our participant subjects. The drawing in question was of a black dog attacking a white dog from behind—to be distinguished from one in which the two dogs appeared in the reverse roles. The sender signed:

first dog black; after dog white.

When the receiver was informed that he had identified the drawing incorrectly, he argued with the sender that the white dog was really 'first' and the black dog 'after' — obviously referring to the relative location of the dogs in the drawing—whereupon the sender insisted that the black dog was 'first' because he was doing the biting.

The picture which emerges, then, is of the deaf signers attempting to improvise means to make up for the limitations of *ISL*. Significantly, even those subjects who did make use of full sentences occasionally resorted to signs indicating location, or to personal pronouns, as for instance:

bear monkey; bear monkey give man you.

Apparently they were aware that the full form is not too reliable a means of making oneself understood in *ISL*.

4. *Sign order in full sentences*

This section treats of only those 20 subjects who used the full form in some or all of their messages. We will examine which rule, if any, was followed by these subjects, in their sentences; the position of the verb has been discussed in a previous section.

If the use of full sentences is due to the influence of Hebrew word order, as has been argued above, the order of signs in the sentences may be expected to follow the Hebrew word order. In Hebrew, the predominant word order in declarative sentences is: subject, verb, direct object, indirect object. As stated, the position of the verb in *ISL* is variable. As for the nouns, it was indeed found that the predominant order was as in Hebrew. Let us symbolise this order as *SOI* (subject, direct object, indirect object).

Of those 20 subjects who used the full form, there was only one who used a different sequence consistently, namely *IOS* (in four messages, two of which were understood correctly; and on one occasion, *SIOS* which was misunderstood). The rest used *SOI*. But often they used other sequences as well. Table 2 presents the forms used by the 9 subjects who used more than one sequence in the course of the experiment. We shall call them the 'inconsistent' subjects. In this and the following cases, doubtful cases have been interpreted in a conservative fashion as *SOI*.

Table 2

The number of messages in which the various sequences were used by inconsistent subjects

Subject number	*SOI*	*SIO*	*OSI*	*OIS*	*IOS*	*ISO*
10	7 (5)[1]	1 (0)				
12	3 (2)	1 (1)				
30	1 (0)	1 (0)			1 (1)	
27	6 (2)	2 (1)	1 (0)			1 (0)
1	2 (1)		1 (0)			
11	1 (0)		1 (0)	1 (0)	1 (1)	
9	1 (1)				1 (1)	1 (0)
4	3 (2)				1 (0)	
16	3 (1)				2 (0)	

[1] In parentheses are the number of messages understood correctly.

As shown in the table, each of the possible six sequences was used at least once. The sequence most preferred, after *SOI*, was *IOS*. This may have something to do with the spatial order in which the figures were arranged in the drawing: the agent always appeared on one side, holding one of the figures, with the recipient on the other side of the drawing—the left-right order being counterbalanced in the various drawings.

Third in frequency was the *SIO* sequence, which is also permissible, although less common, in Hebrew.

Of special interest is subject No. 27, who, in two messages, used both *SOI* and another sequence in the same message:

bear monkey man give; monkey you; bear man give monkey (*SOI, SIO*).

bear monkey give man; first bear; monkey bear give man; bear monkey (*SOI, OSI*).

It should not surprise us that neither of these messages was understood by this subject's partner. The remaining 9 of these subjects who used the full form used *SOI* consistently in a total of 49 messages, 33 of which were understood correctly.

One can only speculate about the possible determinants of the sequence adopted by a signer of a given message. Presumably the sign executed first was the one standing for the figure which happened to be most salient in the signer's mind at the moment of signing. There is some experimental evidence that saliency determines the choice between active and passive sentences in spoken language (Turner and Rommetveit, 1968). A similar factor may therefore be presumed to have operated in our experiment too.

In which way were the messages using various sequences understood by the receiver? The receiver would point to the drawing he thought had been described by the sender. His choice therefore indicates which sign order he imputed to the sender. To illustrate, one of our subjects signed :

man bear monkey give,

which may be symbolised as *ISO*. His partner then indicated a drawing of a monkey handing a man to a bear. Apparently he believed that the sender had put the object (man) first in the utterance, and the agent (monkey) last, with the recipient (bear) between them, that is, he construed the message as *OIS*.

If, as Table 2 shows, there was no consistency within subjects in encoding messages, was there any consistency in the way they were decoded? Here, again, the answer is negative. To give some idea of how the messages were decoded, we report here only the results over subjects.

SOI, when misunderstood, was construed as *SIO* in 10 messages, as *OSI* in 8, as *OIS* in 4, as *ISO* in 2 and as *IOS* in 2.

SIO was understood twice correctly, and once as *SOI*.

OSI was understood as *IOS* once.

OIS as *ISO* once; *ISO* as *OSI*, or as *IOS* (once each).

Finally, *IOS*, unless it was understood as intended, was construed either as *OIS* (2 messages), as *OSI* (1 message) or as *SOI* (1 message).

These numbers do not quite match the data of Table 2 because in four messages the receiver did not indicate *any* drawing: messages in which the order was *SOI, SIO, OSI* and *IOS* respectively. Further, because subject No. 27, in two of his messages, used two orders (see p. 112) there was no simple interpretation of how these were construed by the receiver.

H

There seems to be no clear pattern evident here, and, as stated, there was no consistency within subjects.

5. *Degree of understanding between partners*

Some of the data regarding the amount of comprehension achieved was presented in Table 2, p. 112. A more revealing approach is to look at pairs of subjects and ask which proportion of the total number of messages sent by both members of the pair was understood. If both of the pair used the same grammar, better comprehension would be expected than if they did not.

As we have seen, subjects who used the full form can be grouped into two groups: those who were consistent in the order used in the full sentences, and those who were not. As expected, if both members of the pair were consistent, comprehension was better than if one was and one was not. The proportion of messages understood was 0·74 and 0·54 respectively (with four pairs of the first kind and three of the second).

Least understanding was evidenced by the two pairs of inconsistent partners—only 37·5% of the messages of these four subjects were understood.

There were three pairs in which neither of the partners ever used the full form. It is of interest that these achieved a somewhat better degree of comprehension than the 'inconsistent' pairs, namely, 44%. Apparently their more primitive structures worked better than the inconsistent use of full sentences.

It is noteworthy that even those who used the *SOI* order to the exclusion of any other, occasionally failed to understand their partners even when the latter used the *same* sequence: as stated, no more than 74% of the messages were understood in the consistent group. Further, there was not a single subject among those who took part in the experiment, who understood all the messages sent by his partner. It seems that none of our subjects showed complete mastery of the *SOI* sequence. Evidently the experimental task placed a heavy load on our subjects, and their poor performance may have been due partly to their getting confused by its complexity. Much of the variance, however, is accounted for by the degree of knowledge of Hebrew for, as we have seen, it is those who know Hebrew better who tend to use the full form, and the 'consistent-consistent' signers who surpassed others in comprehension belonged to this group.

E. Communication in ISL: an overview of the results

In general, our subjects did very poorly in this experiment and their

114

degree of comprehension was quite low. The reason is that there is apparently no rule which all users of *ISL* employ consistently to distinguish between the subject, the direct object and the indirect object.

One third of our participants did not even combine the corresponding signs in one sentence, and of those who did so, one half failed to use a single sign order consistently. Instead, signers tended to use various *ad hoc* measures to get their meaning across, such as describing the location of figures in the drawing. But these measures are apparently not agreed means of communication, as they were not used consistently and did not ensure comprehension.

A rule can be said to belong to the competence of users of a language only if they are able to use it consistently either in encoding or decoding. In our experiment such consistency was crucial for success in the task imposed on the subject, but no consistency was found. If one sequence (namely, *SOI*) was used much more frequently than any other, this can be attributed to the influence of Hebrew, with which many of our subjects were conversant. Knowledge of Hebrew was indeed found to correlate with the tendency to use a full form (ie, sentences mentioning all three figures and the action going on between them) with the subject in first position. At present, the influence of Hebrew is not sufficiently strong to have all the signers adopt the Hebrew word order; whether it will become the rule of *ISL* in the future remains to be seen.

All this does not imply that the 'original' *ISL* has no syntax. There seem to be at least two rules adhered to steadfastly by all signers: one, concerning the sequence of the noun and its modifying adjective, the second specifying where the verb may *not* appear in the declarative sentence. Paradoxically, *ISL* has these transformation rules, which appear much less crucial for communication than transformation rules for other relations, such as 'subject of', 'object of', which have not appeared in the data.

These findings were not at all what we had bargained for. The starting point of our experiments was the argument that any language must have means of expressing certain grammatical relations—or else it is unsuitable for communication. The data point to the opposite conclusion. The 'original' *ISL* has no means of expressing the subject or the object of the underlying structure, and yet experience shows that *ISL* is an adequate vehicle for everyday give and take of the deaf. The reason is not far to seek. Everyday conversations do not treat of bears carrying monkeys to expectant men. There is no absolute need for rules expressing the grammatical relations discussed here, because

115

the situation is usually such that the meaning is unambiguous. When there is too little redundancy in the situation the signer supplies additional information until he is understood; for example, in our earlier experiment where subjects were presented with a drawing of a white dog biting a black one, one subject not only signed 'white dog', 'black dog' and 'bite', but went on to sign that the black dog ran away.

Note that one does not have to assume any great degree of sophistication on the part of the signer to impute to him such methods. Long experience in communicating in *ISL* will attune him to its resources and limitations, and therefore he will supply the missing information, as in the example given, without much deliberation. But in our experiment the unusual lack of situational redundancy may have made it too hard for some of our subjects to supply enough linguistic context, which explains why communication broke down so often.

Elsewhere (Schlesinger, 1968) it has been shown that adults, using spoken language, may decode an utterance by means of semantic cues without analysing its syntactic structure. The present study seems to indicate that this substitution of semantic for syntactic cues is far from being an isolated phenomenon. Instead, *ISL* seems to resort regularly to semantic cues both in encoding and decoding.

F.   Implications for universals of language

The question of linguistic universals has been formulated in several ways. The 1961 Dobbs Ferry Conference was devoted to 'statistical universals', ie probabilistic statements regarding all languages (Greenberg, 1966). As far as surface structures are concerned only statistical universals can be discovered, but for base structures strict, determinate universality has been claimed (Chomsky, 1965, p. 118). This thesis that the base is universal has important theoretical implications, among others for the language acquisition device and the issue of empiricism vs rationalism raised by Chomsky. This view will now be discussed in the light of our findings on *ISL*.

Different versions of the hypothesis of universality of base structures have been discussed by Bach (1968). According to the version I shall discuss here first there are certain grammatical relations — such as 'subject of' and 'object of' — which appear in the universal base structure.

This particular version is extremely vulnerable because it claims that whatever appears in the universal base appears in the base structure of *every* language. Now, what appears in the base structure of a language must be expressed somehow also in its surface structure. All

116

that is required to refute the hypothesis, therefore, is one language where one of the grammatical relations is left unexpressed in the surface. The conclusion arrived at by the present investigation that *ISL* is such a language thus invalidates this version.

Here it might be argued that the relations 'subject of' and 'object of' really do appear in the base of *ISL* but are expressed in a different manner in *ISL*. Several ways in which signers make themselves understood have been discussed above. The case of a deaf youngster has been quoted who indicated the recipient of the action of biting by signing to his partner which of the dogs (black or white) ran away. However, it is unlikely that a transformational grammar can be written incorporating rules involving such information. It is true, of course, that there is *some* way of expressing what is the 'subject' and what the 'object' even in *ISL*. But when there are no formal transformation rules linking the base structure to the surface structure, there is no reason for a formal *linguistic* base structure. All that one might claim is that the *cognitive* structures of users of *ISL* are the same as those of speakers of other languages: in our experiment the deaf participants, as far as we know, perceived differences between drawings in the same way as we do. The term 'linguistic universals' could, of course, be stretched so as to accommodate these universally communicable cognitive structures, but it is hard to see why one should not simply say, instead, that everything can be expressed somehow or other in every language, at least through the expedient of continuing to talk until the meaning becomes clear.[9]

Is there any way of avoiding the conclusion that the relations 'subject of' and 'object of' do not belong to the universal (linguistic) base structure? Perhaps, one might argue, these relations do indeed appear in the universal base but are left unexpressed in *ISL*. However, the sole justification for the theoretical constructs of the base are their empirical consequences manifested in the surface structure. The above argument, therefore, would leave the proposition of universality without empirical content.

Let us now consider another version of the hypothesis. According to this version, there is a universal set of grammatical relations out of which each language selects a subset for its base (cf Bach, 1968). Thus, all those relations the linguist discovers belong to this universal set, but it is not the case that each language includes every one of these relations in its base. *ISL*, accordingly, includes the relation between the adjective and the noun it modifies (see above), whereas it does not include the relations 'subject of' and 'object of'.

Obviously, this is an extremely weak hypothesis. It is hard to see what facts could possibly be discovered which would disprove it. Any grammatical relation discovered in any language would automatically be included in the universal set, and any non-occurrence of a grammatical relation in one or more languages would be irrelevant to the hypothesis.[10] The hypothesis would become refutable if it were to impose some constraint on the universal set. If, for instance, it could specify two incompatible grammatical relations (or two incompatible sets of grammatical relations), A and B, such that—on independent theoretical grounds and not as an empirical fact—A and B *cannot* both be included in the universal base, this would have the empirical consequence that if any language includes A then no language could include B. Unfortunately, I have no idea how one might formulate such incompatible relations, or what this incompatibility could possibly mean.

There are, then, two versions of the hypothesis that the base is universal. For the stronger version, findings about *ISL* seem to indicate that the hypothesis is false, while for the weaker version, it is hard to see what empirical content it might have, unless it boils down to no more than a list of relations (see footnote 10). To be of any use, the universality hypothesis would have to be formulated so that it would be empirically refutable, but not strong enough so as to be incompatible with the data of *ISL*, among others. So far I have no suggestion for such a formulation. As long as none is forthcoming, the universality hypothesis seems to have only restricted heuristic value: as a prescription to aspire in linguistic analysis to as much universality as possible.

Footnotes

[1] The study on which this paper is based was supported by a grant from the U.S. Department of Health, Education and Welfare, Social and Rehabilitation Service, Project No. VRA-ISR-32-67. I am indebted to Jonathan Shunary who helped in the planning of the experiments and to Ruth Genossar and Tsillah Farkash who served as experimenters; also to

Israel Sella for information regarding our subjects. Thanks are also due to Professor Y. Bar-Hillel and Professor Ch. Rabin, with whom I had an opportunity to discuss an earlier version of the paper, and to Dr J. Morton, for his valuable comments on that earlier version. This of course does not imply that they agree with me in all respects.

[2] It seems that sign order follows word order of the language spoken in the environment in England (Jonathan Shunary, personal communication) and in California, U.S. (Ursula Bellugi-Klima, personal communication).

[3] Although it is doubtful whether one may refer to word classes in *ISL*, it will be convenient to use the customary terms *noun* and *verb* for signs denoting things and actions respectively.

[4] A similar order has been reported by Tyler (1871), Wundt (1921), and Geylman (1957), with regard to the English, German and Russian sign languages, respectively.

[5] It might be argued that in these particular drawings the action of handing over is presumably less salient than the agent of the action, and that therefore the agent came first. However, in our previous experiment where more 'dramatic' actions were described (such as a car crashing into a tree, a man hitting a boy, etc.) the same rule was observed.

[6] This and the following examples are taken from the protocols, with one change: in order to facilitate comparison, we have 'translated' all the messages as if they refer to an identical drawing, namely, the one where the bear hands the monkey to the man. Punctuation marks have been included to increase intelligibility.

[7] In the following, any utterance containing signs for monkey, bear and man, as well as for a verb, are counted as full sentences. Doubtful cases such as those discussed in the preceding section were also included, as were utterances with two verbs, such as 'bear lift monkey, give man'.

[8] Although no subject who rated low on knowledge of Hebrew used the full sentence form more than twice, the reverse was not the case: there were two high-rating subjects who never used the full form. Hence the Spearman rank order correlation between rated knowledge of Hebrew and frequency of use of full form, although significant at the 5% level was not very high: 0·48.

[9] McNeill (this volume) accepts this distinction between cognitive and linguistic structures. We seem to differ only insofar as that I argue that, since the hypothesis of what he calls 'strong' linguistic universals is stronger than that of cognitive universals (which he calls 'weak linguistic universals'), the burden of the proof lies with those who espouse the former.

119

[10]   It would, of course, not be empirically vacuous to specify a limited set of grammatical relations actually found in the bases of the languages of the world. It seems, however, that those in search of the universal base are looking for something of greater theoretical import than such an inventory. I take it as their intention to state something about the nature of language with implications for the structure of grammar and the problem of language acquisition.

References

BACH, E. (1968), Nouns and noun phrases. In E. Bach and R. T. Harms (eds.), *Universals of Linguistic Theory*. New York: Holt, Reinhart and Winston.

CHOMSKY, N. (1965), Aspects of the Theory of Syntax. Cambridge, Mass.: MIT Press.

COOPER, R. L. (1967), The ability of deaf and hearing children to apply morphological rules. *J. Speech and Hearing Res.* **10**, 77-82.

DOLINSKY, R. and MICHAEL, R. G. (1969), Post integration in the recall of grammatical and ungrammatical word sequences. *J. Verbal Learning and Verbal Beh.* **8**, 26-29.

FRASER, C., BELLUGI, U. and BROWN, R. (1963), Control of grammar in imitation, comprehension and production. *J. Verbal Learning and Verbal Beh.* **2**, 121-135.

GEYLMAN, I. (1957), The hand alphabet and speech gestures of deaf-mutes. In E. Smith (ed.), Workshop on Interpreting for the Deaf, Indiana, 1964. (Translated from the Russian.)

GREENBERG, J. H. (ed.) (1966), *Universals of Language* (2nd edn.), Cambridge, Mass.: MIT Press.

JESPERSON, O. (1922), *Language, Its Nature, Development and Origin*. London: Allen and Unwin.

REINECKE, J. E. (1938), Trade jargons and Creole dialects as marginal languages. *Social Forces* **17**, 107-118. (Reprinted in D. Hymes (ed.), (1964) *Language in Culture and Society.* New York: Harper and Row, pp. 534-542.)

SCHLESINGER, I. M. (1968), *Sentence Structure and the Reading Process.* The Hague: Mouton, pp. 113-114.

TURNER, E. A. and ROMMETVEIT, R. (1968), Focus of attention in recall of active and passive sentences. *J. Verbal Learning and Verbal Beh.*, 543-548.

TYLER, E. B. (1958), The gesture language. In Cresswell (ed.), *Primitive Culture.* New York: Harper and Row.

WUNDT, W. (1921), *Völkerpsychologie, Die Gebärdensprache,* **1**, Ch 1, pp. 143-257.

7

Social and Natural in Semiotics

A. A. Leontiev

Institute of Linguistics of the Academy of Science,
Moscow
USSR

A. Social evolution

B. Between behaviourism and nativism

C. Language as a tool

> *The fact that somebody comes along and says, "Oh, I believe*
> *that language has a biological basis" is too easy a way out;*
> *between you and me, we can all say that and then disregard*
> *it, and it's a familiar trick.*
>
> Norman Geschwind.

The aim of this paper is not to introduce any new facts, but to review and reconsider some theoretical notions and principles based upon facts already known. An attempt is made to show that under a different methodological approach the same causes give birth to different effects.

A. Social evolution

Take the word 'semiotics' from the title of this chapter. Its usage has become lately a sort of signal that the author on principle does not qualitatively demarcate different types of sign systems, and in particular communicative systems of animals and human language. We believe it expedient to remember the initial meaning of this term, bringing back to mind the words of Ferdinand de Saussure (1922) about semiotics, or semiology, being "a part of social psychology, and consequently of general psychology . . . It is a psychologist's task to establish the place of semiology". In accordance with Saussure's opinion, we understand semiotics as a discipline studying the role of signs in the development and functioning of human cognition. In other words, semiotics is a branch of psychology dealing with symbolic (symbolic by nature and sign-governed) behaviour.

The principal distinction between the symbolic behaviour of human beings and the communicatively conditioned behaviour of animals lies in the *psychological* peculiarity of the 'human' sign, the idea of which is completely alien to modern semiotics: "The highest form of psychological intercourse which are characteristic of man become possible only due to the fact that man reflects reality generalising it with the help of thinking" (Vygotsky, 1956).

An animal might also seem capable of generalisation since it can carry out functional identification of materially different signals and functional discrimination between materially identical signals. Is it permissible, however, to put a sign of equality here? Is it permissible to think the word has a fixed meaning so far as it substitutes something, ie 'is standing for', some other non-speech signal (cf for this matter the widely known theories of Osgood, 1957)? Exactly such understanding is usually typical of the notion of meaning while the 'social character' of the word or of the meaning of the word is understood as its being common for many people, as the usage 'pressed' upon individuals by society, or as the limits of the varying usage of this word brought about by intercourse with other people. Hence, the meaning ceases to be a social fact and its social aspect proves to be particularly superficial, reduced to the common principles of substituting non-speech signals in various individuals by the word.

A grave misunderstanding seems to arise here from the idea of mankind as a totality of individuals or biological beings who live by themselves in a biological world and only from time to time associate with other individuals to achieve some ends. This, however, does not agree with reality: the social *nature* of a human being introduced in its definition as a biological species, 'homo sapiens'.

"All individuals related to a definite species belong to this species precisely because they are connected by a complex of certain common characteristics inherited from a common ancestor" (Komarov, 1944, p. 207). A newly born animal reproduces in its biological nature changes accumulated in the whole history of the species. Specific features of the species, first of all morphological ones, that is peculiarities of the structure of the animal's body, are realised in every individual. The progressive development, the evolution in the world of animals consists of improvement in the biological adaptation of the animals belonging to the given species to the conditions of life of this species.

The evolution of the species 'homo sapiens' on the other hand has proceeded in some other different sphere than the biological, the species characteristics being accumulated not in the form of morpho-

123

logical changes, but in some other form. It has been a sphere of social human life, a form of the fixation of the achievements of human activities in the social and historical experience of humanity (cf Leontiev and Leontiev, 1959). The experience of the species is now reflected not in changing, let us say, the human hand, but in changing the implement used by this hand; it is reflected in ways and modes of using this implement which are fixed and generalised in it.

Therefore the tempo of evolution of human beings is not to be compared with that of animals; man never faces Nature like the animal eye to eye and even Robinson Crusoe was not all alone on his island and had at his disposal many centuries of Mankind's experience. Man learns from the errors—and still more so from the successes—of other people while each generation of animal can learn solely from its own.

As soon as we accept the idea about human evolution being first of all the evolution of its artificial organs (cf Piéron, 1958), it becomes evident that the *subject* of this evolution as well as of interrelations with Nature in general is a humanity as a whole—'socium', and not an individual. It is mankind as a whole, but not a separate human being, who interacts with the biological environment; therefore such laws of evolution as, for example, the law of natural selection become invalid inside the human society. Not in vain the name of the very principle of morality denying applicability or 'naturalness' of natural selection—we mean humanism—is derived from the name of human beings.

All this applies not only to the practical labour activity of the man, conditioned by the *instruments of labour,* but also to his theoretical and, in the first place, to his cognitive activity conditioned by what L. S. Vygotsky (1960, p. 225) called 'psychological tools'—by *signs* : "Included in the process of behaviour, the psychological tool modifies the whole flow and the whole structure of psychic functions in the same way as the technical tool modifies the process of natural adaptation, giving shape to labour operations."

This being so, it is philosophically as well as psychologically not correct to speak about the man as about a *biological* being and ignore the fact that it is the socium (or, more precisely, the individual as a representative of the socium and as a bearer of both social and biological features), and not the individual as such, that comes forward as the subject in his interaction with Nature, with the surrounding world. Meanwhile we run across exactly such 'biologised' understanding in the problem of 'innate' speech ability.

Let us remind ourselves of Lenneberg's point of view. According to him, heredity provides the individual with the 'language-readiness' in which we detect the 'latent language structure'; the acquisition of language by man is a process of 'actualisation', of transformation of the latent structure into the real one. "Social settings may be required as a trigger that sets off a reaction. Perhaps a better metaphor still is the concept of resonance" (Lenneberg, 1967, p. 378). It is of interest that the individual is regarded as *causa sui*—the motive of his linguistic development is seen exclusively in an inner 'need' and by no means in 'arbitrary extrinsic factors', such as, for instance, the influence of the grown-up people around the child.

Lenneberg's book presents splendid biological, anatomical, physiological and psychopathological arguments while it deals with the acoustic aspect of the language and with articulation. However it is very significant that Lenneberg is compelled to operate with separate observations and theoretical speculations as soon as he comes up to structures of higher levels, for instance to syntactical structures. Thus, there appears a vacuum between the factual arguments and the methodological conclusions of the author, admitting very different reasoning and interpretation of the initial data.

B. Between behaviourism and nativism

According to Lenneberg (1967, p. 379), the individual contains in *himself* all prerequisites for his further linguistic development and the society serves for him only as a *social environment* conditioning this development, but not causing it. This development has two levels: "There are two distinct levels that are relevant to language: in the formation of the latent structure and in the actualization process from latent to realised structure".

Are these levels really different for Lenneberg, Chomsky, Katz and other supporters of the theory of 'innate ideas'? They see two components in the behaviour of human beings: the biological and the other, which could be called 'bio-social'. The latter is regarded as a superstructure over the former—in the spirit of behaviourism. It is true that they criticise behaviourism severely, but in the first place because its adherents apply the simple models developed in animals to the more complicated forms of human behaviour, and because the behaviourists tend to explain too much by 'conditioning', which, if not a social factor, is in any case external (cf for example, Chomsky, 1959). The specific 'social' characteristics, including those of the linguistic behaviour of human beings, are based first of all on the principle of 'rules', the roots of which are again in the biological predisposition.

One can however suppose that there exists a primary difference in the psycho-physiological organisation of both specific and non-social processes in human beings and in animals (such as perception; cf Lenneberg's (1967, p. 332) typical statement: "It is clear that there is no formal difference between man's concept-formation and animal's ability for responding to categories of stimuli"). Still another supposition is that even truly biological behaviour—for instance, in animals—can also be based on the principle of 'rules'. These two problems are not posed by the theorists of 'innate ideas'. In general, one comes to believe that the proper psychological analysis is much substituted in this theory by logical and philosophical analysis. Be that as it may, its supporters do not distinguish physiological mechanisms which are specific for the behaviour of the man, ie the biological and the 'bio-social' components of behaviour are practically the same for them—physiologically.

Meanwhile the mechanisms providing for the proper human abilities do exist and some abilities, such as a musical ear, have been investigated recently by A. N. Leontiev who, following the physiologist A. A. Uchtomsky, developed the notion of a 'functional organ' which is formed during the lifetime as a result of specific activities of various physiological mechanisms united in a unified *functional system*. It should be remembered that this broader notion put forward by P. K. Anochin (1968, p. 79) implies a "broad functional unity of differently localised structures and processes on the basis of an ultimate (and lasting) effect". One of the most important peculiarities of 'functional organs' is their plasticity: "Responding to one and the same task they can have different structure" (A. N. Leontiev, 1965, p. 206), which provides for a wide range of possibilities to compensate disturbed functions. These considerations of A. N. Leontiev go back to the well-known thought of Vygotsky (1960, p. 393) that "the human brain possesses a new principle as compared with the animal localising principle due to which it became the brain of the man, the organ of human mentality".

According to Vygotsky, Leontiev, Luria (cf Luria, 1963), the specific human psychic abilities are served exactly by this sort of mechanism *formed* in the life of the man in the society *by* the society (we shall consider the method of this formation shortly). This mechanism is by no means capable of being reduced to mechanical actualisation of the innate principles of development inherent in the individual. Consequently, the alternative from which Lenneberg *et al* proceed (cf: "The individual does not serve as a passive vehicle or channel through which information is transmitted"—Lenneberg, 1967, p. 378) is no more correct than the opposition of 'rationalistic' and 'empirical' points of view popularised by Chomsky. 'Rationalism' is not the only alternative to 'empiricism' and other approaches are possible, one of which is shared by myself.

C. Language as a tool

I have just mentioned the *formation* of functional organs as a contrast to the actualisation of innate structures. It is essential to emphasise now that the process of the development of psychic functions and properties for which the 'functional organs' are responsible differs fundamentally from both the process of developing the biologically inherited behaviour and the process of acquisition of individual experience. It is realised in a specific form of the *assimilation* of social and historical experience, the assimilation of collective knowledge of the society by every individual. "The individual entering Life . . . faces the world of objects embodying human abilities formed in the process of developing social and historical practice . . . To discover this human side of the surrounding objects, the individual is to be somehow active towards them, and at that adequately active (although, certainly, not identically) as compared with the activity which has been crystallised in them. This is, without doubt, true . . . for language as well. The other prerequisite consists in conditioning the relations of the individual to the world of human objects by his relations to the people: these relations are to be included into the process of intercourse . . . The individual, the child, is not just thrown into the human world, but is introduced to this world by the surrounding people who guide him in it" (Leontiev, 1965, pp. 185-6). This means that the society participates in the formation of human properties not only in the form of 'language environment' but as an *active forming force*— and much more as such.

The aforementioned character of specifically human types of activity as conditioned by tools and signs presents the reverse side of this process of active 'socialisation' of inborn 'natural' processes as the result of objects and phenomena of the outer world being included in these processes together with human abilities materialised in them. If the 'natural' type of interrelations with the surroundings—which is typical of the animal—is governed solely by the individual experience (the species experience being given), the 'social' type of interrelations with the surrounding world—which is typical of the man—is governed in the first place by the social experience materialised in the tool or in

127

the psychological tool (in the sign) in the shape of its *function*—ie in the shape of the abilities and knowledge that can be formed and realised with the help of this tool. The 'natural' processes which are 'socialised' by the inclusion of implements and signs are in themselves 'innate' or—more precisely—can be actualised in the animal world only by the *signalling* and not the *forming* influence of the surroundings; the fact that they include 'social elements' such as tools brings about a new method of physiological maintenance of these processes, being specifically human.

Apparently, already in the early stages of its ontogenesis, the activity of man has a specific psycho-physiological feature which does not yield to any interpretation in the popular terms of the theory of 'innate ideas'. "The system of a child's activities is conditioned on every given stage by both the degree of his organic development and by the degree of his mastering the tools. Two different systems develop jointly, forming practically the third system—the new system of a specific kind" (Vygotsky, 1960, p. 50).

Coming back to Lenneberg's book we find there an indication that there is only a 'substantive' distinction between the formation of ideas in man and the generalisation of stimuli in animals. According to Lenneberg (1967, p. 333) it is displayed in 'word tagging' the processes of cognition: "concepts are superimpositions upon the physically given; they are modes of ordering . . . sensory data". This is the basis of Morton's thought in his contribution to the present volume.

What has been said about the role of tools and signs in the formation of specifically human behaviour can be applied in a great degree also to the processes of perception and other components of human cognition. First, the factor of experience is important not only in the outer sensory link of the system of perception processes, as it is usually assumed, among others, by the psycholinguists (cf Osgood, 1957): its principal role consists in the arrangement of the effector link of this system (cf A. N. Leontiev, 1965; A. A. Leontiev, 1961; Zinchenko, 1966 *et al.*). Most important here is the fact that language becomes a conditioning link in perceptual activity and governs this activity. "The process of verbal denotation in recognising . . . is understood as a process included in the activity of perception itself, and not as an especial process separated from perception by the following processing of its product through thinking" (Leontiev and Ghippenreiter, 1968, p. 19).

Thus, language does not simply facilitate, specify, and intensify the categorisation of the outer world by the individual. It is a force which *forms* this categorisation and imparts a principally new element in it. It is true that "the child must reorganise his way of viewing and imaging things, in order to use language to describe what he knows" (Bruner, 1966, p. 323); but this reorganisation occurs *with the help* of language. A century ago Steinthal said: "Es muss sprechen, um zu denken" (Steinthal, 1871, p. 360). In order to perceive one also must be able to speak—at least, if we mean the human mode of seeing things, projecting the knowledge of their objective properties on them. To be able to distinguish an object from the surroundings as a bearer of such objective properties, it must be cognised; to be cognised, it must be named.

This was perfectly clear to the great Russian linguist and philosopher of language A. A. Potebnya who, very unfortunately, is hardly known beyond his country. With his words I would like to conclude this chapter: "Language is more than an external implement and its purpose in cognition and activity is more comparable with the significance for man of such organs as the eye and the ear . . . *Between the thing and cognition there always comes in the sum of acquired abilities and tradition*" (Potebnya, 1905, p. 643 and 646).

References

ANOCHIN, P. K. (1968), *Biology and Neurophysiology of Conditioned Reflex.* Moscow (in Russian).

BRUNER, J. S. (1966), An Overview, Bruner, J. S. and Oliver, R. (eds.), *Studies in Cognitive Growth.* New York: Wiley.

CHOMSKY, N. (1959), Review of B. F. Skinner's 'Verbal Behavior' *Language* **35**, 26-58.

KOMAROV, V. L. (1944), *The Theory of Species in Plants.* Moscow (in Russian).

LENNEBERG, E. H. (1967), *Biological Foundations of Language,* New York: Wiley.

I

LEONTIEV, A. A. (1961), Psycholinguistics and the Problem of Functional Units in Speech. In *Problems of Language Theory in Contemporary Foreign Linguistics.* Moscow (in Russian).

LEONTIEV, A. N. (1965), *Problems of Psychical Development* (2nd ed.). Moscow (in Russian; and English translation is in print).

LEONTIEV, A. N. and GHIPPENREITER, Y. B. (1968), On Dealing with Visual Sensory System in Man. In *Psychological Investigations.* Moscow (in Russian).

LEONTIEV, A. N. and LEONTIEV, A. A. (1959), The Social and the Individual in Language. *Language and Speech* **2**, 193-204.

LURIA, A. R. (1963), *Human Brain and Mental Processes.* Moscow (in Russian).

OSGOOD, C. E. (1957), A Behavioristic Analysis of Perception and Language as Cognitive Phenomena. In J. S. Bruner et al (eds.), *Contemporary Approaches to Cognition.* Harvard University Press.

PIERON, H. (1958), Le développement de la pensée conceptuelle et l'hominisation. In *Les processes de l'hominisation.* Paris, CNRS.

POTEBNYA, A. A. (1905), *Notes on some literary problems.* Karckov (in Russian).

SAUSSURE, F. DE (1922), *Cours de linguistique generale* (2nd ed.). Paris: Payot.

STEINTHAL, H. (1871), *Abriss der Sprachwissenschaft,* **1.** Theil, Berlin.

VYGOTSKY, L. S. (1956), *Selected Psychological Writings.* Moscow (in Russian).

VYGOTSKY, L. S. (1960), *Evolution of High Psychic Functions.* Moscow (in Russian).

ZINCHENKO, V. P. (1966), Perception as Action. In *Proceedings of the 18th International Congress of Psychology, Symposium 30,* Moscow.

8

Syntax and Semantics

Ruqaiya Hasan

Sociological Research Unit,
University of London Institute of Education

A. Relevance and creativity in competence
B. The semantic level represents the meaning structure of language
C. Semantics and form
D. Syntactic categories are semantically motivated
E. Universality of syntactic categories

An obvious statement regarding language is that it is a symbolic system serving the purposes of communication. Of course there are other symbolic systems, some of which, it may be argued, are better adapted to certain types of communication. Nevertheless, language remains the most popular system for it is the most encompassing and the most widely effective of all. These statements are obvious to the point of being cliches; their only interest lies here in their relevance to the notion of semantics. In a linguistic model, the recognition of the level of semantics is called forth precisely because language is a system —or to use Vinogradov's formulation (quoted in Vachek, 1966, p. 28) 'a system of systems'—and because its use, par excellence, is for communication. The systemic nature of language argues for the recognition of a set of consistent relations governing the value(s) of various elements of the system. Such consistency of relations, which is essential to the very definition of the elements of a system, cannot be accidental; it must arise from some characteristic fundamental to the system as a whole. In a language system such consistency can be traced back ultimately to its communicative function. This same function also implies that a point of contact between language and the extra-linguistic universe must be postulated since it is essential to most language communication. Whatever the areas of disagreement amongst linguists—and these tend to be numerous—it is generally accepted that in a linguistic model it is the semantic level which provides such a contact. Thus 'naming' and 'reference', two of the concepts from the semantic level, simply result from attempts to define the nature of this contact. It would seem therefore that two problems central to any discussion of semantics are: one, how is the semantic level related to other levels of a linguistic model, and two, what is the nature of its contact with extralinguistic reality? I am concerned here only with some aspects of the first of these problems, concentrating in particular on the relationship of the semantic level to the formal levels of grammar and lexis.

Following Lamb (1964), I see this relationship as a hierarchic one: for encoding, the semantic level dominates the levels of grammar and lexis. The latter two levels stand in a representation relation to it; that is to say, in the production of a message, a certain concatenation of semantic components is selected, which in its turn dictates the selection of the grammatical and lexical categories suitable for encoding the semantic components. Semantics is thus a dynamic linguistic level: its categories are the input, whose ultimate output — a string of meaningful noise—is mediated through the categories of grammar and lexis. This view of semantics puts meaning before the actual selection of the set of meaning-encoding categories, structures or symbols; at the same time it claims by implication that the only linguistic level capable of handling the notion of meaning in language is that of semantics. Like most simplified statements, the view that in some sense the apprehension of the meaning-to-be-encoded must precede— however infinitesimally—the actual encoding of it, is open to mis-understanding in various ways. Let it be added at once that this view does not entail that linguistic meanings are immanent or independent of language (see pp. 133-141 for a fuller discussion). Nor do I mean to claim by this statement that we have all reached that state of cool rationality in which we always think before we speak, if the word *think* is used in its most frequent sense. I intend to claim only that some apprehension of the meaning structure of the message must be available, at whatever level of consciousness, before it can be encoded in the formal categories of language. That, in the present state of our knowledge, we do not know what specific form such an apprehension takes is not sufficient argument against holding the view; it has at least the merit of agreeing with the speaker's intuition. The reference here is to such indirect expressions of the speaker's intuition as conveyed by a statement such as 'I wanted to say something but didn't know what to say', which does not mean 'Unfortunately, I ran out of deep structures'. If anything, it must mean 'I didn't apprehend the meaning appropriate to the occasion; hence I did not use my language mechanism'. Again when we have the unmistakable feeling that the way we are saying something does not really mean what we mean to mean (!!), it is perhaps an indication that some component of the meaning structure of the message has not been adequately mapped on to the language categories and that meaning is a stage distinct from and prior to that of its encoding. In listening to natural speech, one is struck by the fact that most speakers are not aware of having produced ambiguous sentences—though perhaps an exception should be made with regard to linguists, who seem to be almost pathologically obsessed with ambiguity! When the ambiguity of a sentence just uttered is pointed out to a speaker, his reactions indicate that he was far from being aware of even the potentiality of ambiguity; in producing his sentence the speaker is concerned primarily with the meaning. So far as he is concerned, the encoding categories are identified by their relation to these components of meaning. Naturally, then, they remain unambiguous for him, unless some extraordinary circumstance arises to shift his focus to the encoding categories. As Lashley has shown (Lashley, 1951; quoted from Sol Saporta, 1961, p. 193), 'elements of the sentence are readied or partially activated before the order is imposed upon them in expression'; it is not fanciful to suggest that this partial activation of the elements of sentences takes place due to the prior apprehension of meaning.

A. Relevance and creativity in competence

The notion of competence (Chomsky, 1965, p. 4) is a commonplace of linguistics today; the ideal speaker of a language has an internalised knowledge of the entire set of rules governing the grammatical, lexical and phonological patterns of his language. Theoretically, therefore, he has the ability of producing any pattern at any time. If we consider the production of speech under normal circumstances, which appears to be qualitatively different from the recall of material learnt for specific purposes, an interesting question presents itself: what is the device that regulates a speaker's choice of a particular sub-set of patterns at a particular time, in exclusion to the rest? It would seem that the speaker matches sense with situation, producing just that set of sentences which is relevant, judged by some standard of relevancy. Asked *Where are you going?* no ideal speaker replies *I ate fish and chips for dinner last night.* This ability to produce relevant sentences is no less central to linguistic competence than the ability to produce grammati-

133

cal sentences. After all, we would not consider a person's knowledge of a foreign language complete if he were in the habit of producing irrelevant sentences, even if these sentences happened to be always grammatically correct. This aspect of a speaker's competence should be reflected somewhere in a linguistic model, also because it permits novelty and creativity in language use in a non-trivial sense. Linguists have recently been fascinated by the discovery that a competent speaker can produce and understand an infinity of novel sentences, and that in theory a sentence can be infinitely long, which they have equated with creativity in language. However, a much more fascinating fact is that the majority of the so-called novel sentences are novel neither in their grammar nor in their lexis or phonology. Their novelty lies most often in a novel concatenation of non-novel meaning components. This is quite obviously the case since otherwise both encoding and decoding would be impossible. We tend also to ignore a rather important aspect of creativity in language; it is in general not recognised that many sentences which are non-novel can be integrated in a speech interaction which is radically different from that in which they might have been said or heard before. It seems to me that the novelty of *the king of Patna loved the princess of Ruritania* is trivial even though it is quite certain that this sentence has never been heard. By comparison, it is an interesting fact that a non-novel sentence such as *little girls love dolls,* which is not even ambiguous, has a variety of possibilities of being integrated in a number of radically different speech interactions, this integration in each case creating a novelty. I believe I am right in claiming that this is a characteristic specific to human language alone.

To return to the discussion, the postulate regarding relevancy presupposes that the speaker knows what the sentence not yet articulated is about. Now, the only linguistic level that can handle the notion of what a sentence is about is the level of semantics. It would therefore seem reasonable to suggest that the semantic level functions as the regulative device in natural speech production. The speaker's apprehension of the meaning to be encoded guides his selection of appropriate encoding categories from the formal levels of language. Consequently, where the meaning to be encoded so demands, speakers of a language will produce complex patterns with an ease which suggests that our notion of complexity in linguistic patterns stands in need of some serious revision. Given the appropriate occasion, sentences with double negatives are no less easily produced than those with a simple positive. Of course, one may maintain that the apprehension of meaning has nothing whatever to do with language, *per se,* and that it somehow comes about through a cognitive structure, largely independent of language. If so, we need to explain how such a cognitive structure can be acquired. Is the cognitive structure of a congenitally deaf person the same as that of a normal speaker's? If this is not the case (see p. 139), then could this difference not be attributed to the non-availability of language? At the same time it should be noted that once the semantic level is denied the capacity of specifying what a sentence is about, the notion of depth for grammatical or lexical categories will be rendered meaningless, since their depth is the function of their interaction with the semantic level (see pp. 145-151). In the last resort, sentences lend themselves to certain transformations or not depending on whether they encode certain semantic components or not. So *the boy frightened the dog* and *the boy admired the girl* lend themselves to different sets of transformations in as much as the deep syntactic functions assigned to *the dog* and *the girl* differ from each other.

B. The semantic level represents the meaning structure of language

1. *What are semantic components?*

If the semantic level has the capacity of specifying what a sentence is about, then it must also represent the meaning structure of a language. It is important here to emphasise that the meaning structure of language is not co-extensive with the total meaning structure with which a normal human being must operate. Not every abstraction, symbol or object to which the epithet 'meaningful' is applied is necessarily a part of the semantic level of language; the possibility should be granted that something may be meaningful without being a semantic component. A smile, a scowl or a clap are culturally meaningful, but these gestures themselves are not semantic components. The components of the semantic level may be characterised as that sub-set of meaningful abstractions and relations whose meaningfulness can be determined language-internally. This is how the term 'semantic component' is used throughout this paper. Thus the lexical item *smile,* a symbol of the code English language, realises a set of semantic components, which are themselves language-determined abstractions referring to the extra-linguistic gesture of smile. They are not replications of an extra-linguistic process, object, or state, etc but have to be seen as theoretical constructs, with no concrete existence. Thus a fragment of the semantic components realised by the lexical item *smile* could be represented as follows:

135

SMILE: [**process of reaction; ascribed to animate participant;**[1] **limited to the ascribed participant; attitudinal modification; . . .**]

All of these components are abstractions and none may be pointed out individually in the real world of our experience. The actual layout of the information is here not central to our discussion; other, and perhaps better, modes of presenting the same information may be found. However, there are certain points I would like to make regarding the substance of the information.

The set of semantic components realised by any one item or category is partially ordered; that is to say, the presence of some component(s) may argue for that of some other(s). For example, wherever, in a set, we find the component **process**, this implies that somewhere within the set will be the components specifying **participant** and **modification**, as in the above case. The two last mentioned components are, however, not ordered with respect to each other. Thus the components of a given set may be seen as a kind of dependency structure involving relations of hierarchy (eg **process** *vis-à-vis* **participant** and **modification** here) and of simultaneity (eg **participant** *vis-à-vis* **modification** here). One may raise the question whether attitudinal modification can be regarded as a component of the semantics of *smile*; after all there can be messages without any modification of the process such as *the baby smiled*. I would suggest that such sentences notwithstanding, **attitudinal modification** is part of the semantic description of *smile*. In our example *the baby smiled*, this part of the meaning of the item is latent. Should the concatenation of meanings to be encoded in the sentence so require, an item will be selected to realise the circumstance explicitly. In making **attitudinal modification** a part of the semantics of *smile*, it is being claimed that there is a fundamental difference between *the baby smiled happily* and *the baby smiled in his sleep,* which can be expressed in a bracketing thus: (*the baby*) (*smiled happily*) and (*the baby smiled*) (*in his sleep*). The circumstance *happily* is integral to the process, while *in his sleep* is not. Further, it enables us to show why *tremendous* in *a tremendous smile* is interpreted differently from *tremendous* in *a tremendous fright*. It follows from this discussion that all the semantic components constituting the description of any one item or category need not be manifest in any one given string in which the item appears; however, the semantic components that remain latent still function as a restrictive as much as if they were manifest.

Attached to each component of such a description, I visualise a (set of) realisational statement(s). In the linguistic model, such statements bridge the gap between the semantic and the formal levels, much as the realisational statements attached to the categories of deep grammar bridge the gap between deep grammar and surface string.[2] For example, take the first semantic component in our analysis of 'smile', **process of reaction,** whose realisational statement would allow any of the three following possibilities:

1. select verb as predicator[3] of a clause as in *smile* in *the baby smiled*; or 2. select noun as head of a nominal group as in *smile* in *a happy smile*; or 3. select deverbal adjective as epithet modifying a head as in *smile* in *the smiling baby*.

Which of the three possibilities will be selected in any given case will be determined by other properties of the message to be encoded. Note that I am not implying here that such selection is consciously undertaken by the encoder; simply, that in some sense and at some level of consciousness, the human brain must be aware of what it is about to do. Whichever of these three possibilities is selected, the entire set of semantic components descriptive of the item will apply equally. That is, so far as the semantics of the item *smile* is concerned, it is not radically altered by the formal status assigned to the item in any given case. If from the total semantic description of an item any component is removed, such a removal will permit an odd or meaningless concatenation of the item in a string. Thus all strings such as *the chair smiled, the chair's smile* and *the smiling chair* will result from a removal of the component **process ascribed to animate participant,** while *the boy smiled the baby* and *the smiled baby* will result from the removal of the component **process limited to the ascribed participant.** The string *the baby smiled expensively* will be permitted if the component **attitudinal modification** were removed.

2. *Universality of semantic description*

It is perhaps evident from the above examples that the validity of the semantic description of any item depends ultimately on whether it is in accord with the facts of the language, which implies that the semantic description of an item in language A is not necessarily the same as that of its translation equivalent in a language B. In order for an item to function as the translation equivalent of some item from another language, partial overlap of meaning is sufficient. Consider for example the English lexical item *elapse*. Let us assume that somewhere in its semantic description, there will appear a component which may be formulated as: **process ascribed to temporal units.** If this component is ignored, we might get a sentence such as *the boy elapsed* (Chomsky,

1965, pp. 76-77). Compare this with the situation in Urdu. According to authoritative dictionaries[4] the nearest translation equivalent of *elapse* is *guzarnaa*. However, the component **process ascribed to temporal units** would not appear to be a part of its semantic description since the Urdu sentences[5] corresponding to the following English ones are acceptable: *much time elapsed, the boy elapsed* (= died), *that opportunity elapsed* (= was gone). One may maintain, of course, that in Urdu there is one graphic item but it has many senses, like the English graphological item *spring* (*spring* as opposed to autumn, *spring* as a specific type of jumping, *spring* as stream, *spring* as in furniture). These senses of the item *guzarnaa*, it may be claimed, are the same as that of the English items *to elapse, to die, to disappear,* but it is quite clear that such a segmentation of the meaning range covered by the Urdu item is conditioned by the fact that one's starting point was English. Were we to start with, say, Chinese, the segmentation would be different. To a speaker of English the fact seems self-evident and universally true that the processes referred to by *elapse* and *die* are conceptually different; perhaps, to the Urdu speaker it seems equally self-evident and intuitively true that the process referred to by *guzarnaa* in each of the cited examples is the same in some respect: in each case it signifies **passing out of existence mysteriously.** Thus cattle and animals may *die* as well as men, but it is only man's privilege *to elapse.* In the parody of an Urdu elegy, a line such as *alas, folks! my parrot has elapsed*[6] has at least two layers of meaning precisely because the translation equivalents of the items *to elapse* and *to die* are at once similar and dissimilar in meaning. One may grant the possibility that the total inventory of semantic components of all languages would be identical; this remains to be proved. There is however no doubt that the meaning structure of all languages is not identical; that is to say, the manner in which these components combine in a given language is not the same as in any other language.

3. How far is concept-formation independent of language?

The view that *guzarnaa* has many meanings each of which is identical with some discrete member from a list of English verbs presupposes that the area of meaning is universally the same. The foundation of the notion of universality for the area of meaning is laid upon the belief that man is everywhere capable of forming certain specific concepts and of establishing certain specific relations between phenomena around him. According to this view the faculty for the abstraction of concepts and relations is independent of language (Lenneberg, 1964).

Further, for a set of reasons, these universal concepts and relations will be reflected in all languages. I should like to suggest that while it is certain that a set of concepts and relations can be formed—indeed must be formed—in the absence of language, it is by no means easy to indicate just where the line between language-independent and language-modified concepts can be drawn. Consider, for example, the sentence *I am taller than myself*. Let us grant that this sentence is universally odd; one would have to think of some extraordinary situation in which it could be uttered appropriately; for example if one were standing in front of a distorting mirror one might conceivably make such a declaration humorously. Let us grant also that the source of its oddity lies in the faulty generalisation conveyed by the statement. A somewhat parallel non-verbal realisation of such a faulty generalisation would be the efforts of a small child to fit two objects of the same shape, size and volume into one another. A universal rule may be postulated that no entity may be compared with itself in terms of one single property. So *the moon is brighter than the moon* is universally odd for the same reasons as *I am taller than myself*. However, sentences such as *I am taller than I used to be* and *the August moon is brighter than the December moon* are not odd linguistically, irrespective of whether they are factually correct or not. The propositions conveyed by these two sentences are obviously not in violation of the universal rule postulated above. If we analyse these propositions we shall find that so far as language is concerned, the entities being compared are not the same. For the purposes of language, *I-now* and *I-then* as well as *August moon* and *December moon* constitute distinct entities. One might reasonably expect that the concept referred to by the first person pronoun *I* can be formed independent of language; what seems doubtful is that any specific modification of the concept can take place independent of language. Here it might be pertinent to add that in her research on the syntactic peculiarities of the language of the congenitally deaf (being carried out at University College, London), Maris Sheppard finds that all elements of 'modality' are used either scantily or incorrectly by her subjects. Thus the use of the 'modals' such as *can, must,* the selection of 'attitudinal adverbs' such as *luckily, unfortunately,* etc are either rare or nonsensical in the texts. Her sample consists of nearly 6000 clauses (a clause is roughly equivalent to a simple sentence). If it is accepted that 'modality' is that component of language through which the speaker's self and attitude are made accessible to his listener (Halliday, 1970), then the implication of Sheppard's findings could be that in some sense the concept of self in the normal speaker is so modified by the availability of language that it makes little sense to compare it with that concept of self which is fashioned without the aid of natural language, as in the case of the congenitally deaf.

A consideration of the two examples of comparison raises at least two questions: first, what qualifies as the same entity so far as language is concerned; and secondly, if the boundaries of the entities recognised in language are created by language itself, in what sense may any concept involving any entity be regarded as free of the influence of language? It may be noted in passing that the notion of co-referent cannot be used to explain why *I am taller than myself* is odd while *I am taller than I used to be* is not. Some other notion is needed to show that *I* and *myself* in our example refer to the same linguistically defined entity while the two *I*'s do not. The referent of these pronouns is not the concrete person, the speaker, in the real world, but some abstraction therefrom. Nor is this relation the same as that of synonymy. Compare *occulists are generally better trained than eye-doctors* (Chomsky, 1965, p. 77) with *occulists are better trained than themselves,* of which only the latter will be regarded as odd by *all* speakers of English, whereas it is possible to interpret the former as a definition of *occulists* by comparison with *eye-doctors*. Parallel examples would be *windows are larger than casements, lads are heftier than boys, ladies are more refined than women*. It does not matter if the definitions are false; sentences presenting factual inaccuracy of the instantial kind cannot be shown to be odd linguistically (Ellis, 1966, p. 92, footnote 27). Perhaps the very factor which allows the encoding of factually inaccurate messages forms the basis of that characterising flexibility in human language which allows it to cope with all conceivable situations (cf Marshall this volume; Morton this volume). I would go so far as to claim that factual misrepresentation of even universally acknowledged facts cannot qualify a sentence as odd, or else we would be in the absurd position of maintaining that *the earth is flat* is an odd sentence. The examples of definitions presented above are linguistically acceptable because as Lyons points out (Lyons, 1963, p. 74; 1968) synonymy does not imply total overlap or identity of reference. *Money* and *wealth* would be regarded as synonymous by most English speakers, yet it is certainly odd to ask *have you any wealth that I could borrow?* This is not to deny that synonymous pairs are subject to certain restrictions but so are pairs related by antonymy. It is no more odd to say *my brother is an occulist and an eye-doctor* than it is to claim *my brother is fat and thin.*

A related point can be made by reconsidering *I am taller than I used to be.* This sentence must contain at least two generalisations, for the proposition conveyed by *this bottle is larger than it used to be,* literally interpreted must be universally wrong. Everywhere man must distinguish between animate organisms and inanimate objects, since the reasons that make the latter example a wrong assertion also account for the wrongness of *I am shorter than I used to be.*[7] Granted that the propositions conveyed by these sentences are universally wrong, does this also imply that they are linguistically odd? It was suggested in the last paragraph that this is not the case. When we have sentences, which when literally interpreted present an impossible proposition, as in *I shall be sorry when I am dead,* they are not counted out of hand as odd; one assigns them some interpretation which fits the possible facts of the universe of discourse as known to us. Thus given the lines of a popular song *But I was so much older then; I am younger than that now,* the native speaker does not treat them as a set of wrong propositions. The exclusion of such sentences from language is not only a misrepresentation of the facts of language as known to the native speaker; it also has the effect of reducing language to what Weinreich (1966, p. 399) described as "humourless, prosaic, banal prose". One would be closer to accounting for the native speaker's intuition, if following Bernstein (forthcoming), one said that the lines in question convey an 'individuated meaning'—a meaning that is highly specific. In such instances the encoder combines the known and old mechanisms of language in such a way that they convey a new concatenation of meaning. Herein lies the source of most of the rhetorical figures of speech as well as of art in literature (Hasan, 1970a).

C. Semantics and form
It was claimed above (p. 132) that the levels of grammar and lexis stand in a representation relation to the semantic level. As levels of linguistic description, grammar and lexis are thought of as complementary to each other, so much so that the two could be seen as the two end-points of a continuum (Halliday, 1961, p. 247; Lyons, 1968, p. 153). For this reason they are sometimes referred to as 'demi-levels' (Ellis, 1966, p. 80) belonging to the formal level. Formal level in this sense may be equated roughly with the lexemic stratum in Stratificational grammars (Lamb, 1966a, pp. 18-27) as well as with the syntactic component in Transformational grammars. The need for recognising

141

grammar and lexis as two separate levels arises from the fact that there comes a point in the total description of language where relations of different kinds have to be postulated to account for the pattern formations. An obvious manifestation of such a fundamental difference between the two levels is expressed in a statement such as: 'in grammar one can make a relatively small number of statements to cover a great many things, while in lexicon one has to record as many individual facts as there are lexical items' (Chao, 1968, p. 57). It would be inaccurate, though, to suggest that no generalisations may be made at the lexical level (see pp. 143-5). Within the level of grammar can be recognised two kinds of relations: the syntactic and the morphological. The difference between the two can be made clear by reference to the notion of 'rank' (Halliday, 1961). The concept of rank is needed to account for the fact that there are units of different sizes in language. Since this notion is basic to that of structure, no matter what one's linguistic model, most linguists make use of the concept either explicitly or implicitly. Syntax may be defined as that body of relations which specifies the conditions under which units of a smaller size are concatenated to form the structure of a bigger unit. For example 'phrase' is an instance of a unit of smaller size than 'clause', and part of the syntax of a language is concerned with stating the relations which allow the concatenation of, say, a nominal 'phrase' and a verbal 'phrase' in the structure of a clause. Morphology has traditionally been regarded[8] as the grouping of members of units of the same size on the basis of some similarity in their own form *or* in the manner of their operation in surface structures. Thus morphological groups as such are not semantically motivated; for example noun declensions in Latin are morphological as also gender in French and Urdu. This point is discussed in some detail below (see pp. 151-2).

1. *Semantics and lexis*

It is often not accepted that both the levels of grammar and lexis stand in the same general relation to the semantic level. This might well be because the reference of lexical items is often thought of as a simple 'thing-sign-for-thing' relation, leading one to the false conclusion that the categories of the lexical level do not lend themselves to statements of formal relations. One consequence of holding this view is that whatever in language cannot be described grammatically is then relegated to the level of semantics, so that 'linguistic description minus grammar equals semantics' (Katz and Fodor, 1963, p. 483). Semantics thus becomes largely an account of the lexicon of a given language. This view can be quite easily refuted by comparing the semantics of the two clauses *the boy loves the girl* and *the girl loves the boy*. The lexical items in the two clauses are identical; the difference in the semantic description of the two can be shown only by reference to the syntactic functions assigned to the items. A distinction is made sometimes between 'being meaningful' and 'having meaning' (Lyons, 1968, p. 412). It is said that a word always has meaning whereas a sentence is meaningful; that is, in the case of the sentence the possibility is allowed that it may not be meaningful, so that being meaningful is not a prerequisite of a sentence but it is a prerequisite of a word. The assumption is that faced with, say, *slithy* an English speaker will not recognise it as a word, but faced with, say, *the chair smiled* he will recognise it as a sentence though perhaps commenting that it has little or no meaning. This distinction seems to me to be spurious.

An important fact regarding lexical items[9] is that a majority of them realise a concatenation of semantic components syncretically. For example, supposing that the semantic components **human, female, young, peer** are realised by the lexical item *girl*, there is no specific part of the item which could be said to realise discretely any particular semantic component. Compared with this the majority of sentences realise sets of concatenations of semantic components discretely, with the result that whichever part of the semantic input is encoded correctly (ie follows realisational statements attached to the semantic components), that part of the sentence conveys some meaning while other parts do not. So *the chair smiled* is like *the baby smiled*; both are statements regarding a participant to whom a process of reaction is ascribed. To the extent that the realisational statements attached to the semantic description of *smile* are not followed (see pp. 136-7), the sentence is odd and ungrammatical. Note that it is uncommonly difficult to find a one-word sentence which has no meaning. Where we have a lexical item in which some discrete part realises some discrete semantic component, we can have the same types of defect in it as are possible in a sentence. For example, consider the item *discap* which is faulty in the same way as *the chair smiled*. It may be noted that the mistake in *discap* cannot be explained morphologically or syntactically, since neither syntax nor morphology has any means of predicting where *dis* can be selected as opposed to *un* as a prefix; only a consideration of the formal patterns at the lexical level will provide a reason for such a decision. The order of the elements of word structure, that is prefix ^ root, is observed just as in the sentence *the chair smiled* the order of subject ^ predicate realising the category 'declarative' is observed. A string of lexical items which does not realise any of the semantic components specific to any sentence-type will not be perceived as a sentence by any speaker. Thus *has flat who been in frying fish this?* (= *who has been frying fish in this flat?*) will not be recognised as a sentence by any speaker of English. Similarly, a speaker will correct *discap* to *uncap* but a sequence such as *cdaips* will be a nonlexical item to him, similar to our scrambled non-sentence. There seems to be no reason for making a distinction between having meaning and being meaningful, since in the last resort these characteristics of the lexical item and the sentence arise from our own mode of defining them. It seems to be a part of our definition of the lexical item that it should correctly realise some correct concatenation of semantic components; otherwise there is no reason why *slithy* could not be regarded as a lexical item having little or no meaning. If we build the same kind of requirement into our definition of sentences, then, *ipso facto,* we would not get a sentence which has little or no meaning. Thus it is neither an accident nor an immanent fact that lexical items are always meaningful.

A consideration of the source of error in *discap* will throw some light on some of the formal relations that obtain between units of the lexical level. In English, we have a lexical set some of whose members may be listed as: *cap, button, clasp, cover, close, fold, wind, tie,* etc. Let us refer to this as lexical set 1. A lexical set may be defined at the primary level of delicacy as a grouping of items which have the potentiality of realising at least one semantic component in common. The more delicate the lexical set, the greater the number of semantic components common to the description of the members of the set. This largely forms the basis for their collocability (ie privilege of co-occurrence) with items from other lexical sets. For example, in the semantic description of set 1, there must appear a component which may be formulated as **process of bringing together to form one body**, and all members of the set will collocate with items from sets 2-5, whose typical items could be stated as 2. *material,* 3. *clothing,* 4. *parcel,* 5. *string.* Set 1 is not syntactically defined; there does not appear to be any syntactic category such that it could be realised by some member of set 1 but not from set 6: *cut, slice, snap, shred, mince,* etc. A general statement regarding set 1 may be made: that when the reversal of the process referred to by any member of it is required, the prefix *un-* can be attached to the item. This explains the difference between *she uncovered the baby's head* and *she discovered the baby's head* (!!). It also explains why one may *uncap a bottle* but the *uncapping of* *stories* is not permitted. Since deverbal adjectives can only have the prefix *un-*, if required, both *unbuttoned* and *unsliced* are permissible items. However, the semantics of *un* in the two items is different: *unsliced* bread is bread that has never been sliced while an *unbuttoned* coat is a coat which must have been buttoned. The cover verb for the reverse processes of set 1, is *undo*, so that one can *undo* what one has *wound, tied, bundled, buttoned*, etc, but one may not *undo* what one has *sliced, shredded, cut, minced*, etc. It is hoped that this discussion, although brief, shows that there is no inherent reason for denying that formal categories and relations can be established for units at the lexical level and that this level stands in the same general relation of representation to semantics as does syntax.

2. *Semantics and syntax*

It is somewhat paradoxical that syntax, where the deep categories have been shown to be semantically motivated (Fillmore, 1968; Halliday, 1967a, 1967b, 1968, 1969a; Lamb, 1966a, 1966b; Lyons, 1967, 1968) is often excluded from consideration in the discussion of semantics while lexis (where this notion has not been postulated) is quite frequently equated with semantics. Sometimes the question is asked with reference to a given sentence: is this sentence unacceptable semantically or syntactically? with the possible implication that the two are in opposition. As I have endeavoured to show, purely semantic unacceptability is indeed rare (see p. 141) for the simple reason that given the right environment an acceptable string will be assigned a meaningful interpretation, no matter how odd its literal meaning may appear to be in isolation. The formal oddity of a string can be shown if one has access to a delicate description of language. Consider our sentence *the chair smiled*. According to the systemic model[10] the oddity of this sentence can be explained syntactically. A brief word first about some aspects of syntactic description in the systemic model. The syntax of a language is here presented in the form of a network of systems. The idea basic to systems is that of environmentally determined choice, so that the point where one starts, determines the range of choices available. Briefly, a system is a grouping of some syntactic features of a given language such that they are mutually exclusive. So, given that one's starting point is the unit clause (a clause is roughly the same as a simple sentence), the range of choices available is to be found in the set of systems applicable to the unit, such as those of 'mood', 'transitivity' and 'theme' to mention but three. Now the primary terms of the system of 'mood' are 'indica-

K

tive' and 'imperative': no clause may at once have both these features. Supposing a clause has the feature 'indicative', there is then the possibility that it may either have the feature 'declarative' as in *the chair smiled* or 'interrogative' as in *did the chair smile?* Each systemic feature is related to some semantic component; the more delicate the system, the more specific the semantic component related to its terms. Thus the semantic component related to the feature 'indicative' may be labelled **discourse unit** while those related to 'declarative' and 'interrogative' may be labelled **statement** and **question** respectively, both these being more specific than the label **discourse unit**. Attached to each term of the system is a realisational statement, which specifies the form of the surface structure realising the syntactic features. For example in the case of the feature 'declarative', the realisational statement requires that the elements subject and predicate be placed in that order in sequence. So, *the chair smiled* is a declarative clause whose surface structure is $S^\wedge P$, where S is represented by *the chair* and P by *smiled*. One component of the meaning of this clause is precisely this; as stated earlier (see p. 143) it is a statement, as is *the baby smiled* or *all those people who objected to the decision taken by the board walked out*. So far as the system of 'mood' is concerned *the chair smiled* is a well-formed clause; to this extent it is also non-odd.

The source of its oddity lies in that the realisational statements attached to certain features from the system of 'transitivity' are not followed accurately. This system deals with process-participant relations.[11] Process may be regarded as the pivot of 'transitivity' choices, for the process type determines what participant roles may be selected within the clause. If the feature 'reaction' is selected, it is essential not only that the verb realising the predicator of the clause be a member of the class which refers to processes of reaction, but also that a particular participant role be selected. This participant role, following Halliday (1968, p. 185ff), may be labelled 'affected'. The definition of the term 'affected' is purely syntactic (which is not to deny that it has a semantic value as well). The 'affected' is that participant, realised typically by an animate nominal phrase, without which an 'indicative active' clause with the feature 'reaction' would be meaningless or unacceptable. This 'transitivity' function may be mapped onto the subject or the (conventional) object or complement in the surface structure of the clause. This depends on some other syntactic feature(s) of a given clause. Thus in *the baby smiled, the baby* is the 'affected' while both in *the dog frightened the boy* and *the boy loved the girl, the boy* has the function of 'affected'. Note that it is possible to say

146

the boy loved with a passion almost fanatical in its fervour. It is beside
the point for the definition of the term 'affected' that the latter clause
will always imply *loved someone*; the relevant point to our discussion
is that the last example above is acceptable while *loved the girl with
a passion almost* . . . etc, unless elliptical, will be regarded as unacceptable. In clauses with the feature 'reaction' the participant 'affected'
can be realised only by an animate nominal phrase; wherever this
requirement is not met, we will have an odd clause. Thus the reason
for the oddity of the clause *the chair smiled* and *the dog frightened
the wall* is the same: both are odd because the 'affected' participant
the chair and *the wall* happen to be inanimate nominal phrases. Moreover both are odd both syntactically and semantically.

D. Syntactic categories are semantically motivated

Syntactic peculiarity results in semantic peculiarity because, as claimed
earlier (see p. 143), syntactic categories are semantically motivated.
They do not come to have some semantic value by accident; as Bazell
(1964) has implied, one cannot squeeze out more from a category than
one puts into it in the first place. This claim is not tantamount to the
statement that meaning determines a syntactic category. If that were
the case the clauses *I don't like apples* and *I dislike apples* would have
to be regarded as representing the same syntactic category; moreover,
one would really be in a quandary since one would not have any
criterion for deciding which of the components of the meaning of a
given item determines its syntactic status, there being no reason for
regarding any particular component of the meaning of that item as the
crucially defining one in any given instance. Although both *I don't like
apples* and *I dislike apples* have the semantic component **negation** in
common (along with some others), only the former is an instance of the
syntactic category 'negative'. This asymmetry between syntactic
categories and semantic components arises from the fact that a given
semantic component may have alternate formal means of realisation,
while a given syntactic category has only one given typical semantic
value. So, the semantic component **negation** can be realised either by
the syntactic category 'negative' or by the selection of a lexical item in
whose semantic description appears the component under focus. A
total one-to-one correspondence does not exist between the units of
semantics and the units of form; otherwise one could do without one
of the levels. The realisation of some given semantic component is,
therefore, a necessary but insufficient requirement for the definition of
any syntactic category. This requirement (that every syntactic category

147

should have a typical semantic value) arises from the fact that language is a code (see p. 140); in the absence of this characteristic not only would the syntactic symbols of the code defy decoding but it would also be impossible to describe the grammar of any language, at least in the sense in which the term 'grammar' has been traditionally used. The point regarding the typical semantic value of a syntactic category can be illustrated quite easily: thus typically, the syntactic category 'negative' realises **negation**; 'declarative', **statement**; 'interrogative', **question**; 'imperative', **order**; and so on. I would suggest that there are at least two additional requirements for the definition of a syntactic category. In the first place, if the typical semantic value of a category is modified it should be possible to state explicitly the environment in which such a modification is possible; moreover it should be possible to make such a statement in terms of some formal property to be present in the item under focus. This condition would hold constant for all instances of the given category. For example, consider the category 'negative', whose typical semantic value has been stated as **negation**. However, when we have a clause such as *I don't dislike apples*, the semantic value of the category 'negative' is modified; this value may now be labelled **reserved negation**. The environment in which the negative category will have such a semantic value can be stated in terms of the formal properties of the process in the item: if the process of the clause is realised by a verb in whose semantic description the component **negation** occurs, the negative category will always have the value 'reserved negation'. Other examples of this type are: *they don't distrust John, they did not disarm the country, he never disagrees with anything*. It is often maintained that double negation is tantamount to absence of negation. Note, however, that **reserved negation** is neither identical with **negation** nor with its absence; *I don't dislike apples* does not mean *I like apples*, as is evident from the fact that one may have sentences such as *I don't dislike apples but I don't like them either*. Again, the typical semantic value of 'declarative' is **statement**, but when we have a clause such as *politicians are clever?* with a high-level followed by a high-rise intonation, the semantic value of the category 'declarative' is modified to that of **question**. There is however a difference between **questions** realised by the 'interrogative' and **questions** realised by a 'declarative' with such an intonation: the former is an **unmarked question**, simply calling for some information; the latter also presupposes some specific attitude on the part of the interlocutors. The distinctions of meaning to which attention is being drawn here are admittedly very delicate, but a competent speaker of

English must be aware of these distinctions, otherwise the two pairs of clause types would not be used in a regular manner. The fact that the typical semantic value of a syntactic category may be modified in formally stateable environments does not prove that semantics is irrelevant to the definition of categories of syntax; rather it allows us to extend and make explicit the area of formulable distinctions in meaning available to the patterns of a given language. Strangely enough, it was Bloomfield who remarked upon the fact that the meanings conveyed by the categories of natural language are "far more accurate, specific and delicate" than any that can be conveyed by non-linguistic means (Bloomfield, 1933; quoted from Sol Saporta, 1961, p. 242). The accuracy, specificity and delicacy of meanings conveyed by natural languages is possible largely because the semantic values of categories in language can be modified.

The second additional requirement, and probably the strongest, for the definition of syntactic categories may be formulated as follows: a syntactic category **A** should be systematically relatable to another syntactic category **B**. Ultimately this systematic relation between two (or more) categories arises from an inherent relation obtaining between the typical semantic values of such categories under focus. As an example, we may consider the categories 'volitional' and 'causative' in Urdu (Hasan, 1970b) instances of which would be *the cook weighed the rice* and *the master made the cook weigh the rice*,[12] respectively. The typical semantic value of the former category can be stated as **process capable of being voluntarily undertaken,** while that of the latter is **process instigated by some participant other than actor.** It is clear that only clauses which are instances of the 'volitional' category can also be 'causative'. The Urdu clause, *this year, excessive rainstorms caused the crops to ruin,*[13] despite mentioning a cause, is not syntactically 'causative', just as despite **negation,** the clause *I dislike apples* is not 'negative'. Unless a process can be undertaken voluntarily, the possibility of causing it to be undertaken does not exist. It is for this reason that *they made him come across an advertisement* is odd. Such relationship between the syntactic categories allows the syntax of a language to be presented as a network of systems where some category functions as the environment in which some other categories constitute a possible range of choices. This relationship also forms the basis of transformations and arrangement of items into agnate sets.[14]

E.   Universality of syntactic categories

It scarcely needs to be pointed out that this kind of relationship

149

between two (or more) semantic components of a given language does not arise from the language itself. It is a matter of extra-linguistic reality that a process, capable of being undertaken voluntarily, is also one which can be caused to be undertaken. This might encourage the belief that if syntactic categories are semantically motivated—as they must be if they are deep—then it follows that such categories are universal. Such a belief would be correct only *if* all languages were of necessity bound to reflect in their semantic structure the same set of relations between extra-linguistic phenomena *and if* there were no others means but syntax of realising such sets of relations. However, languages vary in what relations between their semantic components would be realised lexically or syntactically, nor is it to be taken for granted that they all reflect the same set of relations between extra-linguistic phenomena. In the description of languages, quite often the same pair of labels is attached to a pair of categories in two distinct languages. This, it turns out, is a matter of convenience and does not furnish an adequate reason for concluding that the relations between the members of the pairs so labelled is identical. The reasons for using the same labels are not always the same. In Urdu, the verb capable of realising a causative process has a specific form; thus *khilaanaa pilaanaa* are the causative forms of *khaanaa* (to eat) *and piinaa* (to drink). Consequently in the surface structure of an Urdu causative clause, there is only one non-discontinuous verbal phrase realising the predicator as in *maalik nee baavarcii see caval tulvaaee* (the master made the cook weigh the rice) where *tulvaaee* realises the predicator. In English the majority of verbs do not have a distinct causative form. Consequently, even if *make . . . weigh* is regarded as one predicator, the surface structure of the English clause will be said to contain either one discontinuous verbal group or two discrete ones, depending on which analysis one favours. The clauses in the two languages would seem to be labelled 'causative' primarily because of their semantic value. On the other hand, the label 'agentive passive' is applied to the English clause *the window was washed by John,* as also to the Urdu clause *jon see khiRkii dhoii gaii.* This labelling, it would appear, is based on the peculiarities of the surface structure of the two clauses. The semantic value of 'agentive passive' in the two languages is different: for English it may be stated as **the actor of the process constitutes new but not unexpected information** (Halliday, 1967b, p. 217); for Urdu the value of the category is **potentiality of the process being carried out,** so that the translation equivalent of the Urdu clause in English is not the agentive passive *the window was washed by John* but *John was able to wash the window* (Hasan, 1970b; Kachru, 1966). Moreover in English the category 'passive' presupposes that of 'transitive'; that is to say, no clause which is not 'transitive' may be 'passive'. This requirement does not hold for Urdu; here a clause may be 'passive' irrespective of whether it is 'transitive' or not. So, a clause such as *beecaree buuRhee see itnii duur na calaa gayaa* (*the poor old man was not able to walk that far*) is an 'intransitive agentive passive' clause. It follows from the semantic value of the agentive passive in Urdu that it presupposes the category 'volitional', so that a passive clause such as *LaRkii see baRii Galtiyãã ki gaĩĩ* (*the girl was able to make many mistakes*) is odd while in English *many mistakes were made by the girl* is not. The comparison of the English and Urdu passives[15] also provides an illustration of what was meant by the statement that not all languages reflect in their syntax the same set of relations between extra-linguistic phenomena. It may or may not be true that a certain set of relations between and abstractions from extra-linguistic phenomena will be universally reflected somewhere in all languages. I am inclined to think that this claim as such is of no great interest to the description of individual languages unless it were also claimed that each such specific abstraction and relation will universally have the same formal mechanism for its realisation. The latter is, quite patently, not the case and there is no reason for suggesting that the deep categories of syntax are by definition universal, much less that the syntax of languages is universal.

Universality does not form part of the definition of a syntactic category, the crucial criteria being the three in conjunction: that (a) it should have a typical semantic value, (b) its typical value should be modifiable only under certain stateable formal conditions, and (c) that it should be systematically related to some other categories of the same level. These criteria are in consonance with the statement that syntactic categories are semantically motivated. This is the ultimate basis of the distinction between syntax and morphology. Purely morphological categories are not semantically motivated, which is one of the reasons why they are not mastered as easily as other parts of the language. Two-year-old Jonathan insisted on *foots*; when corrected consistently to *feet*, he compromised at *feets*. An instance of a morphological category in Urdu is 'gender'; as in French, all nouns in the language are either 'masculine' or 'feminine'. The value of this pair of terms for these two languages is however different from that which they have for English. Thus an Urdu masculine noun is not one which is **animate** and **male**; such disparate items as *box, pamphlet, man,*

151

pillowcase, pen and *formality* are masculine (the Urdu items for these are *Dabba, resaala, aadmi, Galaaf, qalam* and *takkaluf,* respectively). Thus the items labelled masculine in Urdu do not share any particular semantic component in common; what determines their status as masculine is the manner of their operation in surface structure. Depending on what syntactic function is assigned to an item labelled masculine or feminine, certain items of the surface string will have a certain specific form: thus *laRkaa aayaa* (the boy came), *laRkii aaii* (the girl came); *kitaab kaa safa* (the page (masculine) of the book (feminine)), *aadmi ki kitaab* (the man's (masculine) book (feminine)); *aadmi nee eek Dabba xariidaa* (the man (masculine) bought a box (masculine)), *aadmi nee eek Dibiya xaridi* (the man (masculine) bought a little-box (feminine)), and so on. It is of interest here to note that often what may be regarded as a purely morphological category, upon consideration turns out to be a category which can be defined by reference to deep lexis or syntax. Such an example would be the lexical set I discussed earlier (see pp. 144-5). Again, the set of verbs in English to which the suffix *-able* can be attached so that the resultant item can function as an epithet as in *admirable* can be specified by reference to syntax. Very simply this suffix *-able* can be used with that set of verbs which can realise the process 'reaction' in an active transitive clause where two participants are required but where the role 'affected' can be mapped only onto the subject. Thus the epithets formed from *love, admire, like, enjoy* and *detest* are *lovable, admirable, likeable, enjoyable* and *detestable.* The clause type specified above can be exemplified by *he loved/admired/liked/enjoyed/ detested it,* where *he* is the affected participant. This explains why one may say *Jim is a likeable fellow* but not *Jim is a puzzleable fellow.* Such findings indicate that we are yet very far, indeed, from having explored the depth of the syntax of even a language so well described as English.

Footnotes

[1] For a fuller discussion of the concept 'participant' see Halliday, (1967a, 1967b, 1968, 1970) and also Fillmore (1968). Roughly, participant roles

are such as actor, affected, causer, beneficiary, etc of a process. An example presenting all these participant roles would be *Marmaduke made Alison sew a dress for his daughter,* where *Marmaduke* has the function of causer; *Alison,* of actor; *a dress,* of affected and *his daughter,* that of beneficiary.

[2]   For a demonstration of how realisational statements bridge the gap between deep grammar and surface structure see Halliday, 1969a. Linear ordering of elements within a unit, realising a syntactic category, is specified by such statements. 'Order' is therefore a matter of deep syntax, a view that has been held by linguists in this country at least since Firth. Some relevant comments in this paper will be found on pp. 143 and 146.

[3]   The element 'predicator' is always realised by a verbal phrase; it has the function of realising the process of a clause. Thus the element predicator is realised by the verbal phrases *smiled* and *has been sewing* in the clauses *the baby smiled* and *Alison has been sewing a dress.*

[4]   The dictionaries consulted were *Standard English-Urdu Dictionary* by Maulvi Abdul Haq (Anjuman Press, Karachi) and *Ferozson's English-Urdu Dictionary* (Ferozson's, Lahore).

[5]   The Urdu sentences corresponding to the English ones are as follows: *bahot waqt guzar gayaa, laRkaa guzar gayaa, mauqaa guzar gayaa,* respectively.

[6]   The line comes from an anonymous parody in Urdu and reads: *afsos ke logo, meraa totaa guzar gayaa.*

[7]   It has been pointed out to me that old people do grow shorter as they grow older, but I let the example stand since this information does not materially alter the general point being made here.

[8]   I must accept full responsibility for the definition of morphology being presented here; in particular, the assertion that 'similarity in the manner of their operation in surface structures' characterises morphological groupings is my own interpretation of how the term was used, in effect, in traditional grammars. An illustration of this point is provided on p. 152 in this chapter. Further, one may consider such English items as *toast* and *underwear* whose assignment to the category 'mass noun' (nouns which may not be modified by a numerical such as one, two, three, . . .) is purely morphological. This does not mean that the label 'mass' is therefore morphological, simply that the grouping *toast* and *underwear* with *water* is a matter of morphology, not of syntax. Since morphological groupings are not semantically motivated, they are much more difficult to predict and therefore much more difficult to learn. I still find myself wanting to say *one toast* or *a couple of underwears.* Now, there is nothing in the surface structure of the items *toast* and *underwear* which could

153

be said to be similar except the fact that they both 'behave' as if they were mass nouns; but to maintain that *this* is the similarity in their surface structure is to go round and round in a circle. Rather it is the manner of their operation in the nominal phrase coupled with the fact that no motivation for such behaviour can be found which will explain both cases that makes their grouping morphological. It may be objected that in interpreting syntax and morphology thus, I am substantially re-defining the terms; this may be true but the re-definition presented here seems to me to have the merit of being closer in spirit to how the terms were employed, than a literal interpretation of the terms would be.

⁹ It is useful to make a distinction between what constitutes a graphological word, or a grammatical word, and the lexical item. Despite a large degree of overlap, the three are not identical. Thus the item *spring* in English represents one graphological word while it represents at least four lexical items (cf comments on p. 138 above). Again it may be desirable to regard *man* as one grammatical word belonging to the class *noun*, though lexically a distinction may be made between *man* in *the man came yesterday* and in *man, did you notice what she was wearing?* Thus, 'lexical item' as used in this paper is not the same as 'lexical item' or 'lexical entry' as used in transformational grammars (Katz and Fodor, 1963, p. 495; Katz and Postal, 1964, p. 17; Chomsky, 1965, p. 166), where most often the terms can be equated with graphological word, as in the treatment of *bachelor* by Katz and Fodor, which is said to be *one* lexical item with many meanings.

¹⁰ The discussion of syntax and syntactic categories presented in this paper presupposes the systemic model (Halliday, 1961, 1966, 1967a, 1967b, 1968, 1969a, 1969b, 1970; Huddleston 1965; Hudson *et al.* 1968). The systemic model takes a functional view of language (Halliday, 1970), maintaining that for the theoretical description of language, the distinction between performance and competence is trivial in the sense that no aspect of performance can be theoretically described unless it is systematic and no systematic performance is independent of competence. Irrespective of their validity on other counts, most traditional descriptions of language are not descriptions of unsystematic performance. There is no opposition between competence and performance in language in any interesting sense, unless by performance were meant the motor and neurological processes involved in the production of speech, when it would be a matter of one's definition of the scope of linguistics to decide whether such processes form an integral part of the description of language. The systemic model is thus concerned with the systematics of the use of language. The discussion of the syntax and of particular systems in this paper is of necessity both brief and over-simplified; in particular I have used certain terms for ease of communication which do not appear in the system networks of English. Some examples of such terms are 'active', 'passive', 'transitive'

and 'intransitive'. I am fully responsible for the interpretation of the model as well as for all views expressed on syntax and semantics in this paper.

[11] A detailed discussion of the system of transitivity for English may be found in Halliday (1967a, 1967b, 1968).

[12] The Urdu sentences corresponding to the two here are *baavarcii nee caval tolee* and *maalik nee baavarcii see caval tulvaaee*, respectively.

[13] The corresponding clause in Urdu would be *is saal, baarish aur tuufaan fasl ko barbaad karnee kaa mujib huee* or less formally *is saal, baarish aur tuufaan ki wajeh see fasl barbaad ho gaii*.

[14] An agnate set is a grouping of items which are syntactically related and differ from each other in a regular manner that can be specified syntactically. Thus active and passive form an agnate set.

[15] For a more detailed discussion of the semantic values of the different types of passive in Urdu, see Hasan (1970b).

References

BAZELL, C. E. (1964), Three misconceptions of grammaticalness. *MSLL* **17**, 3-9.

BERNSTEIN, B. B. (1970), A sociolinguistic approach to socialization. In Cumperz, J. and Hymes, D. (eds.), *Directions in Sociolinguistics* (forthcoming).

BLOOMFIELD, L. (1933), *Language*. Henry Holt and Co. New York: (quoted from Sol Saporta, *Psycholinguistics, A Book of Readings*. New York: Holt, Reinhart and Winston, 1961).

CHAO, Y. R. (1968), *Language and Symbolic Systems*. Cambridge University Press.

CHOMSKY, N. (1965), *Aspects of the Theory of Syntax*. Cambridge, Mass.: MIT Press.

ELLIS, J. (1966), On contextual meaning. In Bazell, C. E., Catford, J C., Halliday, M. A. K. and Robins, R. H. (eds.), *In Memory of J. R. Firth.* London: Longmans.

FILLMORE, C. J. (1968), The case for case. In Bach, Emmon and Harms, R. T. (eds.), *Universals in Linguistic Theory.* New York: Holt, Reinhart and Winston.

HALLIDAY, M. A. K. (1961), Categories of the theory of grammar. *Word* 17, 241-292.

HALLIDAY, M. A. K. (1966), Some notes on deep grammar. *JL* 2, 56-67.

HALLIDAY, M. A. K. (1967a), Notes on transitivity and theme in English, 1. *JL* 3, 37-81.

HALLIDAY, M. A. K. (1967b), Notes on transitivity and theme in English, 2. *JL* 3, 199-244.

HALLIDAY, M. A. K. (1968), Notes on transitivity and theme in English, 3. *JL* 4, 179-215.

HALLIDAY, M. A. K. (1969), Options and functions in the English clause. *Brno Studies in English,* pp. 81-88.

HALLIDAY, M. A. K. (1969b), Relevant models of language. *Educational Review* 22, 26-37.

HALLIDAY, M. A. K. (1970), Language structure and language function. In Lyons, J. (ed.), *New Horizons in Linguistics.* Harmondsworth: Penguins.

HASAN, R. (1970a), Rime and reason in literature. In Chatman, S. (ed.), Proceedings of second style in language. New York: O.U.P. (forthcoming).

HASAN, R. (1970b), The verb 'Be' in Urdu. In Verhaar, J. W. M. (ed.), *The Verb 'Be' and its Synonyms.* Foundations of Language, Supplementary Series, 7.

HUDDLESTON, R. (1965), Rank and depth, *Language* 41.

HUDSON, R., HUDDLESTON, R., and HENRICI, A., and WINTER, E. O. (1968), *Sentence and Clause in Scientific English,* University College, London, Communication Research Centre.

KACHRU, Y. (1966), *An Introduction to Hindi Syntax.* Department of Linguistics. Urbana: University of Illinois.

KATZ, J. J. and FODOR, J. A. (1963), The structure of a semantic theory. In Fodor, J. A. and Katz. J. J. (eds.), *The structure of language.* New Jersey: Prentice Hall Inc.

KATZ, J. A. and POSTAL, P. M. (1964), *An Integrated Theory of Linguistic Description.* Cambridge, Mass.: MIT Press.

LAMB, S. M. (1964), A sememic approach to structural semantics. *Transcultural Studies in Cognition* **66,** 57-77.

LAMB, S. M. (1966a), *Outline of Stratificational Grammar.* Washington D.C.: Georgetown University Press.

LAMB, S. M. (1966b), Epilegomena to a theory of language, *Romance Philology* **19,** 531-573.

LASHLEY, K. S. (1951), The problem of serial order in behaviour. In Jeffress, L. A. (ed.), *Cerebral Mechanism in Behaviour.* New York: John Wiley (quoted from Sol Saporta (1961), *Psycholinguistics, A Book of Readings.* New York: Holt, Reinhart and Winston).

LENNEBERG, E. H. (1964), A biological perspective of language. In Lenneberg, E. H. (ed.), *New Directions in the Study of Language.* Cambridge, Mass.: MIT Press.

LYONS, J. (1963), *Structural Semantics,* Publication of the Philogical Society XX, Basil Blackwell, Oxford.

LYONS, J. (1967), A note on possessive, existential and locative sentences, *Foundations of Language* **3,** 390-396.

LYONS, J. (1968), *Introduction to Theoretical Linguistics,* Cambridge University Press.

SAPORTA, S. (1961), *Psycholinguistics.* New York: Holt, Reinhart and Winston.

WEINREICH, U. (1966), Explorations in Semantic theory. In Sebeok, T. A. (ed.), *Current Trends in Linguistic Theory.* Hague: Mouton and Co.

VACHEK, J. (1966), *The Linguistic School of Prague.* Indiana University Press.

157

9

The Integrated Study of Language Behaviour*

Thomas G. Bever

Department of Psychology,
Rockefeller University,
New York

A. Why we are where we are

B. Why some are nativists

C. Language as a communicative system

D. Conclusion

A. Why we are where we are

The previous chapters in this volume have presented a mélange of dissatisfactions with many aspects of the contemporary study of language. A review of the intellectual history that has led us to our current confusion may help us understand the nature of the issues we face today. I shall start with quotations from the work of a psychologist particularly concerned with a description of language behaviour which emphasised that sentences are the natural unit of linguistic analysis:

> "The sentences cannot be isolated from speech behaviour by any automatic empiricist procedures which operate solely on the 'observable facts': rather the sentence is given definition in terms of intuitions about sequences of words.
> We can define the sentence as . . . *the linguistic expression of the voluntary arrangement of a whole mental image in its components, set in logical relations to one another.*" (p. 240)

This kind of definition has several consequences. The most impor-

* Research supported by PHS 1 GM 16737. I am indebted to A. Jonch and N. S. Sutherland for advice on the manuscript.

158

tant is that superficial word order does not uniquely determine the internal relations.

"How is the logical structure maintained in those sentences which are not statements? . . . And furthermore, how are the main members of a statement related to one another if the sentence undergoes some kind of linguistic transformation, that nevertheless leaves its sense untouched? If I change the sentence 'Caesar crossed the Rubicon' into the form 'The Rubicon was crossed by Caesar', has the subject 'Caesar' thereby become the object and conversely has the former object, 'the Rubicon', become the subject? Or if I say 'the crossing of the Rubicon was carried out by Caesar' has the original predicate now changed into the subject?" (p. 259)

This difficulty is overcome by distinguishing between two levels of linguistic analysis:

"If one maintains that in the two sentences 'Caesar crossed the Rubicon' and 'The Rubicon was crossed by Caesar' the subject has changed, then one has thereby assuredly lost sight of the 'subject' in the Aristotelian sense as that which undertakes the predicate and has replaced it with the behavioural viewpoint, namely that the 'subject' must be the topic. The acting person in both cases naturally is Caesar. But he is the topic of the action only in the first and not in the second sentence. The first is a statement about Caesar, the second about the Rubicon." (pp. 260-261)

Finally, the 'logical' internal relations among the sentence-parts are not merely 'formal' relations, but are also taken to be psychological:

"The logical and the psychological do not constitute a union with separable components; rather the logical relations among the sentence-members are primarily psychological: logic has abstracted them from the psychological course of thought, in order to investigate their laws in their particular and most perfectly isolated form." (p. 260)

Though this analysis of the study of language is similar to recent linguistic discussions of language structure (cf Chomsky, 1965), its author was Wundt, writing at the turn of the century. Unfortunately, Wundt did not combine his insightful views on language with his well-known experimental zeal; if he had, the study of language would now be much more advanced as an experimental science. Wundt categorised the study of language as part of *social* psychology, for which experimental techniques were considered to be inappropriate. One could study the nature of language only through the sort of philosophical considerations and personal introspections exemplified in the above quotations. Such structures as 'mental images' or 'voluntary expressions' were not thought of as amenable to direct study by experimenting on behavioural processes. It was necessary to study language and other higher order mental capacities primarily by means of introspective intuitions.

In the hands of Wundt's students (notably Titchener in the U.S.A.), introspection became a systematic basis for attempts to use personal intuitions as a primary source of psychological data. It was eventually realised that a general science based on introspections would always be limited: one man's 'image' of peanut butter could be another man's 'image' of horseriding. That is, introspections become so idiosyncratic that they cannot be used as the basis for a science.

Many reacted against such a *'mentalist'* enterprise and joined the ranks of operationally-obsessed behaviourist psychologists. For thirty years the psychological study of sentences lay fallow, submerged in the dogmatic behaviourist requirement of an experimental basis for all psychological data. The particular consequence of these strictures for language study was that linguists and psychologists avoided any considerations of abstract, 'logical' structure. To see the remarkable contrast to earlier views, one can compare Leonard Bloomfield's 1914 book *The Study of Language* with his 1933 book, *Language*. The former is an open exploration of Wundt's considerations, while the latter rejects such views as 'unscientific mentalism'.

The development of 'Generative Grammar' in 1957 represented a return to the earlier structuralism of Wundt, albeit with more powerful and more precise descriptive devices than were originally available (Chomsky, 1957). In Chomsky's reformulation, the possible internal 'logical' relations among words and phrases are described by a set of elementary phrase structure rules and a lexicon. This latter component generates representations of particular logical structures, such as that shown in (1).

1. Actor   = Caesar
    Action = Cross
    Object = Rubicon
    Tense   = Past

The internal structure and external form of each sentence are related by a set of 'transformations', which organise the phrases into particular sequences (as in 2).

2. a. Caesar crossed the Rubicon.
    b. The Rubicon was crossed by Caesar.
    c. It's Caesar who crossed the Rubicon.
    d. It's the Rubicon that Caesar crossed.
    e. It's Caesar that the Rubicon was crossed by.
    f. What Caesar did was cross the Rubicon.
    g. What happened to the Rubicon was that it was crossed by Caesar.

Such a descriptive model accounts for the fact that superficially different sentences can have the same set of internal relations, the differences being contributed by differences in the transformations which map the internal structures onto their external forms.

This model of grammar set the scene for the difficulties and perplexities raised in many of the other chapters. The basic data which such a grammar describes are intuitions about the grammaticality of certain sequences (eg 3a is grammatical while 3b is not) and the relations between sequences (eg the structure in 3c is related internally to 3a, while that of 3d is not (even though 3c and 3d are superficially similar).

3. a. Caesar crossed the Rubicon.
    b. *Caesar the Rubicon crossed.
    c. The Rubicon was crossed by Caesar.
    d. The Rubicon was crossed by midnight.

Such intuitions are assumed to be stable reflections of actual linguistic structure. The fact that the psychological nature of such introspections is totally obscure does not undercut the claim that the intuitions are valid data, so long as no claims are made about the psychological processes which they imply.

B. Why some are nativists

Grammarians have made the distinction between grammar and speech behaviour particularly clear by emphasising that grammars account for 'linguistic knowledge' but not for the processes which deploy that knowledge. Psycholinguists have attempted to capitalise on the insights

---

*This symbol indicates that the sentence following is not an acceptable English sentence.

of linguists by incorporating grammars, unmodified, into their models of speech behaviour. However the grammarian's intention was to account only for the structural properties implied by our basic knowledge of sentence grammaticality. The interaction of grammaticality with other aspects of behaviour, for example, social function, semantics, general psychological systems, human communication, biological systems and innate structures, was explicitly left open by generative grammarians.

Of course, like the psycholinguists of the early 1960s, we all find linguistic grammar tantalising. A grammar's descriptive precision and the centrality of the facts about language which it describes encourage us to incorporate it directly into the explanation of all aspects of language behaviour. The frustration involved in such attempts is also reflected in the previous chapters.

While linguists themselves make no claims about the psychological properties of linguistic rules, they have produced detailed arguments that human infants learn language as a consequence of highly specific inborn structures, 'pretuned' to extract human language from their environment, and not to extract other kinds of communication systems. That is, the structure of human language is not learned (and presumably formed) by some 'general purpose' learning capacity in the child, but by means of highly specific innate structures (Chomsky, 1965; Katz, 1967; Lenneberg, 1967).

It is useful to consider the kinds of facts which motivate linguists and psychologists to make such strong claims. The child learns the elements of his first language by the age of three without apparent specific instruction and appears to acquire an intuitive knowledge of the internal, 'abstract' structure of sentences even though he is never presented with their explicit expression. This developmental pattern in language acquisition is incompatible with those theories of learning and cognitive structure which assume that the environment reinforces the child for particular overt acts, and which account only for the incorporation of originally overt stimuli and responses. On such a view the unreinforced appearance in the child of 'abstract' logical structures (for example, the concepts in 1) is particularly puzzling.

1. *Speech production*

Furthermore, the patterns of language learning do not show the steady incremental convergence towards adult language predicted by the view that language learning proceeds by the steady mastery of individual sentence constructions. There are abrupt shifts in the manifest speech performance of the child, which imply drastic structural reorganisations of his linguistic knowledge. Firstly, there are several developments which characterise learning to speak, regardless of the language that is being acquired (the speech production data are reviewed in Slobin, 1970). The child starts out speaking individual words which appear in many instances to indicate relational interactions rather than mere naming. For example (6a) could mean any one of the full sentences in (6b-f), depending on the situation.

6. a. Doggie.
    b. There is a dog.
    c. I want the dog.
    d. Listen to the dog.
    e. I'm scared of the dog.
    f. Is that a dog?

There is clearly an early point in the child's linguistic development when a single word carries relational intention. Presumably limitations of expressive capacity restrict the pronounceable output to one-word utterances, even though relations between several words are intended.

When these limitations are overcome and the child advances to two-word utterances, several interesting characteristics appear in his speech. First, there is a universal 'actor-action', 'action-object' word order for two-word utterances containing transitive verbs. That is, utterances like (7a) always mean (7b) and utterances like (7c) mean (7d). In utterances with intransitive verbs, each child goes through a

7. a. mommy kiss
    b. 'mommy is kissing somebody' (or 'should be doing so')
    c. kiss mommy
    d. 'somebody is kissing mommy' (or 'should be doing so')

phase of using one characteristic word-order or the other, but the order varies from language to language and from child to child as in (8ab).

8. a. glass fall
    b. fall glass

(It is striking that these phenomena also occur in inflected languages, such as German and Russian.) Finally, when the child can produce three-word utterances his language passes through a series of sentence forms, each of which is distinct from adult constructions. For example, the way in which a child asks questions goes through several stages

(Bellugi, 1967). The stage at which the child says sentences (9a) does not represent a *gradual* convergence towards the external appearance of the adult question form (9b). Rather, the child is using a specific

9. a. What Harry said?
    b. What did Harry say?

rule (*place the WH-word first* in questions). Similarly, the development of the child's expressive mastery of the past participle of English strong verbs goes through stages like those in (10a-c) (see Cazden, 1968). At the stage when the child produces utterances like (10b) his

10. a. Harry went
     b. Harry wented
     c. Harry went

ability to talk is temporarily worse (ie, less adult-like) than at a younger age because he is *overgeneralising* the rule that past participles for weak verbs are formed by adding *-ed* to the stem. The conclusion from all these facts is that the child's early speech production is based on certain structural hypotheses. He thus acquires discrete abstract rules for talking rather than mastering his language by the steady accumulation of specific constructions.

2. *Speech perception*

The development of the child's ability to understand sentences has been studied less, but there are striking similarities to the development of talking ability (reviewed in Bever, 1970b). At the age of two years, the child uses a perceptual strategy that a 'noun-verb' sequence is interpreted as 'actor-action'. For example, the sentences in (11) are correctly acted out (significantly more often than chance) by two-year-old children. The child's correct performance on sentences like (11c)

11. a. *The horse kisses* the cow
     b. It's *the horse kisses* the cow
     c. It's the cow *the horse kisses*

shows that he does not merely take the first noun of a sentence to be the actor, but rather appears to analyse the 'noun-verb' sequence as a kind of primitive *gestalt* even when it does not occur first in a sentence. Further evidence for this possibility is shown by the fact that the two-year-old child performance is 50% correct on passive sentences like

(12a). Apparently the *is* in (12a) blocks the 'noun-verb' *gestalt* since, if it applied, children would always *reverse* the interpretation of passives incorrectly taking 'the cow' as actor (cf R. Bates, 1969, for further discussion). Furthermore, the fact that semantically improbable sentences (12b) are performed better than chance at age two years supports the interpretation that the child is using a structural strategy rather than a semantic one.

12. a. The cow is kissed by the horse
     b. The dog pats the mother

In the interpretation of complex sentences with more than one *noun-verb* sequence the young child takes the first such sequence as the most significant, and tends to ignore other parts of the sentence. Thus in comprehension and repetition studies young children tend to respond to the italicised portion of the sentences in (13).

13. a. The horse *the cow kissed* fell over
     b. *The horse kissed the cow* and fell over
     c. *The horse kissing the cow* fell over

At age four the child appears to have given up his dependence on the 'noun-verb' *gestalt* and now interprets sentences using the strategy that the first noun is the actor. Accordingly, his performance on sentences like (11c) and (12a) is *worse* than at age $3\frac{1}{2}$, while his performance on sentences (11a) and (11b) improves (if it is not already at 100%). After this period the child's performance on complex sentences becomes much more like that of an adult: if the child ignores one of the clauses, it is usually the subordinate clause which is dropped, regardless of the order of presentation in the sentence.

In brief, the mechanism for understanding sentences appears to go through discontinuous phases without any specific training or reinforcement of the perceptual mechanisms preferred at each age. As in the case of the development of speech production, at certain ages the child's performance can deteriorate, suggesting that linguistic perceptual development involves the reformulation of perceptual rules rather than the perceptual mastery of a gradually increasing number of different constructions.

3. *Neurological dominance*

There are certain gross neurological developments between 2 and 5 years which suggest a structural shift in the neural organisation related

165

to language capacity. It is well-attested (see p. 15) that in normal adults, linguistic capacity is relatively localised in one brain hemisphere (usually the left). For example, clinical evidence shows that lesions in the left hemisphere are more likely to cause aphasia than lesions in the corresponding area of the right hemisphere. Similarly, Kimura (1967) showed that most normal adults repeat more of the digits presented to the right ear (functionally enervating the *left* hemisphere) than of those presented simultaneously to the left ear (enervating the *right* hemisphere). (See Bever, 1970c, for a review of these and related phenomena.) Lenneberg (1967) presents evidence that this neurological specialisation of linguistic function is not 'fixed' until the age of 12-13, since before that age aphasia resulting from lesions to the left hemisphere is quickly overcome, suggesting a 'transfer' of the function to the right hemisphere. The relative persistence of aphasia from left-hemisphere lesions sustained after that age suggests that the relative equipotentiality of the two hemispheres has been lost.

More recent research indicates that while there is some lability of dominance, which is perhaps not firmly developed until age 12, there is also a predisposition for the left-hemisphere to be dominant in speech even in the very young child. First, Wada (1969) has reported a greater anatomical development in neonates of left hemisphere brain areas involved in speech behaviour. Second, Teuber and Twitchell (Teuber, in press) have found that children with signs of early lesions in the left hemisphere have retarded verbal development compared with children showing signs of early right-hemisphere lesions. Such investigations suggest that the young child does not have total freedom to select which hemisphere is to be specialised for language; there is a genetic predisposition for the left hemisphere.

We have found a relation between the development of certain perceptual strategies for dealing with speech and the development of an ear-preference. Those children between three and five who show a strong ear preference also show a strong tendency to utilise the strategy that the first noun in a speech sequence is the actor. This suggests that there is an intimate relation between the differentiation of such strategies and the emergence of lateralisation (Bever, 1970c).

Some of our recent investigations show that environmental stimulation plays a critical role in the emergence and 'fixing' of the neurological predisposition for the left hemisphere (Bever, Palmer, Sumner and Moran, in preparation). We examined two socio-economically matched populations of boys at age four years, eight months (4/8) on simple measures of hand, ear and eye dominance. The experimental group had participated in a diffuse 'cultural enrichment' programme (see Rees and Palmer, 1969, for a description of the programme) starting at 2/8 for some boys and 3/8 for others. A control group was tested (on standard measures of intellectual capacity) at the same intervals as the experimental groups but received no enrichment. At age 4/8 the experimental groups showed more hand/ear/eye consistency (ie preferring the right hand, right eye, and right ear to the same extent) and more children showed an overall preference for the right side (associated functionally with the left hemisphere, at least for the hand and ear). That is, while there may be a predisposition for the left hemisphere to be dominant, certain environmental stimuli can stimulate the emergence of its structural integration with sensory-motor processing.

In conclusion, the development of the ability to talk, and to listen, and of the neurological dominance underlying language all start out at age two with certain predispositions, either inborn or previously acquired. Shifts occur in each of these aspects of linguistic organisation as a consequence of interacting with the linguistic and cognitive environment. Such facts support the claim that language-learning depends on specific mental and physiological structures rather than on 'general intelligence'.

Some scholars have taken the linguists' claim that language is 'innate' to include the claim that inborn linguistic predispositions are not themselves derived from other general properties of human neurology and cognition, but are limited to their linguistic expression. It is not a necessary part of the claim that there are innate structures underlying linguistic universals that those structures are not reflected in other aspects of human behaviour. Of course, it is also not obvious what a 'general purpose' learning model would be like, despite the attempts of many psychologists to frame one. Insofar as a general learning theory predicts the impossibility of abstract linguistic structures, it is inadequate to account for the learning of human language. However, failure of one type of allegedly general purpose learning theory to account for language learning does not prove that some other general learning theory will not account for it.

C. Language as a communicative system

The previous chapters discuss specific ways in which we should modify our preoccupation with the acquisition of pure grammatical structure so as to set the psychology of language in a broader perspective. Leontiev urges that we view both social structure and language as functions of the basic 'urge' for socially motivated and organised communication. Schlesinger makes the related argument that human language is merely one example of possible human communication systems. Wales narrows the argument further by discussing specific psychological mechanisms that may underlie highly intricate grammatical structures. Hasan maintains that grammatical structure itself cannot be studied or understood in isolation either from the semantic structure of language or from the semantic properties of specific lexical items. The two chapters concerned with the biological basis of linguistic structure both suggest that we must be cautious in assuming that every universal property of languages is necessarily 'innate'. Campbell points out that many behavioural properties recruited by human language are also utilised by presumptively more primitive communication systems. Finally, McNeill attempts to distinguish between different kinds of linguistic universals as a function of the extent to which they are derived from general (non-linguistic) cognitive properties of human beings.

Viewing all of these arguments together we can see that they represent attempts at a delimitation of the role of 'syntax' in language which we should take into account when studying its universal properties in adults and its development in children. We could represent this delimitation as a kind of conceptual algebra which describes what we must factor out from language behaviour before attributing it to a specific linguistic structure rather than to a linguistic expression of a

14. (Structure of Language Behaviour) — $(SU + HCS + PN + SS + BUC + CS) =$ (specifically linguistic structures)

general psychological structure (where SU = social urge; HCS = common properties of all human communications systems; PM = psychological mechanisms; SS = semantic structures; BUC = biological universals of communications systems; CS = common properties of all human cognition systems).

Of course such conceptual articulation is possible only when the items are mutually exclusive and functionally independent (ie when what is represented by one term is not affected by what is represented by any of the other terms). Unfortunately, such independence is the exception rather than the rule; we cannot add and subtract aspects of behaviour as though they were integers. Rather we must view language as an organizing communication system within which different mental and neurological mechanisms interact and modify each other. In discussions and research we may refer to each mechanism as though it had isolable properties, but this must be viewed as a necessary idealisation and a scientific metaphor rather than a reflection of the true state of affairs.

Dissatisfaction with the current devotion to syntactic phenomena in language behaviour is a natural outgrowth of the progress and speed of the structuralist revival that has occurred within linguistics. It is indeed time to expand our horizons beyond the treatment of syntax to more inclusive treatments of language behaviour. However, we must tread carefully lest our enthusiasm to describe all available 'facts' about language leads us into the same kind of behaviourist swamp that engulfed the last structuralist period between 1920 and 1950. We can avoid this danger and bring the study of language into line with other areas of behavioural science if we recognise that language behaviour is itself a function of a variety of interacting systems, none of which is logically prior in its influence on language behaviour.

In this sense the study of language is like the study of an animal within biological science. Consider for example the description of a rabbit: it includes such items as the fact that the rabbit engages in hopping behaviour, is herbivorous, has a specific normal body temperature, has a certain kind of liver, has a unique genetic structure, lives in holes in the ground, and so forth. All of these facts are part of the description of what a 'rabbit' is; yet none of them alone is an exhaustive or sufficient description of 'rabbit'. All of the physiological and behavioural subsystems of the rabbit exist simultaneously and can modify each others' structure and function. Thus, while we can study the function of the rabbit's liver as though it existed in total isolation, there are certain points where our description of the liver must take into account other subsystems of the animal—eg, the body temperature, normal heart rate, the behavioural patterns accompanying elimination of body wastes and so on. Of course, certain aspects of the animal might appear to be so remote as to be functionally distinct from each other; for example, one might think that there is no mutual influence between the length of the rabbit's ears and the function of his liver. However, interactions between each subsystem set up for isolated description cannot be ruled out *a priori,* but must be examined empirically. For example, one might argue that the length of a rabbit's ears is involved in increasing body surface to increase control over body temperature (cf the fact that desert-rabbits' ears are particularly oversized). Thus after all, there is an interaction between ear length, and *all* internal organs via temperature regulation. An animal is a coherent whole in which no component is entirely distinct from any other.

169

An analogous line of argument holds for the study of language. During the past few years we have concentrated on the study of the structure and acquisition of the syntactic aspect of language; we have made the simplifying assumption that the interactions between syntax and other aspects of language behaviour are sufficiently remote so that theoretical conclusions about the structure of syntax will not turn out to be spurious when placed in a larger context. However, as we consider other subsystems of language behaviour it is becoming clear that the attempt to study syntax *in vitro* has certain limits which we may have already exceeded.

In the remainder of this discussion I shall review three aspects of the interaction of syntactic structures with other behavioural aspects of language. First, there are many sources for the unacceptability of potential sentences in addition to structural 'ungrammaticality': in some cases linguists may mistakenly construct a syntactic theory to rule out particular utterances as 'ungrammatical' which in fact are unacceptable due to non-grammatical facts about their use. Second, the role in laboratory studies of particular grammatically defined structures is greatly influenced by the subject's task: thus certain structures which are necessarily primary in linguistic descriptions play a secondary role in many other kinds of speech behaviour. Finally, the nongrammatical mechanisms of speech behaviour in the child can be seen to play a part in the formation of the child's grammar itself. As a result the linguist may claim as a structural 'grammatical universal' a property of language which is really due to extra-grammatical properties of the language-learning child.

1. *The multiple source of sequence unacceptability*

Linguistic grammars are descriptions of a range of structural facts about speech sequences, the most basic of which is that some are grammatical and that some are ungrammatical. The intuitions of native speakers about the acceptability of potential sentences is the main source for such facts. For example, the sequences in (15) are clearly ungrammatical, while those in (16) are clearly grammatical.

15.　a.　*I believe it that John to be a Martian.
　　　b.　*Paul Bunyan falled the trees as fast as J.
　　　　　Apple seed growed them.
　　　c.　*Me Tarzan, you Jane.
　　　d.　*White man speak with forked tongue, steal land, sell firewater braves.

*This symbol indicates that the sentence following is not an acceptable English sentence.

16. a. I believe John to be a Martian.
    b. P. Bunyan felled the trees as fast as J.
       Appleseed grew them.
    c. I'm Tarzan, you're Jane.
    d. The White men spoke with a forked tongue, stole the land
       and sold firewater to braves.

These cases are perfectly clear and will be agreed upon by all native speakers of English. Thus the factual basis of grammars can be quite solidly grounded in intuitions about acceptability of sequences.

However, there are many bases for unacceptability judgements in addition to the violation of grammatical constraints. First, there are cases in which sentences are unacceptable because they appear to place an inordinately heavy load on the system of speech perception. For example (a) is far less acceptable than the grammatically parallel (b) in each of the pairs below:

17. a. ?The horse raced past the barn fell.
    b. The horse ridden past the barn fell.

    a. ?The pitcher tossed the ball tossed the ball[1]
    b. The pitcher thrown the ball tossed the ball.

    a. ?They didn't like even considering discussing continuing selling buildings.
    b. They didn't like even considering a discussion of continuing to sell buildings.

There are also cases in which sentences are unacceptable because they are impossible to utter (at least without special practice which allows one to circumvent the usual system of speech production):

18. a. ?Peter Piper picked a peck of pickled peppers.
    b. Peter Johnson picked a lot of ruined peppers.

    a. ?She sells seashells by the sea shore.
    b. She hawks mollusks by the sea shore.

    a. ?Rubber baby buggy bumpers bug Bugs Bunny.
    b. Metal baby carriage bumpers upset Bugs Bunny.

? This symbol indicates that the acceptability of the sentence following is questionable.

Certain sentences are unacceptable because they involve inherent contradictions:

19. a. *All bachelors are married.
     b. No bachelors are married.

     a. *The king isn't a king.
     b. The king isn't a prince.

Other sentences are unacceptable because they have presuppositions which are either generically or factually false:

20. a. *Why don't all the married bachelors get divorced?
     b. Why don't all the married men get divorced?

     a. *Why doesn't the present king of France abdicate?
     b. Why doesn't the present premier of France resign?

Certain sentences are unacceptable given the conversational context in which they occur; thus, following (21c), (21a) is unacceptable while (21b) is acceptable:

21. a. *The river is three miles south of the house.
     b. The house is three miles north of the river.
     c. Where is the house?

The personal context in which a sentence is uttered can influence its acceptability: (22a) is unacceptable spoken to one's sergeant but perfectly acceptable when spoken to one's psychiatrist. Conversely (22b) is unacceptable when spoken to one's grandmother (at

22. a. My eldest male sibling enjoys rhythmic relaxation in his abode.
     b. My brudder frugs in his pad.

least for the author) but entirely acceptable when spoken to (certain of the author's) contemporaries.

Finally, there is a set of sentences which might be spoken and understood but which are felt to be unacceptable (15, 23). Unlike the previous kinds of unacceptability we may agree that such sentences

---

* This symbol indicates that the sentence following is not an acceptable English sentence.

are unacceptable but we cannot find any particular aspect of speech behaviour that makes them so. It is not the case that they are hard to understand or say, that they are meaningless, or that they violate

23. a. I hope it for to be stopping raining when I am having leaving.
    b. In English article precedes noun.

certain contextual conventions. They are simply unacceptable English sentences, no matter what the situation. It is cases like these, which have no obvious source for their unacceptability, that are classified as 'ungrammatical'. When we cannot find any other behavioural or contextual reason for the unacceptability of an utterance we conclude that it is *structurally* incorrect and modify the theoretical grammar accordingly, so that it marks such sequences as 'ungrammatical'.

Unfortunately, most of our judgements about the acceptability of a given sequence combine several features of the different systems of speech behaviour. I tried above to give examples of each kind of unacceptability that would be maximally clear; most real cases are compounded. Even if we can all agree that a particular sentence is unacceptable, it is much more difficult for us to agree *why* it is unacceptable. Yet this agreement is crucial, since a syntactic analysis of a language is intended to account for 'pure' structural acceptability judgements, and not for acceptability judgements caused by non-syntactic, semantic, psychological or contextual factors.

Although intuitions about sequence acceptability do not directly reflect the structure of the language in all cases, such intuitions are the main data the linguist can use to verify his grammar. This fact could raise serious doubts as to whether linguistic science is about anything at all since the source of the data is so obscure. However, this obscurity is characteristic of every exploration of behaviour. Rather than rejecting linguistic study, we should pursue the course typical of most psychological sciences; give up the belief in an 'absolute' intuition about the acceptability of sentences and study the laws governing the process involved in producing such intuitions.

The effect of stimulus context on the absolute judgement of the stimulus has become a part of almost every branch of psychology. One of the most basic laws governing the interaction between stimuli is the *law of contrast*; for example, the well-known phenomenon of feeling that the ocean is cold on a hot day while the same ocean at the same temperature feels warm on a cool day. One's 'absolute' judgement of a stimulus can be affected by the difference between the stimulus and its context. This influence by contrast clearly can affect 'intuitions' about structural grammaticality. For example, in the sentence triples in (24), (b) compared with (a) may be judged 'ungrammatical', but contrasted with (c) they will probably be judged as 'grammatical'.

24.   a. Who must telephone her?
        b. ?Who need telephone her?
        c. *Who want telephone her?

        a. He sent money even to the girls.
        b. ?He sent money to even the girls.
        c. *He sent money to the even girls.

        a. I wouldn't like John to win the race.
        b. ?I wouldn't like for John to win the race.
        c. *I wouldn't force for John to win the race.

That is, not only are there several kinds of systematic bases for the unacceptability of sequences, but even the judgement of structural grammaticality is itself subject to contextual contrast.

The fact that linguistic intuitions are subject to the same kind of influences as other types of human judgement does not invalidate many results from linguistic investigations. Many intuitions about sentences appear to be strong enough to resist contextual effects. We can expect that these intuitions will remain constant even when we have developed an understanding of the intuitional process (eg, the relationship between actives and passives; the fact that 'John hit the ball' is a sentence of English, etc). However, recent linguistic theoreticians have placed increasing dependence on relatively subtle intuitions (see Lakoff, 1968; Kiparsky and Kiparsky, in press; Ross, 1968; MacCawley, 1968), whose psychological status is extremely unclear. Since there are many sources for intuitional judgements other than grammaticality, and since grammaticality judgements can themselves be influenced by context, subtle intuitions are not to be trusted until we understand the nature of their interaction with non-grammatical factors. We require a science of linguistic introspection to provide a theoretical and empirical basis for including some acceptability judgements as syntactically relevant and excluding others. If we depend too

? This symbol indicates that the acceptability of the sentence following is questionable.
* This symbol indicates that the sentence following is not an acceptable English sentence.

much on acceptability intuitions without exploring their nature, linguistic research will perpetuate the defects of introspective mentalism as well as its virtues.

2. *The role of theoretical linguistic structure in actual speech behaviour*

The role the structures postulated by linguistic theory actually play in behaviour is a baffling problem. A transformational grammar describes every sentence as having an internal and an external phrase structure, and a set of transformations which map the former onto the latter. There is no clear evidence, however, how the formally defined transformations are utilised in either speech perception or memory, although there is evidence that the internal and external structures are utilised directly in these processes. Nevertheless, some perceptual models have attempted to incorporate a grammar as part of the processing mechanism. For example, 'analysis-by-synthesis' models of speech perception postulate that a grammar is used to generate possible sentences as part of ongoing speech perception; when the sentence generated by the grammar matches the just-heard stimulus sentence, the perceptual mechanism marks the stimulus sentence as having that grammatical structure (see Halle and Stevens, 1963). This kind of

25.

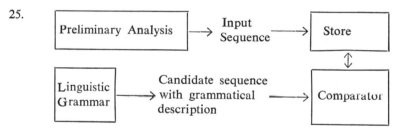

perceptual model predicts that sentences whose grammatical description involves many transformations should be correspondingly complex perceptually. For example, passive sentences should be more difficult to understand than active sentences. This particular prediction was borne out by many different kinds of experimental studies, and it appeared as if the 'psycholinguistics' of the 1960s was to be a period of exciting interaction between linguistic theory and psychological experimentation, in which theoretical claims from linguistics could be directly verified by experimental psychology (cf, Miller, 1962).

Unfortunately, clear success was limited only to the very first experiments, such as the study of the relative perceptual complexity of the passive construction. Many examples appeared of sentence constructions in which more grammatical transformations resulted in sentences which were in fact *simpler* to understand, as in the examples (b) in (26).

26. (Sentence pairs in which (b) has more transformations than (a) but is perceptually simpler)

    a. The dog was called by someone.
    b. The dog was called.

    a. The cat that is small is on the mat that is made of grass.
    b. The small cat is on the grass mat.

    a. That John left the party angrily and quickly annoyed Bill.
    b. It annoyed Bill that John left the party angrily and quickly.

While everybody was willing to agree with the claim that sentence perception involves in part the discovery of the internal, 'logical' relations inherent to each sentence, it was not at all clear how the grammatical structures used to describe intuitions about sentences are themselves deployed in actual sentence processing (Fodor and Garrett, 1968). Such an observation raises the general question: which linguistically-postulated structures are primary in actual speech behaviour and which are abstracted from behaviour?

There are three structures which are manifest in most linguistic theories (even those that are not 'generative'), the phoneme, the external phrase structure, and the internal 'logical' structure. Our current research suggests that these three structures are the residue of an internal abstraction process, rather than structures which are themselves actively used in all normal speech processing. There is strong empirical *linguistic* evidence for the 'reality' of each of the three linguistic structures: each structure is necessary for the description of certain indisputable facts about sentences. However, observational and experimental investigations indicate that the role of these structures in speech behaviour is dependent on the particular activity. In general, these linguistic structures appear in behaviour as organising concepts rather than as primary behavioural entities.

(a) THE NONPERCEPTUAL AND NONARTICULATORY REALITY OF THE PHONEME. Consider first the phoneme, the basic sound unit in language. The word *bats* is made up of four such units, which correspond (in this case) to the individual letters in the spelling of the word. There is a great deal of intuitive confirmation of such a subdivision of the acoustic stream of speech: the presence of spoonerisms in speech, of alliterative and rhyming folk poetry, and the natural development of phonemic alphabets. In formal linguistic study the phoneme is the basic segment for analysis of the sound patterns unique to each language. In English, for example, the rule for the regular formation of the plurals is as stated in (27).

27. To the singular form add
(a) $/s/$ if it ends in a voiceless consonant except those in (c)
(b) $/z/$ if it ends in a voiced consonant or vowel except those in (c)
(c) $/ehz/$ if it ends in a sibilant or fricative consonant

For example, after the word *bet* (case (a)) the plural ending is pronounced '-*s*' as in *bets*; after the word *bed* (case b) it is '-*z*' as in *bedz*; if the singular form of the word ends in a vowel (eg, *bay*, case b) then the plural is also pronounced as '-*z*' (as in *bayz*). Finally, after the word *bush* (case c) the plural ending is pronounced '*ehz*' as in *bushehz*. ('Fricative sounds' are phonemes that involve a marked turbulence of air in their production; eg, the last sound in 'bush, butch, budge, rouge, bus, buzz'.)

These three rules account for all the regular plural forms in English in an elegant and straightforward manner. The large number of acoustic-articulatory phenomena in languages that are equally well described in terms of phonemes is the basic descriptive motivation for postulating their existence. Unfortunately, attempts to determine the acoustic (or articulatory) definition of the objective constancies associated with each phoneme have been frustrating and unsuccessful. The physical realisation of each phoneme is modified by the surrounding phonemes. The acoustic (or articulatory) definitions must take into account sequences of several phonemes at the same time so that the interdependencies can be included in the description.

A more natural unit for objective definition of the basic units of speech perception and articulation is the *syllable*. Not only do we feel that we talk in syllables (rather than stringing phonemes together) but it is also possible objectively to describe the physical properties of the articulatory and acoustic boundaries of syllables. Such boundaries are marked by changes in articulatory movements and corresponding changes in the acoustic intensity of the speech signal. The relative clarity of the objective definitiveness of the syllable is also reflected in

M

the fact that it is possible to speak all syllables in isolation, but impossible to speak most phonemes in isolation.

Unfortunately the description of linguistic phenomena such as plural formation cannot be naturally described in terms of unsegmented syllables, but must depend on the subdivision of the syllable into phonemes. There are approximately 5,000 unique syllables in English. The rule for plural formation would have to list the different kinds of syllables that take the different plural forms (in $/-s/$, $/-z/$ and $/-ehz/$) in the rule like (28).

28. To the singular form add
    (a) $/s/$ if it ends in '-bet, -bat, -but, . . . -sip, -sap, -sup . . .'
    (b) $/z/$ if it ends in '-bed, -bod, -bud, . . . -sib, -sab, -sub . . .'
    (c) $/ehz/$ if it ends in '-bef, -baf, -buf, . . . -sis, -sas, -sus . . .'

While such a representation in terms of syllables would be slightly more economical than listing all the singular words themselves, the major generalisation would be lost that it is the sound *at the end* of the syllable that determines the sound of the plural. This fact could be captured by describing syllables in terms of the sounds that they end in, and stating the rules as listed for the phonemic analysis, as above. But this description would be equivalent to the phonemic analysis itself since it would merely be a circuitous way of referring to the phoneme in question as 'the last sound of the syllable'. Of course, rule (28a) and (28b) would in fact be impossible to state in an unsegmented syllabic system: neither $/s/$ nor $/z/$ are themselves syllables, and therefore could not be used as theoretical terms. One would actually have to list separately the pluralisation process as the formation of a new plural syllable from each singular syllable as exemplified in (29). That is, using unsegmented syllables, plural formation would be a process made up of thousands of rules.

29. | singular form | plural form |
| --- | --- |
| -bet | -bets |
| -bat | -bats |
| -bit | -bits |
| . | . |
| . | . |
| . | . |
| . | . |

Thus we appear to be in a dilemma. While the syllable is the natural unit for the description of linguistic data, the phoneme is the natural unit for the description of linguistic regularities. This dilemma can be converted into an empirical question about the relative role of the phoneme and syllable in actual speech behaviour. To examine this, Harris Savin and I (Savin and Bever, 1970) compared the amount of time it takes for a person to react discriminatively to a syllable beginning in a particular phoneme depending on whether or not he knows the entire syllable to listen for or just the first phoneme of the syllable. We found that it takes about a fifteenth of a second *longer* to identify the syllable when only the first phoneme is known than when the entire syllable is known. Yet all the responses are completed before the middle of the vowel. Listeners are conscious primarily of syllables, and secondarily of the phonemes. We take this result as an empirical reflection of the fact that phonemes are themselves entities which are abstracted out from speech perception and production. The role of such units is to 'mediate' the acoustic and articulatory regularities in the language. Phonemes are 'psychologically real', but their level of conscious reality is *derived* from the primary acoustic/articulatory speech unit, which is the syllable.

(b) THE ABSTRACTNESS OF SURFACE PHRASE STRUCTURE. Another theoretical structure postulated by all linguistic theories is the external phrase structure (or 'parsing structure') which ascribes a hierarchical analysis to the relations between adjacent words and phrases. The phrase structures in (30a) and (30b), indicated by parentheses, represent such hierarchical relations among sequences. Like the phoneme, phrase structure organisations of sentences are critical to the formulation of linguistic rules which capture generalisations about sentence organisation. The phrase structure analysis of sentences is behaviourally reflected in our perception and production of the placement of relative pauses, as well as agreeing with our intuitions about the relative closeness of the associations between adjacent words. Analyses like those in (30) represent empirical data in language behaviour. Phrase structure hierarchies are also indispensable to linguistic analysis; they represent the notion of *phrase type*, which is the theoretical term referred to in linguistic rules (eg, 'noun phrase, verb phrase, adverbial phrase', etc). Each phrase type subsumes a wide variety of distinct constructions, each of which is treated as the same by grammatical rules.

30. a. (they (fed him (dog biscuits)))
     b. (they (fed (his dog) biscuits))

31. NP_1 V NP_2 $\rightarrow$ NP_2 be $V+$ed by NP_1

Consider the formulation of the passive rule in English if the notion of the constituent 'nounphrase' (*NP* in (31)) were not a possible concept. One consequence would be that each of the passive sentences in (32) would be formed from the active structure by a separate structural rule.

32. a. *The wine* was produced by a *German mouse.*
    b. *The alcoholic beverage* was produced by a *German mouse.*
    c. *The wine* was produced by *a mouse of German extraction.*
    d. *The fermented juice from a bunch of grapes* was produced by *a German mouse.*
    e. *The wine* was produced by *a mouse born in Germany.*
    f. *The liquid in a bottle, made from the juice of undried raisins,* was produced by *a rodent born in Germany that has whiskers and is crackers about cheese.*

The notion of 'nounphrase' (italicised in the examples in (32)) allows a simple and intuitive statement of the linguistic regularities. In brief, there are both behavioural and formal motivations for the analysis of sentences into phrase structure hierarchies.

The question remains, however, as to the role of such hierarchies in ongoing speech behaviour. Traditional and current theories of speech perception agree that the most straightforward (and first) step in the comprehension of sentences is the analysis of the surface phrase structure. (Full comprehension of the meaning is presumed to require 'deeper' or 'more abstract' operations on the allegedly easily perceived surface structure.)

To test experimentally the claim that the first and easiest step in sentence perception is the isolation of surface phrase structure we have examined the displacements in the reported location of a single click presented during sentences (see Garrett and Bever (1970) for a review of this research). Our first studies demonstrated that the reported location of a click is attracted towards boundaries between explicitly signified clauses (Fodor and Bever, 1965; Garrett, 1965). For example, clicks objectively in the positions marked '*S*' in the sentences in (33) were reported as having occurred in or toward the points between the clauses, marked '*R*'.

33. a. (The reporters (who were watching George)) drove to the car $\quad\quad\quad\quad\quad\quad\quad\quad\quad\quad\quad\quad\quad\quad\quad\quad\quad S \quad\quad R$
    b. (To catch the reporters) George drove to the car. $\quad\quad\quad\quad\quad\quad\quad R \quad\quad S$

Such results demonstrate the claim that the clause units are primary segments of speech processing: a click is mislocated as occurring at the boundaries of such units, presumably reflecting their perceptual coherence or *gestalt*.

These experiments left open the question as to whether it is the external or internal organisation of sentences that is the basis for perceptual segmentation. Our studies confounded the two levels of sentence organisation, since clause boundaries like those in (33) are points at which a surface structure boundary difference coincides with a logical structure difference, as pictured in (34). (Square brackets represent the segmentation of internal structure sentences.)

34.　a.　[[The reporters who were watching George]　drove the
　　　　　2 1　　　　　　　　　　　　　　　　　　　1　　　　　　　car]
　　　　　　　　　　　　　　　　　　　　　　　　　　　　　　　　2

　　　　　　Actor – reporters　　　　　　　　Actor – reporters
　　　　　　Action – watch　　　　　　　　　Action – drove
　　　　　　Object – George　　　　　　　　　Object – car

　　　b.　[[To catch the reporters]　　　George drove the car]
　　　　　　2 1　　　　　　　　　1　　　　　　　　　　　　　　　2

　　　　　　Actor – George　　　　　　　　　Actor – George
　　　　　　Action – catch　　　　　　　　　Action – drove
　　　　　　Object – reporters　　　　　　　Object – car

To show whether internal structure boundaries are the basis for perceptual segmentation we examined the location of clicks in sentences which differed in their internal structure segmentation without any corresponding differences in their surface phrase structure. We found that the internal phrase structure organisation differences were reflected in corresponding differences in click locations, as shown in

35.　a.　[The general desired　[the troops to fight the enemy]]
　　　　　1　　　　　　　　　　2　　　　　　　　　　　　　　　2 1

　　　　　　Actor – general　　　　　　Actor – troops
　　　　　　Action – desired　　　　　　Action – fight
　　　　　　Object – it (S_2)　　　　　　Object – enemy

　　　b.　[The general defied　[the troops]　to fight the enemy]
　　　　　1　　　　　　　　　　2　　　　1　　　　　　　　　　2

　　　　　　Actor – general　　　　　　　Actor – troops
　　　　　　Action – defied　　　　　　　Action – fight
　　　　　　Object – troops　　　　　　　Object– enemy

181

(36). This demonstrated that logical structure organisation can act alone as the basis for perceptual segmentation, at least as reflected in the location of clicks.

36. a. The general desired the troops to fight the enemy.
      R   S

   b. The general defied the troops to fight the enemy.
                       S   R

These results left open the possibility that surface phrase structure could also act as the basis for perceptual segmentation. In cases like (33) the click-displacement effects might have been due to the internal structure organisation. To test surface structure effects separately, we have repeatedly examined the location of clicks in sentences with differences in surface structure that do not correspond to internal structure sentence boundaries. The results indicate that such phrase structure divisions within clauses do not attract clicks. For example, there was no difference in the pattern of responses to clicks in (37a) and (37b). (The phrase structure difference is indicated with the parentheses.)

37. a. Sam walked (up the highway) . . .
   b. Sam (looked up) the address . . .

These results suggest that the first step in the conscious organisation of heard sentences is the segmentation of speech into distinct logical structures rather than the organisation of the entire surface phrase structure. Listeners are first conscious of the segmentation of sequences into structural units that correspond to the units of meaning, namely internal structure sentences.

Of course, our negative results on the effect of surface phrase structure might merely have shown that click location is not a true behavioural indicator of segmental processes. Our studies on minor phrase structure distinctions all required subjects to report the sentence and click location immediately following the stimulus sequence. One might argue that the delayed response 'washed out' any perceptual effects of surface phrase structure. If this were so one would expect no change in the effect of surface structure on click location if subjects waited even longer before reporting their responses. In a separate experiment (Bever, 1968) I required subjects to wait five seconds before writing down the sentence and indicating the click location. Contrary to the prediction, distinctions in minor phrase structure like that in (37a) and (37b) *do* affect the location of the clicks when listeners delay their reporting (eg, the location response patterns are relatively as shown in (38a) and (38b)). That is, listeners develop a *greater* appreciation of surface phrase structure as they hold the sentence in memory.

38.   a.   Sam walked up the highway.
R   S

   b.   Sam looked up   the address.
S   R

The conclusion from these studies is that in immediate sentence processing listeners segment together only those surface structure phrases that correspond to internal sentences. Complete surface phrase structure details are organised as part only *after* the listener has comprehended the sentence, not as the very first perceptual step. It would appear that surface phrase structure, like the phoneme, is a secondary, derived construct so far as the immediate conscious organisation of speech stimuli is concerned. This is perhaps more startling than our claim about the abstractness of the phoneme, since surface phrase structure appears to be one of the few aspects of linguistic phenomenology which traditional and modern grammarians agree as 'obviously real'

What then of the many percepts which do reflect phrase structure, such as stress and intonation? What of the 'set' experiments, in which subjects learn surface structure patterns as an aid to perceiving novel sentences which repeat those patterns? What of the studies of eye movements during reading which suggest that details of surface phrase structure guide where readers look? Is it not the case that these phenomena justify the claim that surface phrase structure is perceptually primary? It is my belief that all of these demonstrations of the 'behavioural reality' of surface phrase structure depend on giving listeners an opportunity to 'abstract out' the phrase structure analysis. Accordingly, they do not demonstrate that surface phrase structure organises immediate processing when the structure is not known beforehand. Rather, the existing phenomena show that, *once known*, the surface phrase structure of a particular sequence can interact with basic sensory processes and sensations.

The most obvious case is the formation of phrase structure set. Mehler and Carey (1968) found that subjects perceive a sentence like (39) in noise better after a series of five sentences with similar surface

183

structure than after five sentences with a dissimilar phrase structure like (40).

39.   They are (smiling authors).

40.   They (are fixing) airplanes.

Such a result does not demonstrate that such details of surface phrase structure are ordinarily responded to in perception. Rather, it demonstrates that listeners can isolate and expect such a particular phrase structure after repeated presentation.[2]

The perception of stress patterns might be taken as empirical evidence for the use of phrase structure hierarchies in immediate processing. Such percepts as in (41) have been taken as the factual basis

41.   a.   The fat (general's wife) (the fat wife of a general).

      b.   The (fat general's) wife (the wife of the fat general).

for cyclically applying stress assignment rules such as (42) in English (see Chomsky and Halle, 1969).[3] ('1' indicates strong stress, '2' intermediate stress and '3' weak stress.) These rules apply first to the

42.   Apply stress 1 to the initial constituent of a phrase and lower other stresses. This rule applies to successively more inclusive phrase constituents.

43.

$$((fat)\ ((general's)\ (wife)))\quad (((fat)\quad (general's))\quad (wife))$$

a.   fat   general's wife   fat general's wife

b.   *fat*   *general's wife*   *fat general's wife*

smallest constituent as shown in (43) and then to successively more inclusive constituents (43a, then 43b). The kind of intuitions about stress shown in (41) might be taken as empirical support for the immediate perceptual organisation of the phrase structure in (41) since, at first, stress would appear to be an aspect of speech that is perceived directly. The fact that phrase structure is required to describe the stress pattern and that stress is an immediate percept would appear to justify the claim that phrase structure is an immediate percept. However, in studying intuitions of stress as in (41) linguists require a good deal of personal introspection and reflection to decide on stress

184

patterns, except for the intuitions about the placement of the primary stress. This reflects the fact that only primary stress is reliably observable as an intensity variation in the acoustic analysis of speech. This was shown by Lieberman (1963), who found that if the articulatory information is removed from utterance but intensity and intonation preserved, linguists could not agree on the position of any stress levels below the primary one. The subjective assignment of stress patterns that reflect minor differences in phrase structure depends on independent knowledge of the phrase structure and reflective consideration of it.[4] The complete stress pattern is not itself perceived immediately and cannot be taken as evidence for the claim that all the details of surface phrase structure are perceptually primary.

Our own experimental demonstration of the role of surface phrase structure in guiding eye fixations has a similar explanation (Mehler, Bever and Carey, 1967). We found evidence that there is a rule of eye-fixation which describes the relative frequency of the part of a sentence we look at directly as a function of its phrase structure (44). This rule

44.   Fixate on the initial half of a constituent.

applies to successively more inclusive phrase structure constituents. We tested the predictions made by (44) on sequences whose phrase structure was ambiguous, as in (45), with a preceding context to force the interpretation one way or another.

45.   They were lecturing doctors.

The cross-subject comparisons of relative number of eye-fixations at each point were in accord with the predictions made by (44). This would appear to support the claim that surface phrase structure plays an immediate role in sentence perception; it interacts with the ongoing placement of eye-fixations, which surely implicates it in the very first stages of perception. However, the design of our experiment required that the subjects be pre-set to expect one of the interpretations of the ambiguous sequences. This presetting involved several preceding sentences containing direct presentation of the ambiguous phrase in a context which disambiguated it (eg, a preceding sentence might be 'The lecturing doctors spoke clearly . . . '). Our subjects were explicitly pretrained in each case on the critical phrase with a particular phrase structure. The influence of the phrase structure of the critical phrase on eye-fixations merely demonstrated the role of phrase structure in the recognition of pre-set structures.

The conclusion from these arguments is that the complete surface phrase structure of a sentence is not necessarily perceived as the first step of sentence perception. Rather, surface phrase structure *can* be used if listeners are pre-set for it, and it can be appreciated if listeners are encouraged to process further a sentence after first hearing it.

(c) HOW MANY DEEP STRUCTURES ARE REALLY INSIDE THE MIND? A third linguistic structure figuring prominently in current descriptions is the syntactic organisation of the grammatical relations between phrases, which is internal to every sentence. Like the phoneme and phrase structure, internal or 'deep' syntactic structure is used in linguistic descriptions both for empirical and theoretical reasons. Consider the sentences in (46). It is clear that the logical relations between 'the cat', 'interest' and 'the dogs' are constant despite the obvious differences in the surface form of the different sentences in (46). The

46. a. The cat interested the dogs.
    b. The dogs were interested by the cat.
    c. It's the cat that interested the dogs.
    d. It's the dogs the cat interested.
    e. It's the cat by whom the dogs were interested.
    f. The cat happened to interest the dogs.
    g. It's true that the cat interested the dogs.
    h. The dogs happened to be interested by the cat.
    i. The cat succeeded in interesting the dogs.
    j. The cat seemed to interest the dogs.
    k. The interesting of the dogs by the cat really occurred,
    l. The cat's interesting the dogs really happened.
    m. What seemed to happen was that the cat interested the dogs.
    n. It's the dogs that the cat happened to interest.
    o. Interesting the dogs was easy for the cat.
    p. It was easy for the cat to interest the dogs.
    q. The dogs were easy for the cat to interest.
    r. It's interesting the dogs that the cat did.
    s. What the cat did was interest the dogs.
    t. What interested the dogs was the cat.
    u. What the dogs were interested by was the cat.
    v. It's the cat the dogs were interested by.
    w. It's by the cat that the dogs were interested.
    x. The cat happened to seem to be able to interest the dogs.
    y. What the cat seemed to do was interest the dogs.
    z. The interesting of the dogs by the cat happened yesterday.

aa.   Being interested by the cat happened to the dogs.

.

.

.

.

z^n Fssst.

concept of grammatical relations, such as actor, action, object as in (47), is inherent to every sentence independent of the explicit construction of the sentence.

47.   actor $=$ cat
      action $=$ interest
      object $=$ dogs

The systematic representation of the logical relations among the phrases in each sentence could take different forms. A grammar could label the internal relations which the parts of the sentences have in relation to each other separately for each type of sentence construction. For example, (48a) and (48b) articulate the separate relations among the phrases within active and passive construction. The systematic separate representation of the logical relations for all clause construction types would appear to be impossible, since there is no known limit on the complexity of such structures which are inherently allowed

48.   a.   In an active sentence the first noun phrase is the actor and
           the last is the object.
      b.   In a passive sentence the first noun phrase is the object
           and the last is the actor.

by a language. Consider the number of different statements of the logical relations needed just for the different sentence constructions in (46). Furthermore, statements like (48a) and (48b) fail to represent directly the fact that there are sets of *related* sentences which differ in their construction, but which share certain internal phrase relations (as do all the sentences in (46)). Finally, formulae like those in (48) *presuppose* that each sentence is independently marked as to what construction type it is. Yet this requirement makes formulae like (48) circular rather than explanatory.

These empirical failings of stating the grammatical relations with a different formula for each construction type are avoided if a grammar contains rules for relating one construction type to another. For example, the active and the passive construction could be related by a

187

'co-occurrence transformational' formula as in (49). The relation in (49a), stated formally in (49b), can explain the fact that (48a) and (48b)

49. a. To every transitive declarative sentence there corresponds a passive sentence in which the noun phrase order is reversed, in which the verb is placed in the past participle form and followed by the word *by*, in which a form of the verb BE follows the first noun phrase and is inflected with the tense of the original sentence.

  b. NP_1 Verb + tense$_i$ $NP_2 \Longleftrightarrow$
    NP_2 Be + tense$_i$ Verb + ed by NP_1

are related. Such formulae relate sentence constructions with different surface orders of the phrases but they do not themselves change the logical relations (cf Harris, 1955).

The need to represent the logical relations inherent in every sentence is not maintained out of idle caprice, nor merely out of the desire to represent directly speakers' intuitions about such relations. The set of semantic and syntactic restrictions on possible phrase combinations are stated across such relations. For example, the sentences in (50a) and (50b) are unacceptable for the same reason, despite their superficial differences; namely no inanimate noun (eg, 'sandwich') can be the

50. a. *The dog interested the sandwich.
    *The sandwich was interested by the dog.

object of the action 'interest'. To state this restriction without reference to the concept 'object' one would have to refer to each of the different constructions separately, since the ordinal position of the 'object' can vary in each construction (as in (46a-z)). Clearly, the statement of such restrictions in terms of underlying logical relations is vastly simpler (and more to the point) than statements in terms of actual sentence construction (even if the latter form of description were possible).

Formulae like (47) represent in a compact manner the logical relations for all sentence constructions. The assignment of the logical relations could be stated on only one of the construction types since the transformations like (49b) do not change the logical relations. It should be noted that neither the active nor the passive sentence is the more 'basic' in the formula in (49); the formula merely states a two-way mapping which specifies how to transform one sentence construc-

* This symbol indicates that the sentence following is not an acceptable English sentence.

tion into a corresponding sentence of the other construction. The question remains as to which construction type should be used as the 'basic' one on which the logical relations are stated. The active form is the most appropriate since all combinations of phrases can appear in an active construction, if they can be combined into a sentence at all. Certain active sentences do not have corresponding passive forms (sentences with intransitive verbs, eg, 'the dog slept', do not have corresponding passives, eg, *'was slept by the dog'); but no (non-idiomatic) passive form fails to have a corresponding active. Thus if we assign the logical relations in a sentence with reference to the active form, as in (48a), the statement need only be made once for all the possible logical relations in the entire language. If the passive form were basic and the relations stated as in (48b), then an additional statement would be required for sentences which have no passive version at all, such as sentences with intransitive verbs. Arguments of this sort can be marshalled from all construction types showing that the simple active form of sentences is the most appropriate structure to use as the 'basic' construction representing the logical relations among the phrases.

The decision to represent the logical relations in sentences based on the active form leads to a natural ordering of the application of rules in the formation of all sentence constructions. The grammatical representation of each sentence always includes the active form to which it corresponds (if it is not an active sentence itself) as the canonical representation of its logical relations. A natural consequence of the ubiquity of the active form in every construction is to derive the other forms by means of transformations like (49b). Such transformations now have directionality, mapping the active sentence onto successively more distantly related constructions. The structure of grammar of this kind is presented in (51).

51.

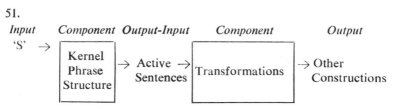

It follows from the organisation of grammar in (51) that the structure to which transformations apply is an abstraction from the simple

* This symbol indicates that the sentence following is not an acceptable English sentence.

active form of the sentence rather than the active sentence itself. If the passive reordering rule applied to a fully formed declarative sentence like 'The cat interested the dogs' then an incorrect form like (52) would result, in which the verb inflection agrees in number with the *original* singular surface phrase structure subject, *cat*.

52. *The dogs was interested by the cat.

53. The cat sg past interest the dog pl.

The generalisation that the first noun phrase determines the number of the verb inflection can be maintained only if the passive reordering rule applies *before* the inflection rule. This has the consequence that the passive reordering transformation applies to an abstract structure that has not yet had agreement inflections applied to it, as in (53). That is, the transformations do not apply to an *actual* sentence, but to an abstract schematic representation of the logical relations among the phrases of the sentence. A grammar of this kind is outlined in (54). This was the form of a transformational grammar proposed by

54.

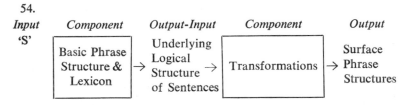

Input 'S'	Component	Output-Input	Component	Output
	Basic Phrase Structure & Lexicon →	Underlying Logical Structure → of Sentences	Transformations →	Surface Phrase Structures

Chomsky in 1957 and refined in 1965. Basic phrases are generated in a schema which represents their logical interrelations. A set of transformations map such schemata onto actual sentences.

Certain transformations impose serious rearrangements on the external form of a sentence, such as the passive (55). Other transformations change specific lexical items (56) and others adjust the final form of the sentence (57).

55. NP_1 tense V NP_2 → NP_2 tense Be V+ed by NP_1 (passive)

56. NP tense Be V_x+ed by NP → NP tense Be V_x+ed preposition$_x$ NP (preposition is 'in' if V is 'interest', 'at' if V is 'upset', etc)   ('pseudo-passive')

57. NP + no_i tense V . . . → NP + no_i V + tense + no_i . . .
                                                                       (number and tense agreement)

Sample derivations with these transformations are presented in (58)-(60).[5]

58. The cat sg. past interest the dog pl.
    The cat sg. interest sg. past the dog pl.   (number
                                                  agreement)
59. The cat sg. past interest the dog pl.
    The dog pl. past Be interest+pp. by the
    cat sg.   (passive)
    The dog pl. Be+past+pl. interest+pp. by
    the cat.   (number and
                                                  tense agreement)
60. The cat sg. past interest the dog pl.
    The dog pl. past Be interest+pp. by the
    cat sg.   (passive)
    The dog pl. past Be interest+pp. in the
    cat sg.   ('pseudo-passive')

    The dog pl. Be+past+pl. interest+pp. in
    the dog sg.   (number and
                                                  tense agreement)

One of the first studies of the 'psychological reality' of such a grammar centred on the role of the underlying phrase structures of sentences as the active schemata used in sentence memorisation. A series of experiments suggested that, in memorising lists of sentences, we tend to encode them in terms of their individual internal structures, with additional information specifying the transformations that must apply to yield their surface structure (Miller, 1962; Mehler, 1963). One demonstration of this was the fact that passive sentences are harder to remember than active sentences. This was allegedly due to the passive sentence (eg (48b)) having one additional fact to be memorised over active sentences, namely the information that the passive transformation applies as well as the (obligatory) number and tense agreement transformation.

In a recent experiment we examined the validity of the behavioural claim that the active (58), the passive (59) and the 'pseudo-passive' (60) require an increasing amount of space in memory, corresponding to the relative number of transformations involved in their derivation, as summarised in (61) (Bever and Hurtig, forthcoming). Subjects were asked to examine each sentence in a heterogenous set of nine for five seconds, and to write out all the sentences after each of five trials. We found that active sentences (58) were the best recalled, passive (59) the

191

next best and pseudo-passives (60) were the worst recalled, just as predicted.

			transformations
61.	a.	The cat interested the dogs	(number and tense)
	b.	The dogs were interested by the cat	(passive, number and tense)
	c.	The dogs were interested in the cat	(passive, pseudo-passive, number and tense)

This kind of evidence, obtained by many researchers, widely supports the claim that the encoded form of sentences corresponds at least in part to an analysis of the logical relations on the one hand, and informations about transformations used to derive the surface form of the sentence on the other hand. These experiments verified analyses made by syntactic theory, using a straightforward interpretation of the interaction of memory and syntax. The notions of 'internal structure' and 'transformation' became psychologically respectable, and we all looked forward to further experimental studies of the role of these structures in behaviour.

Developments in syntactic theory, however, suggested that the internal representation of most sentences was far more abstract than had first been thought. For example, further consideration of a 'pseudo-passive' sentence like (61c) indicated that to derive it from the passive form of the sentence fails to capture many linguistic regularities (Postal, 1968).[6] First, certain syntactic forms can exist in the 'pseudo-passive' construction which cannot exist with the passive itself. For example (62a) is perfectly grammatical while (62b) is not (on the interpretation that John is the actor and there is no contrastive stress). Yet how could (62a) exist as a derivative of a *non-existent* form like (62b)?

62. a. John was interested in himself.
  b. *John was interested by himself.

In addition to such formal difficulties it was noted that there is a strong intuitive feeling that the first noun phrase of such 'pseudo-passives' (*dogs* in (61c)) is an actor, while this is not characteristic of

* This symbol indicates that the sentence following is not an acceptable English sentence.

passive constructions themselves. Furthermore, the second noun phrase of the corresponding 'active' sentences (*dogs* in (61a)) also appears to be an actor, which is not characteristic of ordinary actives. Compare (63a) with (61a). In (63a) *dogs* is the object of an action carried out by *cat*, while in (61a) *dogs* is not an obvious object of the same kind and *cat* certainly does not 'carry out' an action 'upon' *the dogs*. This difference can be seen in sentences (63b) and (63a). Clearly (63b) is unacceptable because *rock* cannot be an actor, while its initial position in (63c) does not imply that it is an actor. Thus the generalisation in (48a) would appear not to be correct if sentences like (61a) are interpreted as closest to the active form.

63.   a.   The cat bit the dogs.
     b.   *The cat interested the rock.
     c.   The rock interested the cat.

In sum, there are formal and intuitive reasons for considering that 'pseudo-passives' (61c) rather than 'pseudo-actives' (61a) most closely represent in external form the internal relations, according to which the first appearing noun phrase is an actor, as in (48a). In this analysis the apparent 'active' form of such constructions (61a) is itself derived from the abstract structure closest to 'pseudo-passive'. That is, the deep phrase structure generates a form like (64), and an exchange transformation (66) would form the 'pseudo-active' structure as in (65).

64.   The dog plural past interest in the cat singular.

65.   The cat singular past interest the dog plural.

66. $NP_1 V_x prep_x NP_2 \rightarrow NP_2 V_x NP_1$ (where $V_x prep_x$ is 'interest in, upset at, . . .' etc.) (*exchange*)

There are other cases in which actor and object are exchanged by a transformation like (66) to produce apparent active sentences that are in fact derived from other forms. For example, (67b) is derived from a form like (67a) and (67d) from one like (67c), (67f) from (67e) and so on (note that for these examples one does not need to argue which form is the basic one; in either case they motivate the existence of a non-passive rule which exchanges actors and objects). That is, in addi-

* This symbol indicates that the sentence following is not an acceptable English sentence.

tion to the passive rule there is a general subject/object exchange rule, like (66) which applies with verbs like *interest, upset, dry*, etc.

67. a. Everyone teases her easily.
     b. She teases easily (for everyone).
     c. The raisins dried in the sun.
     d. The sun dried the raisins.
     e. We suggest from graph three that . . .
     f. Graph three suggests (to us) that . . .

Thus there are many reasons to include a rule in English grammar which can explain the relation between the 'pseudo-passive' and the corresponding active. Both would appear to have the order of logical relations reversed from the general case. If one analyses the 'pseudo-passive' as closest to the basic form and derives the corresponding 'active' from it by the exchange rule, then this anomaly is avoided, since the 'pseudo-passive' orders the phrase relations in an order most closely corresponding to the canonical order assumed in (48a). The relative transformational complexity of the sentences in (61) on this analysis is presented in (68).[7]

			transformations
68.	a.	The dogs were interested in the cat.	(number and tense)
	b.	The cat interested the dogs.	(exchange, number and tense)
	c.	The dogs were interested by the cat.	(exchange, passive, number and tense)

In the light of these arguments what are we to make of the earlier experimental demonstrations that *the* underlying syntactic structure as presented in (61) is the basis on which sentences are memorised? We are now faced with two competing linguistic analyses, both of which have certain formal and empirical arguments in their favour, but which mark different sentence constructions as the closest to the underlying logical structure. One way of resolving this conflict would be to take the memory experiments as evidence for claims about which analysis is correct. On this criterion the analysis in (61) rather than (68) would be considered correct since it best predicts the sentence memory results. However, the motivations for both of the above analyses are also empirical, albeit non-experimental since they are based on intuitions

194

about linguistic facts. Our dilemma is not one that can be resolved by trying to ignore some of these facts merely because they are not 'substantiated' by results. We must instead specify the circumstances under which the different analyses are behaviourally relevant.

It might be argued that the analysis in (68) is relevant only to the most reflective aspect of linguistic behaviour, namely the behaviour of producing linguistically relevant intuitions. In this sense one might wish to argue that the analysis in (68) is an artefact of linguistic technique. However, this is not the only kind of behaviour in which the structural analysis in (68) appears. In a separate experiment with the same sentence materials as above, we asked subjects to recall the sentences after a relatively long period of time, from an hour to several days. Under those circumstances we found that the order of recall success was predicted better by the analysis in (68) than in the previous experiment (combined with the hypothesis that the smaller number of transformations makes a sentence easier to recall). Given a long period of time subjects apparently shift from using the analysis of sentences in (61) to one more like that in (68). We have also found that this shift can be triggered in part by giving each subject prior experience with a range of sentence constructions for each individual sentence like those in (68), before he is asked to pick out one of them to memorise. That is, anything which encourages the subject to place the sentences that he is memorising in a broader linguistic context stimulates him to use a 'deeper' linguistic analysis for the representation of those sentences.

This is analogous to the differences between the linguistic considerations which underlie the two analyses. The first analysis in (61) was based on a relatively narrow range of facts, while the later analysis in (68) was based on attempts to take into account more sentence relations and uses transformational rules needed for entirely different kinds of sentence constructions, eg (66). If our view is correct, subjects can implicitly carry out such linguistic analysis on sentences they are given to learn and develop 'more abstract' organisations of the sentences as they reflect on the sentences or put them into a broader perspective. That is, subjects can intuitively recapitulate the stages of linguistic arguments that I reviewed above, first motivating an abstract organisation among sentences (as in (61)) and then a more abstract organisation (as in (68)). Under the right circumstances (having more time or more experience with the range of sentence types) both subjects and linguists make use of a deeper analysis of the logical forms internal to the sentences.

195

THE STUDY OF LANGUAGE BEHAVIOUR

(d) GRAMMARS, LEVELS OF ABSTRACTION AND THE ACQUISITION OF STRUCTURE. This result poses a problem for our understanding of the relation between the structure of a language and the individual speaker's knowledge of that structure. The halcyon days are gone when one could speak of the extent to which a given speaker/listener was using *the* grammar of his language in his behaviour. Rather, we find that different (and sometimes incompatible) structural hypotheses about sentence structure are brought out by different sorts of behavioural tasks. This changes the original goal of discovering *the* grammar of English, to discovering the set of possible (ie *natural*) grammars which speakers (and linguists) invent. This set is itself primary data for the study of the human processes of abstraction. That is, we can consider linguistic investigations as providing a range of possible grammatical organisations of sentences. If we find that more than one such organisation has behavioural validity (as (61) and (68)), then we have a central problem for psychological explanation: what is the nature of human abstraction which makes certain structural organisations of sentences natural, and what are the laws governing which natural organisation appears in different tasks?

The moral from the studies of the behavioural reality of the phoneme, phrase structure and underlying structure is clear. The descriptive role of such linguistic constructs justifies their use, and is alone sufficient evidence for their 'psychological reality'. But the behavioural manifestation of such constructs depends on the task and the way in which speakers approach the task. Just as we must develop a science of the phenomenology of sentence intuitions, we must also develop a theory of the interactions of internal structures with actual behaviours, if we are to progress in our understanding of language. In this sense we are indeed returning to experimental mentalism. But our position is somewhat stronger than that of the mentalists at the turn of the century. Unlike them we have a detailed theory of the set of possible internal structures of language and a range of techniques for their study. Rather than having to concentrate on individual personal images and introspections, we can study experimentally the interrelations between sentences and behavioural effects of sentence structures held in common by many speakers and analysed by a general linguistic theory.

The existence of different behavioural organisations of relations among sentences in adults raises a parallel question about the acquisition of grammar in children. The facts reviewed earlier suggest that there are certain structural universals which appear in the early

196

development of patterns of talking and listening. However, it is quite possible that the structure of the grammar that mediates between these systems is initially less abstract than the most abstract adult grammar. This would be consistent with our finding that the range of sentence constructions considered and the amount of time spent considering them increase the 'abstractness' of the organisational schema applied to them. Thus, as the child increases his range of perceptual and productive mastery, the grammatical structure he uses to organise his implicit knowledge may also become more abstract. To investigate this possibility we must apply various techniques to ferret out the structural organisation that children maintain as the basis for their linguistic skill. Merely to study the development of the skill itself is not sufficient since, as I have argued, the same manifest skill can reflect quite distinct internal organisations.

3. *The influence of the child's speech behaviour on universals of linguistic structure*

Each system of speech behaviour discussed above plays a role in language as a whole, and therefore constrains the form of the other systems. For example, it is often noted that the perceptual mechanism for speech comprehension must comply with the syntactic structure of the language. Obviously, many specific perceptual rules reflect structural properties unique to each language. For example, we can show experimentally that English listeners search implicitly for a noun when they hear a determiner (words like 'the, a, some . . . ', etc) and clearly such a strategy would play no role in the listening habits of speakers in a language without prenominal determiners. There are also universal structural constraints which are reflected in universal properties of the mechanism for speech perception. For example, the perceptual mechanism is not required to decode sentences with backwards word order.

It is equally true (although less often recognised) that the form of the syntactic system is itself constrained by the limitations of human perception. Clearly the child does not learn grammatical constructions which he cannot understand; in this way perceptually incomprehensible constructions are weeded out of the grammar of a language as they arise. In some cases, structural universal constraints on syntax might allow specific constructions to exist in a language which are ruled out because they are nevertheless hard for a child to understand.

The interplay between perceptual and grammatical complexity is most strikingly revealed in the history of language, in which we can

197

observe cases where a change in one part of a grammar makes certain constructions harder to understand; these constructions are then ruled out of the language by further developments in the grammar. An example of the effect of this kind of interaction on the structure of language appears in the evolution of the constraints on the presence of relative pronouns introducing subordinate clauses in English. Consider the sentences in (69a, b).

69. a. The boy who likes the girls fell down.
    b. *The boy likes the girls fell down.

Sentences like (69b) are ungrammatical, in which the subject relative pronoun is deleted in a relative clause modifying an initial noun. We can find a plausible explanation for this in the child's early strategy of interpreting any 'noun/verb' sequence as 'actor-action' and his tendency to take the first such sequence as the most important part of the sentence. If the relative clause introducer ('who, that') were deleted as in (69b) the child would be misled into concentrating his attention on what is in fact the *subordinate* clause of the sentence since the first 'noun/verb' sequence is not marked as subordinate. Furthermore, there would be complete ambiguity of a sentence like (69b) with one like (70b), derived from (70a).

70. a. The boy likes the girls who fell down.
    b. *The boy likes the girls fell down.

While a certain amount of derivational ambiguity appears in most languages it is plausible that ambiguity as to which clause is the main clause and which the subordinate is particularly difficult for the perceptual mechanism to deal with. Most ambiguities can be resolved by the context in which they occur; nevertheless there would be many instances in which the ambiguity between sentences like (69b) and (70b) would be particularly hard to resolve from conversational context, since one of the basic logical propositions is shared ('The boy likes the girls'). We found that children go through a period of interpreting sentences with the most obvious interpretation even to the point of misinterpreting sentences like 'The dog pats the mother'. Accordingly, ambiguous sentences that are not uniquely biased to a particular interpretation by the context would be particularly hard for the child since there would be no contextually 'obvious' interpretation.

* This symbol indicates that the sentence following is not an acceptable English sentence.

Such constructions would tend to be blocked from occurring in the language if there were an available grammatical mechanism that could block them.

Thus there are two perceptual reasons that one could suggest for the restrictions on the deletion of subject relative pronouns on initial nouns, as in (69b). The first sequence would be misinterpreted as an independent main clause, and the construction would also be highly confusable with the sentences derived from deletion of subject relative on non-initial nouns as in (70b). The restriction against subject relative pronoun deletion on non-initial nouns (70b) has a weaker perceptual motivation — namely that the sequence created by that deletion, although not initial, would itself be a plausible independent clause (eg, 'the girls fell down') and produce a confusing sentence.

At first these arguments may appear hopelessly *post hoc*—we have merely rationalised a perceptual system around the grammatical phenomenon as its explanation. There are several counters to the claim that our explanation is circular. First we are using *independent* evidence from perception in adults and the acquisition of perceptual mechanisms in children to show that such constructions are perceptually difficult. Second, there are other grammatical structural constraints on optional rules in English which can be directly interpreted as maintaining an initial subordinate clause marked as distinct from an initial main clause. For example, there are no restrictions on subject relative pronoun deletion if the form of the verb in the relative clause is itself not confusable with the main verb of a sentence. While (71b) is not an allowed derivation from (71a), (71c) is. On our interpretation (71c) is allowed because in it, the relative clause verb form is uniquely marked (by the ' . . . ing') as in a subordinate construction.

71.   a.   The boy who is running down the street is happy.
         b.   *The boy is running down the street is happy.
         c.   The boy running down the street is happy.

There are similar restrictions on the deletion of complement particles, 'the fact' and 'that' in English. These are freely deleted from many constructions when the subordinate clause does not appear first in the sentence (72a-d). However, *at least one* of these markers must appear when the subordinate clause is in initial position (72e-h). This is not merely a restriction that the subordinate marker must always appear at the beginning of initial subordinate clauses, as is shown by

* This symbol indicates that the sentence following is not an acceptable English sentence.

199

72. a. I know the fact that John is here.
     b. I know that John is here.
     c. I know the fact John is here.
     d. I know John is here.
     e. The fact that John is here is known to me.
     f. That John is here is known to me.
     g. The fact John is here is known to me.
     h. *John is here is known to me.

73. a. I am bothered by the mere fact of John's being present.
     b. I am bothered by John's being present.
     c. The mere fact of John's being present bothered me.
     d. John's being present bothered me.

74. a. I heard the claim of the fact that John is present.
     b. I heard the claim that John is present.
     c. I heard the claim John is present.
     d. The claim that John is present was heard by me.
     e. The claim John is present was heard by me.

the examples in (73d) and (74e). In these cases there are other markers that the initial clause is subordinate (the ' . . . ing' on the verb in (73d) and the presence of the deverbal complementising noun 'claim' in (74e)). The complementising particles 'that' and 'the fact' may be deleted on initial subordinate clauses *only* if there is *some other basis* for uniquely recovering the fact that the initial clause is a subordinate clause. The generalisation underlying all these restrictions is that an initial subordinate clause must be marked as distinct from an initial main clause. Accordingly, the restriction on subject relative pronoun deletion on initial nouns is simply a particular rule operating within the general restriction on the form of English sentences.

The final independent evidence for our interpretation is drawn from the history of English. The modern English restriction on deleting subject relative pronouns on non-initial nouns is less strongly motivated perceptually than the restrictions on deletion following initial nouns. This is reflected in the fact that there was a long period in English when sentences like (70b) *could* occur. (Of course, in Old and Middle English, the form of the relative and demonstrative pronouns used to introduce relative clauses was quite different; the examples given here are merely to illustrate the structural properties of the sen-

* This symbol indicates that the sentence following is not an acceptable English sentence.

tences. See Bever and Langendoen (in press) for a collection of historical examples, and a more detailed discussion of the phenomenon.) That is, the relative pronoun was deletable when it modified non-initial nouns: before the 12-13th Century, sentences like (75b) were optional versions of sentences like (75a). It was only around the 14th Century that such sentences became completely inadmissible.

75. a. Alle mæhtign þæm be gelefes.
    b. Alle mæhtign þæm gelefes.
    (All power to him (who) believes).

Why should this have happened? Why should sentences like (75b) ever have been admissible if they are inconsistent with the perceptual strategies, and why did they then become ungrammatical when they did? In our view, such sentences were acceptable before the 14th Century because the object noun (eg, 'the girl' in (70b) or 'þæm' in (75b)) was often uniquely inflected in a non-subject case ('accusative' in (70b), 'dative' in (75b)). That is, there could have been no confusion that the noun-verb sequence created by deleting the subject relative pronoun was a *subject-verb* sequence, since the noun phrase was often uniquely and explicitly inflected as a *non*-subject noun. Sentences like (70a) were not allowed at this time because in them the modified initial noun was also inflected in subject case and the perceptual confusion would have been as strong as in modern English.

By the end of the 14th Century nominal and adjectival declensions had largely disappeared so that all sentences like (70b, 75b) were now themselves perceptually confusing as in modern English. It was at this time that the restriction against deleting any subject relative pronoun appeared. In our view this development occurred simply as a way of resolving the perceptual difficulty occasioned by the loss of the nominal inflection system. As children learned the language, they gradually constrained admissible deletions of relative pronouns to the modern system, because of the newly developed difficulty in understanding sentences which violated that system.

In brief, the history of the language reveals an interplay between the organisation of the grammatical rules and the perceptual complexity of the sentences generated by those rules. The deletion of subject relative pronouns on *initial* nouns has always been inadmissible as part of the general system of restrictions that guarantee that initial subordinate clauses are distinct from initial main clauses. In Old English subject relative pronouns could be deleted on non-initial nouns because such nouns were often explicitly marked by inflections

o

as non-subject; such a 'noun' could not be misinterpreted as an independent clause subject of the following subordinate verb. When noun inflections were lost from the language this confusion could arise: such sentences became perceptually complex and the restriction on subject relative pronoun deletion was extended to relative pronouns modifying nouns in all positions.[8]

In this example the scope of the particular optional (or 'stylistic') rule that deletes relative pronoun modifiers was modified according to the perceptual habits of the child. This exemplifies how the relative dependence of the child on perceptual strategies of speech constrains the form of structural grammars which are learned. It is obvious that a grammar could not be learned in which every sentence is ambiguous with respect to its internal structure. Similarly, a grammar in which every sentence violated universal perceptual principles could not be learned. But existing grammars do contain sentences *some* of which are ambiguous, and *some* of which strain general perceptual principles. We cannot restrict the universal form of a possible grammar in any way except to say that sentences which it predicts must be, *in general, perceptually analysable.* Surely the notion of relative perceptibility must be measured *vis-à-vis* the actual use of the language and the properties of the child's cognitive structure rather than be reference to 'structural universals of the grammar of a language'. Accordingly, certain universal features of linguistic grammars are due to laws governing their actual use by young children and adults. The fact that the child is simultaneously acquiring a structural grammar and systems for speech production and perception leads to a view of language learning and corresponding principles of linguistic change and linguistic universals which emphasises an interaction between the different systems of language use. Since language learning includes the simultaneous acquisition of perceptual and grammatical structures, the ultimate structure of the grammatical system is partially a function of two kinds of simplicity: simplicity of the structural system itself, and simplicity of the systems for speech perception and production.

It remains for further research to show what perceptual constraints interact with the syntax of non-Indo-European languages. The mechanisms of speech production and, even more important, of structural learning will undoubtedly be shown to have profound effects on the kinds of structures which languages exhibit. I have concentrated on English because we have done little work with other languages. I have concentrated on the effects of the *perceptual* mechanism in syntax because we understand nothing about the mechanisms of language acquisition and speech production. Since we are at the beginning of our investigations I urge the reader to take our examples with a dose of salt; future research will indicate most of the specific claims made here to be superficial and incorrect. But there is no doubt that such interaction between speech behaviour and linguistic structure occurs continuously and is the main source for the life and evolution of every language.

D. Conclusion

One common thread in this volume is a wariness of the monolithic tendencies of the recent revolution in the study of language: each author discusses some particular way in which structural properties of language should be embedded within other systems of language and cognition. I have argued that the concept of language behaviour is like the concept of a particular species—a complex of interacting systems, primarily the systems of speech perception, speech production and speech structure. Such subsystms *mutually* influence each other's internal structure; accordingly, *no* system is more central or explanatory than any other. In this chapter I have presented a sample of theoretical, experimental and historical approaches that can be used to explore the interactions of these behavioural subsystems of language.

There are two conclusions from this view of the study of language. First we must be much more careful than in the recent past to study the nature of our intuitions about sentences. It will not do to multiply formal 'levels' or apocalyptically to attack each others' theories every time a new kind of intuition appears on the horizon. We must first make sure that we understand its nature and its interaction with other sets of intuitions. Not only will this solidify the factual basis of linguistic description, it may offer some understanding of how further to develop experimental phenomenology.

The final point bears on the question of nativism in language and the relation of human language to more primitive communication systems. Nobody in command of his faculties can deny that language is innate in some sense, just as it is innate to a monkey to have digital opposition. But the study of homologues in allegedly primitive forms of advanced behaviour only confuses the problem. Consider the uselessness of comparing the monkey's capacity to hang by his fingers, with his capacity to hang by his elbow and by his prehensile tail. Similarly, evolutionary analogues are equally spurious: one does not seek the explanation of what is uniquely innate in a modern horse by 'subtracting out' what was innate to an *eohippus*. Each species is a coherent organism with its own interacting organisational systems; these interactions necessarily modify and mutate whatever innate structures are shared with earlier related species. Given that all behavioural systems naturally interact within a species it is not clear that one can compare two intact species to isolate what structure is unique to one of them (see Campbell, Chapter 1). Nor can one treat 'structure of language' as independent of the 'structure of cognition' (see McNeill, Chapter 3) since both structures determine certain aspects of each other.

Accordingly, it is not at all clear that homologues of communicative behaviour in non-human animals constitute a basic behavioural substrate on which human language rests. Nor is it clear how the basic perceptual, cognitive and social mechanisms internal to humans independent of language are organised by language behaviour itself. We do not face a problem of describing *what* is innate in human language, either by reference to related dumb species or to the linguistic role of non-linguistic aspects of human cognition. Rather, our problem is to specify *how* the child's desire to communicate recruits and organises human capacities into the species of behaviour that we know has 'language'.

Footnotes

[1] I am indebted to J. Limber for calling my attention to this particular construction.

[2] Notice also that the surface phrase structure difference in these cases is also reflected in an internal structural difference. Mehler and Carey found that such differences did not form an effective perceptual set if they were not also reflected in surface structure differences.

[3] These examples are only intended to give the reader an idea of the *kind* of processes involved in English stress assignment. The reader should consult Chomsky and Halle for a full treatment of the problem.

[4] Note that the finding that phrase structure is not ordinarily assigned as an initial step in sentence perception is further evidence against the

standard "analysis-by-synthesis" model of speech perception. According to that model, the goal of the synthetic component of perception is to generate a "match" of the surface phrase structure of the sentence which is allegedly already computed. The evidence reviewed here suggests that the surface phrase structure is often never fully computed in perception either as the first *or* the final step.

[5] The pseudo-passive transformation (56) was not discussed in print by Chomsky, to my knowledge. However, the analysis of sentences such as (61c) as derived from passives by a rule like (56) is consistent with the syntactic theory as presented in *Syntactic Structures* (and was discussed in classes by Chomsky in 1961). This analysis was later rejected because of the meaning differences between sentences like (61b) and (61c), on the view that sentences with different meanings cannot have different underlying internal structures. However, Chomsky's current arguments (1970) that certain aspects of semantic interpretation depend on surface structure would allow for deriving (61c) from (61b), with meaning differences accounted for by surface structure interpretive rules.

[6] The arguments against the analysis in (61) presented here are stimulated by Postal's work, although the reader should credit Postal with the correct arguments and the author with the incorrect arguments. The main point of the present discussion is to explore the kinds of linguistic arguments there are against the analysis in (61) and in favour of an analysis like that of (68).

[7] At least for the interpretation of (61a) which is synonymous with (61c). The difficulty with these cases is that (61a) is ambiguous, meaning either the same as (61b) or the same as (61c). This suggests that there are two possible analyses of sentences like (61a, ba c).

(61a)—$Base_j$, number and tense
(61b)—$Base_j$, passive, number and tense
(61c)—$Base_j$, number and tense

(61a)—$Base_i$, exchange, number and tense
(61b)—$Base_i$, exchange, passive number and tense
(61c)—$Base_j$, number and tense

On either analysis 'pseudo-passives' (61c) are simpler transformationally than passives (61b), which directly conflicts with the analysis in (61). In the reported experiments the verbs used were not 'cognitive' like *interest* but impersonal like *dry*. A sample set of sentences corresponding to 61a, b, c is: (a) the sun dried the raisins; (b) the raisins were dried by the sun; (c) the raisins dried in the sun.

[8] For the purposes of the present discussion the loss of inflections is left unexplained. See Bever and Langendoen (1970) for further discussion.

HE STUDY OF LANGUAGE BEHAVIOUR

References

BATES, R. (1969), A study of acquisition of language. Doctoral dissertation, University of Texas.

BELLUGI, URSULA H. (1967), The acquisition of the system of negation in children's speech. Unpublished doctoral dissertation, Harvard University.

BEVER, T. G. (1968), A survey of some recent work in psycholinguistics. In Warren J. Plath (ed.), *Specification and Utilization of a Transformational Grammar*, Scientific Report No. 3, prepared for Air Force Cambridge Research Laboratories, July. pp. 1-68.

BEVER, T. G. (1970a), The cognitive basis for linguistic structures. In Hayes, R. (ed.), *Cognition and Language Development*. New York: Wiley, pp. 277-360.

BEVER, T. G. (1970b), The influence of speech performance on linguistic competence. In Levelt, W. and d'Arcais, G. B. F. (eds.), *Advances in Psycholinguistics*, 1. Amsterdam: North-Holland Co., pp. 21-50.

BEVER, T. G. (1970c), The Nature of Cerebral Dominance in Speech Behavior of the Child and Adult. *Mechanisms of Language Development*. New York and London: Academic Press.

BEVER, T. G., LACKNER, J. and KIRK, R. (1969), The underlying structure sentence is the primary unit of speech perception. *Perception and Psychophysics* **5** (4), 225-234.

BEVER, T. G. and LANGENDOEN, D. T. (1970), The interaction of perception and grammar in linguistic change. In Stockwell, Robert P. and MacCulay, Ronald (eds.), *Historical Linguistics in the Perceptive of Transformational Theory*. Indiana University Press (in press).

BEVER, T. G., PALMER, F., SUMNER, J. and MORAN, H. (1970), The influence of early experience on ear dominance and hand/ear/eye co-ordination. (in preparation.)

BLOOMFIELD, L. (1914), *The Study of Language*. New York: Holt.

BLOOMFIELD, L. (1933), *Language*. New York: Holt, Reinhart and Winston.

BLUMENTHAL, A. L., and BOAKES, R. (1967), Prompted recall of sentences. *Journal of Verbal Learning and Verbal Behavior* **6**, 674-676.

206

CAZDEN, C. (1968), The acquisition of noun and verb inflections. *Child Development* **39**, 433-448.

CHOMSKY, N. (1958), *Syntactic structures.* Hague: Monton.

CHOMSKY, N. (1965), *Aspects of the theory of syntax.* Cambridge, Mass.: MIT Press.

CHOMSKY, N. and HALLE, M. (1968), *The Sound Patterns of English.* New York: Harper and Row.

CHOMSKY, N. and MILLER, G. A. (1963), Introduction to the formal analysis of natural language. In Luce, D., Bush, R. and Galanter, E. (eds.), *Handbook of Mathematical Psychology* **2**, pp. 269-321. New York: Wiley,

FODOR, J., BEVER, T. G. and GARRETT, M. (1968), The development of psychological models for speech recognition. Contract No. AF 19 (628) -5705, to MIT, Department of Psychology, January.

FODOR, J. and GARRETT, M. (1967), Some syntactic determinants of sentential complexity. *Perception and Psychophysics* **2** (7), 289-296.

GARRETT, M. and BEVER, T. G. (1970), The Perceptual Segmentation of Sentences. In Bever, T. G. and Weksel, W. (eds.), *The Structure and Psychology of Language.* New York: Holt, Reinhart and Winston (in press).

GESCHWIND, N. and LEVITSKY, W. (1968), Human Brain: left-right asymmetries in the speech area. *Science* **161**, 186-187.

HALLE, M. and STEVENS, K. N. (1964), Speech recognition: a model and a programme for research. In Fodor, J. A. and Katz, J. J. (eds.), *The Structure of Language: Readings in the Philosophy of Language.* New York: Prentice-Hall.

HERZBERGER, H. (1970), Perceptual complexity in language. In Bever, T. G. and Weksel, W. (eds.), *The Structure and Psychology of Language.* New York: Holt, Reinhart and Winston (in press).

KATZ, J. J. (1967), Recent issues in semantic theory. *Foundations of Language,* **3**, 124-194.

KIMURA, D. (1967), Functional asymmetry of the brain in dichotic listening. *Cortex* **3**, 163-178.

KIPARSKY, P. and KIPARSKY, C. (1970), Fact. In Jakobovits, L. and Steinberg, P. (eds.), *Semantics*. New York: Holt, Reinhart and Winston (in press).

LAKOFF, G. On generative semantics. In Jakobovits, L. and Steinberg, P. (eds.), *Semantics: An Interdisciplinary Reader in Philosophy, Linguistics, Anthropology, and Psychology*. New York: Holt, Reinhart and Winston (in press).

LAKOFF, G. (1968), Instrumental Adverbs and the Concept of Deep Structure. *Foundations of Language* **4**, 4-49.

LENNEBERG, H. E. (1968), *The Biological Basis for Language*. New York: Wiley.

LIEBERMAN, P. (1965), On the Acoustic Basis of the Perception of Intonation by Linguists. *Word* **21**, 40-54.

MACCAWLEY, J. (1968), The Role of Semantics in a Grammar. In Bach E. and Harms, R. (eds.), *Universals in Linguistic Theory*. New York: Holt, Reinhart and Winston, pp. 125-170.

MEHLER, J. and CAREY, P. (1968), The Interaction of Veracity and Syntax in the Processing of Sentences. *Perception and Psychophysics* **3**, 109-111.

MEHLER, J., BEVER, T. G., and CAREY, P. (1967), What We Look at When We Read. *Perception and Psychophysics* **2**, 213-218.

POSTAL, P. M. (1970), The best theory. In Peters, S. (ed.), *Goals of Linguistic Theory* (in press).

POSTAL, P. M. (1968), Cross-Over Phenomena. In *Specification and Utilization of a Transformational Grammar*. Scientific Report No. 3. Yorktown Heights, New York, IBM Watson Research Center.

REES, A. and PALMER, F. (1969), Concept training in two-year-olds. Presented at SRCD, March 27.

ROSS, J. R. (1968), Universal constraints on variables. Unpublished doctoral dissertation, MIT.

SAVIN, H. and BEVER, T. G. (1970), The non-perceptual reality of the phoneme. *Journal of Verbal Learning and Verbal Behavior* **9**, 3, 295-302.

THE STUDY OF LANGUAGE BEHAVIOUR

SLOBIN, D. (1970), Universals of grammatical development in children. In d'Arcais, G. B. F. and Levelt, W. (eds.), *Advances in Psycholinguistics* 1. Amsterdam: North-Holland Co.

TEUBER, H. L. (1968), Mental retardation in childhood after early trauma to the brain: some issues in search of facts. Introductory Lecture given at Lincoln Nebraska Conference sponsored by the NINDS, October 13.

WADA, J. A. (1969), Interhemispheric sharing and shift of cerebral function. Ninth International Congress of Neurology, Sept. 1969. Abstract in *Exerpta Medica, International Congress Series*, **193**, 296-297.

Author Index

211

Subject Index